From a
Breton Garden

From a Breton Garden

*The Vegetable Cookery
of Josephine Araldo*

Josephine Araldo
Robert Reynolds

with illustrations by
Gary Bukovnik

Aris Books

Addison-Wesley Publishing Company, Inc.

*Reading, Massachusetts   Menlo Park, California   New York
Don Mills, Ontario   Wokingham, England   Amsterdam   Bonn
Sydney   Singapore   Tokyo   Madrid   San Juan*

Library of Congress Cataloging-in-Publication Data

Araldo, Josephine, 1897–1989
　From a Breton garden : the vegetable cookery of Josephine Araldo / Josephine Araldo and Robert Reynolds ; with illustrations by Gary Bukovnik.
　　　p.　　cm.
　　"Aris books."
　　ISBN 0-201-51759-0
　　1. Cookery (Vegetables)　2. Cookery, French.
I. Reynolds,　Robert.　II. Title.
TX801.A72　1990
641.6'5—dc20　　　　　　　　　　　　　90-363
　　　　　　　　　　　　　　　　　　　　　　　　CIP

Aris Books Editorial Offices and
Test Kitchen
1621 Fifth Street
Berkeley, CA 94710
(415) 527-5171

Text design by Paul Quin
Illustrated by Gary Bukovnik
Jacket design by Copenhaver Cumpston
Set in 11.5-point Garamond 3 by NK Graphics, Keene, NH

ABCDEFGHIJ-VB-9543210
First printing, September 1990

Acknowledgments

This book owes its existence to Josephine, whose life was her faith, her family, and her work. Faith was the powerful force at the core of her being.

Her security was her husband Charles, her daughter Jacqueline, and her grandchildren David, Rick, Mark, and Danny. Jacqueline's support for this book was clear from the beginning. Over the years I have been very moved by the warmth her family extended to me.

It was Josephine who breathed life into what notions I developed about my profession. She was a model of pride in work as a thing unto itself, and she bound those notions into a belief. She inspired in me a love for France that goes deep, and then called me "Frenchie."

Susan Catalano taught me the value of artistic collaboration. She took over my life in San Francisco, put a computer in my hands, and pushed me on a plane to France where the nuts and bolts of the book were tightened. She forgave all my blundering, and said some things are forever.

At the heart of the collaboration was Paul Quin, the book's designer. Acting on the belief that design is an integral part of development, he established links to every part of the project. He understood, he explained, and he was patient. He focused, deliberated, discussed, and above all enjoyed the labor.

Paul kept me focused, clear, and true to a vision I shared with Josephine. He presented our vision to Addison-Wesley. He worked with Robin Cowan, the copy editor, on the integrity of the line editing she wanted to do. He dreamed in Brittany blue with Gary Bukovnik over the artistic contribution of his watercolors. His efforts were a catalyst for responses, worthy of the subject, that everyone returned in kind.

Josephine's editor was John Harris, whom she called "Harry." John was the book's mother hen; he watched his brood, and kept everyone close by. He faced every limitation I came up against and still found inspiration to express the underlying themes. His hair is grayer, but he's happy. John's efforts were backed by his assistant, Greg Kaplan, who attended to the hundreds of details of his job with encouragement and calm. He also helped test recipes.

Cope Cumpston accepted the team that was put together. As Art Director, she was cool and rational, sensitive and open. In the process of forming her own professional opinions, she never wavered in her willingness to listen and to apply high standards. Laura Noorda, as Production Supervisor, heard all the sounds between the notes. She never failed to respond, to tune, and to communicate with clarity. Robin Cowan, the copy editor, responded to every confusion and made clear every intention so that this book could be articulate. She scrutinized the smallest details as well as the overall scope. She worked in ways that made things move forward.

Gary Bukovnik's watercolors are the visual manifestation of the collaboration. They are like the book—a bountiful gift worthy of Josephine's vision. They convey immediately that the experience is pleasing, lush, appetizing, and elegant.

Contents

List of Recipes

Artichokes

Asparagus

Beans

Cardoons

Carrots

Celery Root

Chard

Chestnuts

Cucumbers

Dandelion Greens

Eggplant

Endive

Fennel

Jerusalem Artichokes

Pumpkin

Radishes

Rutabagas

Salsify

Sorrel

Spinach

Tomatoes

Turnips

Watercress

Zucchini

Epigraph

Brittany is a fairyland of the wind, the night, and the moon, which casts over its druidic forests the great, melancholy secret it has told to the old oaks and to the ancient shores.

There is a sort of sacred grandeur about Brittany found nowhere else. That admiration is inspired by respect and piety. Both heroic and mystic, Brittany has mothered a peerless line of saints and heroes . . . the Knights of the Round Table . . . Merlin, the wizard, the idyl of Tristan and Isolde.

But what about gastronomy? I was waiting for that! I have been shouting from the roof tops about the wonderful and unappreciated Breton food . . . Without question the coasts of Brittany offer the most prodigious and inexhaustible varieties of edible fish in the world, and this not counting those caught in the open sea. . . . As for Breton charcuterie, it is a charming, country charcuterie smelling of the open air and aromatic herbs.

The Breton vegetables are world famous . . . mountains of cabbages, cauliflowers, salad greens, and potatoes. Brittany also produces delicious desserts, thanks to its *cordons bleus*, with their inventive talents, and to the abundance of its fruit (strawberries from Plougastel, apples, pears, cherries, nuts, grapes). . . .

Despite the constant buffeting of "Ar Mor"—the ancient name of Brittany—by Atlantic storms, this granitic land produces a number of interesting white wines, some of which are often quite pleasant. . . . But for thousands of years cider has been the Breton national drink. . . .

We assure you that certain Breton vegetables—and some are truly succulent—taste very good in company with a good local cider.

Let us drink a *bolée* (bowl) of cider to those battling the deep green-blue sea!

> Curnonsky
> *Traditional Recipes of the Provinces of France*

How This Book Came to Be Written

The recipes contained in this book reflect the life story of a great French chef and a truly remarkable woman: Josephine Araldo. Her story parallels the story of twentieth-century cuisine. She amassed this collection of vegetable recipes over the span of her career, which began in the 1920s when she was a student at the professional cooking school in Paris known as the Cordon Bleu. I have seen the originals of some of these recipes in her notebooks from that period. They are written in an old-fashioned hand on old pieces of paper. She kept typed versions in manila folders that were filed systematically by heading: soups, salads, sauces, vegetables.

Josephine would talk now and again about her recipes in a light that was startling; she'd refer to dishes such as red cabbage and wild berries. On other occasions she might talk about cabbage, apples, and gooseberries. No one really understood these combinations, but there was a recurring theme. Finally I asked her to tell me the story behind these dishes. And so she told me about her grandmother, La Mère Jacquette, and we came to talk more and more about food, Brittany, and her experiences in Paris with the legendary Henri-Paul Pellaprat, her teacher at the Cordon Bleu. I was transported into a world that existed only in her memory.

The mind is like a muscle; the more it is exercised the better it works. The more we talked about food, the more Josephine remembered. Often we would sit and talk for hours. I remember more than once sitting with her at the house on McAllister Street and talking through the afternoon until the room went dark. Still we continued to talk. Finally, her husband Charles would come and ask if we would join him for some soup (for which he was famous). On these occasions, we would laugh because Josephine wished that she could speak as well as I could, and we joked that I would lend her my way with words and she would provide the subjects for discussion. She loved ideas, and an education was something she most valued. (In her seventies she studied theology at the University of San Francisco.) In our conversations, we wandered in and out of subjects as diverse as religion and food, and always back to Brittany. We became absorbed in stories as children might, and it was a most wonderful treat to be able to spend time like this with Josephine.

Over time, I started to piece together common themes about her grandmother's dishes, the most singular of which were unusual combinations of fruits and vegetables. I eventually wrote a story about them, which I read to her, carefully spelling out the details of a hypothesis. I was determined to help Josephine get her book on vegetables published. I remember that day; she was sick in bed. I sat with my face no more than six inches away from her and I went through what I had written sentence by sentence. After each point I would ask: "Do you understand what I'm trying to say? Am I on the right track? Do you want me to continue?" She kept saying yes. I took her personal history in the form of stories, and wove them into the context of Breton society and French history. I applied a quirky sort of theorizing that I was taught to do as a student of the chef, Madeleine Kamman, in France.

The basic premise of the story I wrote for Josephine is that the cooking of Brittany had been practically subsumed under the heading of French cooking, so that almost all that remained visible were dishes such as *Carottes Bretonnes*, or others like them, that were recorded by chefs in Paris. But Josephine's grandmother learned to cook before the time of Napoleon III. La Mère Jacquette lived through all the events that came to threaten the very existence of the Breton people and their culture. And so I saw that from her grandmother to Josephine and then to us came an example of something pure.

When Josephine decided she wanted me to be her editor and co-author, she presented me with a recipe manuscript. She tossed it to me triumphantly as if to say "Well, my work's done. What's taking you so long!" She wrote the recipes in the same way she operated in the kitchen: Do this, then this, but first remember to do that. My job was to standardize the recipes, give them a consistent voice, fill in gaps, and assign intention when Josephine's notes fell short of clear instruction. This was a daunting task, and I worried that the "flavor" of the recipes would be lost in this process. In Brittany, they say that the best apple brandy doesn't survive the tax man's stamp—the best of it is kept home. I was determined to survive the tax man.

Josephine said the book should be entitled: *From Brittany, France to America.* I took that to mean: beginning in Brittany, passing through France, and on to America. So, I have divided the original manuscript materials into three sections: Pont-Scorff, Brittany; Paris, France; and San Francisco, California. It was not always easy to categorize Josephine's recipes as Breton, Parisian, or Californian. I used my own judgement at times and could not avoid using my own theories to identify what went where. Josephine's own failing health towards the end of the project made it hard to use her memory as a guide. But, as my own editor instantly understood and supported, to have simply organized this book conventionally, by vegetable and not by geography and time, would have failed to articulate the transfer of knowledge from La Mère Jacquette and Pellaprat to Josephine, and from Josephine to her American students.

From a Breton Garden is the story of how simple truths survive. It speaks first an emotional language that is of the heart and not the intellect. This language is French, *la belle langue,* and I borrow English with poetic license to evoke it. The book next speaks an intellectual language to evoke the underlying formal discipline that is the cultural heritage of French cuisine. And finally, this book speaks a spiritual language, evoking the sources of the original mysteries of Brittany and the *Finistère*—the end of the earth—which is Josephine's origin.

This book came to be through the efforts of many people who have told me stories or parts of stories; the rest is my imagination and the recorded memories of Josephine in her eighties. I have woven diverse elements into a sort of tapestry with the voice of Josephine speaking throughout. You will come upon her suddenly. Turn a corner and there she is, unexpected and bright because that is how she was. Her voice is by turns intelligent and technical, simple and earthy, and everything between. Josephine's vision and views are presented here. Brittany colored her perspective in the way that geography always imprints in our minds the first sense of a personal horizon. Brittany became the lens through which this country girl looked at Paris and the United States.

Kernavo is the way Bretons say hello or goodbye. I can hear the voice of Josephine sweetly singing a little folk tune that repeats that Breton word over and over. She sits in her rocker in the sunlight by the window. *Kernavo* is the greeting; it is sung sweetly. I see her in this book, I hear her voice, and I understand clearly her design. There are times when she shines absolutely uninterrupted and unimpeded by my voice. For new students first discovering Josephine in this book, this is a precious gift. Her old friends and students will see their animated teacher, I believe, as they saw her in her kitchen. Some will be able to look at parts of this work and say, that is Robert, here is Josephine. I have tried to sustain the pleasure of being with Josephine, now that she is gone, within the text I have fashioned.

The food writer, Janet Fletcher, interviewed Josephine in her home a few months before she died. Janet asked her what would make her book different from whatever else was available. "I don't know," Josephine shrugged with a bright smile, "I suppose it will have my spirit."

From a
Breton Garden

PART I

Pont-Scorff,
Brittany

The Traditions of La Mère Jacquette

Some of Josephine's story begins in Brittany, France, over a hundred and seventy years ago and has as its focus her grandmother, a woman named La Mère Jacquette. She lived on a farm that bordered the river Scorff. Here Josephine was raised and learned to cook.

The farm is in the town of Pont-Scorff, inland about sixteen kilometers from the ocean at Lorient. La Mère Jacquette was a widow with a small pension, and if not moneyed, she was, as Josephine put it, "land rich." She loved her garden and had a deep understanding of the working of the earth, the seasons, and nature from instinct and intelligence. She passed on this love and understanding to Josephine.

The land she lived in was Brittany, though her country was France. This is an important distinction, for even in the time and memory of Josephine, there were people who spoke French and, by implication, others who did not. The Bretons of La Mère Jacquette's day governed themselves with the simple logic of a country people who had a clear idea of themselves, a people with high spirits and untamed natures. Their lineage traces to before written history. They built the prehistoric monoliths that give Brittany the name, the Coast of Legends, and give to the people who inhabit it the name, the People of the Sun. *Tristan et Isolde* is the tale of these people who have a very long view into the past.

My own understanding of Brittany, beyond what I learned directly from Josephine, comes from books and people I have known. Michelle Vignes, an internationally known photographer who once photographed Josephine, told me of how, as a child from Champagne, she was evacuated to Brittany during the second World War. She attributes her penetrating visual style to the Breton nature she absorbed while growing up there. A contemporary account of the Breton people is told by Eleanor Clark

5

in a story she wrote of the oyster culture that has made Brittany famous. The book is entitled *The Oysters of Locmariaquer*. It is a passionate tale of the "outsiderness" of these people, and tells a fragile story that makes no more sense than the story of the oyster itself. Both have survived since prehistoric times under the most extraordinary of circumstances. Both have in common something barely within human knowledge to cultivate and preserve.

Breton culture was almost completely vanquished by the fickle and devastating consequences of history. In Josephine's living memory, the women of Pont-Scorff needed a go-between to translate from Breton to French. Education in French for Breton children didn't begin until the very latter part of the nineteenth century and the beginning of our own. The imposition of another language shook the very foundation of their culture. French came to Brittany along with industrialization and war, and these forces combined to threaten the Breton people with extinction.

France lost an enormous portion of its male population in the first World War. France still is recovering. The toll among the Bretons was high, perhaps because they were near at hand: there was a direct train from Brest to Paris. Every one of Josephine's seven brothers was killed in that first war. La Mère Jacquette died shortly after. Then Josephine's own mother died; she couldn't sustain the loss of all her sons. Her death, one senses, was of a broken heart. Since her family was gone, Josephine left, too, first to Paris and then to the United States.

Josephine left her native Pont-Scorff in Brittany because there was no future there for her. She got on the same train that took the men to war and went to the same destination—Paris. As with so many Breton girls, her education was in the traditions of cooking. She brought Brittany to Paris, where all of France was gravitating to flood the capital. Reaction to industrialization and war gave the city new life.

From the second half of the nineteenth century through the first half of the present century, Paris food—French food—was nourished and shaped by a sort of professional "family." Individuals emerged as voices of their time, and they represented their visions in the ways that were available to them. The group included César Ritz, a famous hotelier whose roots were in regional cuisines. At the top of his profession, he was a contemporary of Henri-Paul Pellaprat, who directed the professional school. Prosper Montagné created the gastronomic encyclopedia. Curnonsky was the elected *prince des gastronomes,* and he toured France codifying and recording the local cuisines. He had a special reverence for Brittany. His real name was Maurice-Edmond Sailland, and his real importance was such that his judgements were considered ultimate recognition. Such a grouping of individuals might also include figures such as Edouard Nignon. He was a noted Paris chef of Breton origins, whom Pellaprat named "The Dandy."

Regional cuisine was central to their work; it was what they all drew from. Regional cuisine was not perceived in the same way as we think of it today, i.e., as an interesting variation on a national theme. At that time, when French cuisine was at a peak, they drew upon the themes of regional cooking based on ancestral traditions. Their efforts were directed to ensure the future for the firmly established cuisines, which—like culture and language—distinguish the provinces of France.

La Mère Jacquette exemplified regional cooking apart from any other influences, a thing pure unto itself. She had land and a garden; she was not poor; she had the forests to forage. Her thinking was naive, instinctive, and intelligent, if not educated. She also had the experience of years spent in proximity to the soil and the traditions of generations of her *pays,* her country, Brittany. She was Breton, with all it implies of a spirit undaunted, original, believing, and positive.

Curnonsky did not find La Mère Jacquette in his gastronomic wanderings in search of the cuisines of the countryside; Escoffier never tasted her particular version of the stew she cooked in cider to local taste. However, La Mère Jacquette taught Josephine, and one day Josephine walked across the doorstep of Henri-Paul Pellaprat at the Cordon Bleu. He understood and valued the gift she brought him, traditional Breton cuisine.

There were some things that you could fool La Mère Jacquette about; after all she was a simple country woman without formal learning. Josephine loved to tell the story of "The Cord to Catch the Wind." La Mère Jacquette was old, already a grandmother, and the grandsons loved to play tricks on her, as country people do, in general, and the French in particular. One of Josephine's brothers explained to La Mère Jacquette that there existed a special device, a cord to catch the wind, and he wanted her to ask the *avocat,* Monsieur Gornod, about it the next time she saw him. "Alright," she replied. "I will do it." And she eventually asked him. He, of course, looked at her and wondered if she were dotty. He asked questions to verify her sanity: "What have you had to eat today, Jacquette? Are you feeling well, Jacquette?" She recognized these as inappropriate responses to her question and realized that she had been treated foolishly by her grandchildren.

She had a domain, however, where she was no fool. When she walked out her door into the garden, she noticed what was ready to be picked that day. She knew the woods and what grew where and when. She had a nose for finding things in the woods at Pont-Scorff—mushrooms, berries, and herbs, wild things that carried the perfumes of the earth. What was ready in the domestic garden was the lens through which she looked at the wilder garden of the forests around her.

Josephine knew this garden well, too. "You know, Robeirt," she would begin (I use this spelling to convey the curious inflection she would give to my name), "I can see the garden. I can tell you where things are. The currants are along the wall." And she would sketch the path with her finger. "And there is an old apple tree. It was already 125 years old, and it still bore the best fruit. We used to love to eat things out of that garden."

When Josephine spoke of the garden, she placed you there, and it was not difficult to walk with her and her grandmother: We begin in the garden where the red cabbage is ready. From there, on the way to the woods, Jacquette makes note of wild berries whose colors sing to the cabbage. But there must be a special trick to make them marry. She explains that the berry is tart and will lighten the big cabbage, especially if the cabbage is cooked in cider to trick the vegetable into acting like the fruit. But something is still needed. The tongue is satisfied, but something is needed to connect fruit and vegetable, something with smell, aroma. *Et voilà,* what's this, hiding in the woods? Here are wild mushrooms, perfect to give our cabbage and berries an aroma. Jacquette knows how to make use of their perfume to carry the wildness of the forest to her dish.

Back in Jacquette's kitchen, the center of the house, the aroma fills the air, and at last we eat. The distinct flavors of each element—cabbage, berries, and mushrooms—are carried back and forth across the palate, allowing each discrete taste to synthesize into a dish of unsurpassed harmony and flavor. (See Red Cabbage with Blueberries, page 49.)

If there is magic in the tale of Josephine and her grandmother, it is that you too can reach across five generations and take something tangible from it—a recipe, a dish whose origins are found in foraging and the mentality of an old woman who loved her garden. You can eat what she prepared and find it so new as to be stunning. You can feel her spirit, sense her appreciation. You can share with her all the attendant pleasures of company and conversation—the pleasures of the table located at the center of life. The past is not recreated here; it is still alive because its simple truths remain ours.

La Mère Jacquette knew the garden and the woods because as a cook she was committed to the land. She knew about rutabagas and quinces because they arrived together in a season, but beyond this natural juxtaposition of elements, she developed a technique. The rutabagas were boiled, the quinces sautéed. She might cook the mushrooms she added to red cabbage, but she would not cook the berries that went into the dish. La Mère Jacquette's real talent was her understanding of how to make these elements combine. This is what Josephine always referred to when she said, "Any fool can make a roast, but it takes a genius to know what to do with leftovers." Josephine learned this aspect of self-possession from La Mère Jacquette before going to the Cordon Bleu, and she didn't lose it. She would say that simple cooking, provincial cooking, is always the best. "A dish of beans, well-prepared, will affect more people than any rich ingredient that few can afford."

Josephine unlocked the mystery of good cooking. Simplicity. "Do you know what it takes?" I can hear her ask an audience of eager faces whose total attention she commands. She would pause dramatically as though the silence fueled anticipation. She would begin again in a stage whisper, the key for building drama, and then grossly articulate each sound, each word: "It takes common sense." She would laugh a jolly laugh and proceed to demonstrate what she meant.

It's a long way from nineteenth century Pont-Scorff to late twentieth century American television, yet Josephine, ambassador of French cuisine, breezed onto the stage of "The Mike Douglas Show," operating at full tilt. She set out to demonstrate a preparation. Mike Douglas asked her how she could tell what a tablespoon of something was. She stopped, dipped her spoon into the salt, and poured it into his upturned palm.

"You see that measure?" she asked with utter self-possession. He looked carefully at the little heap of salt and said that he did. She slapped the bottom of his hand, as you might see in a routine by the Three Stooges. It sent the salt flying. "Good," she replied, "never forget it. Now, let me teach you a song for when you beat an egg."

Simple Breton Food

Here are most of the foraged recipes of La Mère Jacquette. Josephine explained that many of these were her own reconstructions. They drew their inspiration from what she remembered of her grandmother. These are simple, homey recipes of field and wood. Curnonsky would call this "simple, straight-tasting" cooking.

Artichokes

BOILED ARTICHOKES

L'Artichaut Cuit Entier

The association between artichokes and Brittany is very strong in the minds of the French. Brittany is known for artichokes. Here, they are the best of the best. No matter how they are prepared, artichokes are always happily accompanied by a Breton cider. The nutty taste of the artichoke communicated to the apple and gives a simple, honest pleasure.

INGREDIENTS	SERVES 6

6 large artichokes
Juice of 1 lemon or 2 tablespoons cider vinegar
1 bay leaf
1 sprig thyme
1 sage leaf
1 teaspoon salt

To Prepare the Artichoke for Cooking Whole: Cut the stems of the artichokes to remove any brown or dried flesh, leaving about 1 inch of stem intact if possible. Bend the first few leaves at the base, and trim them off by sliding a sharp knife along the tough part. This leaves the tender part attached. Trim the prickly end of the remaining leaves with a kitchen scissors. Rub the exposed flesh with lemon to keep it from turning dark.

Fill a large pot with cold water and bring to a rolling boil. Drop in the artichokes, making sure they have enough room to stand upright. Add the salt, lemon, and herbs. Cook approximately 25 to 35 minutes. The artichokes are done when the leaves can be pulled off easily and the bottoms are tender when pricked with a knife. Drain them upside down on a towel or in a non-aluminum colander. Serve with hot melted butter or other desired sauce, such as hollandaise, mousseline, béarnaise, choron, vinaigrette, or Green Mayonnaise (see recipe below).

Acidulated Water: Water is acidulated by the addition of lemon juice or vinegar and is used in the cooking water to prevent certain green vegetables from losing their bright green color. There are other techniques for achieving the same end. For example, a tablespoon of white flour added to the cold cooking water coats the vegetable with starch and prevents discoloration.

GREEN MAYONNAISE

Sauce Verte

Josephine recommended this recipe in a number of dishes.

INGREDIENTS	YIELDS I CUP

3 tablespoons parsley
4 tablespoons watercress leaves
4 tablespoons chopped spinach leaves
¼ teaspoon salt
Boiling water
1 cup mayonnaise (see page 94)

METHOD

Put all the leaves in a small bowl along with the salt. Pour enough boiling water to cover and allow to steep for 5 minutes. Remove the greens from the water, blot the excess water so that they are completely dry. Chop and blend the leaves into a mayonnaise and serve with fish, shellfish, and vegetable dishes.

Alternatively, any herbs can be added to the greens, such as tarragon, chervil, or chives.

STEAMED WHOLE ARTICHOKES

Artichauts à la Vapeur

METHOD

Prepare and trim artichokes as you would for Boiled Artichokes (see page 11). Arrange them bottom-side down in a steamer or colander. Do not use aluminum equipment; it causes the artichokes to oxidize. Set the colander in a large pot with a lid and slowly bring the water to a boil. Cover to keep steam from escaping. Steam the vegetable 40 to 45 minutes. The artichokes are done when the leaves can be pulled off easily and when a knife inserted in the base can pierce them without resistance. Serve with the same sauces as listed under Boiled Artichokes.

BRAISED STUFFED ARTICHOKES

Artichauts Farcis

Artichokes prepared this way are also referred to as *artichauts au gras*, this is, artichokes that are fattened and rich. They can certainly be served *au maigre*, or lean, by replacing the meat with breadcrumbs and flavoring with herbs, such as marjoram and parsley (see Deviled Artichokes page 20). It would still be *au maigre* to add some cheese and to bind the breadcrumbs with an egg. The liquid left from braising could be flavored with a little butter whisked in just before serving.

Because of tannin, which is natural to the artichoke, they are not served with red wines; they tend to fight each other. The artichokes are generally served with crisp, dry white wines, or, in Brittany, they are just as often served with cider, *le pur jus*, the pure juice that Josephine always found as good as champagne.

INGREDIENTS	SERVES 6

6 medium artichokes
Juice of 1 lemon or 2 tablespoons cider vinegar
   1 cup breadcrumbs
   1 tablespoon fresh *fines herbes*: parsley, chervil, chives, tarragon, etc., chopped fine
   1 to 2 cloves garlic, minced
⅓ cup grated cheese
   1 egg
   1 small onion, minced, sautéed (optional)
   1 slice bacon or pork fatback per artichoke
   4 tablespoons vegetable oil
   4 tablespoons butter
Mirepoix: 1 carrot, 1 stalk celery, 1 small onion, all finely diced
   1 sprig thyme

1 small bay leaf
½ cup French cider or white wine
1 tablespoon *glace de viande* or ½ cup other meat stock reduced to 1
    tablespoon (page 333)
Salt and freshly ground pepper

Procedure for Stuffing Artichokes: Trim the artichoke stem and the coarsest outer leaves. Blanch in rapidly boiling, salted water acidulated with lemon juice or vinegar. Cook for 5 to 8 minutes (long enough for the center leaves and choke to be removed easily). Cool the artichokes under cold running water. Drain and remove choke. The leaves that are removed can be scraped and added to the filling, or used for other purposes, such as Artichoke Crêpes (page 19). Season the cavity with salt and freshly ground pepper.

Mix together the breadcrumbs, herbs, garlic, cheese, and egg. If desired, you can add a chopped onion that has been sautéed in a little butter to the stuffing. Stuff this mixture into the artichoke cavity. Wrap each artichoke in a slice of bacon or pork fatback and tie with a string.

Preheat oven to 350 degrees. In an oven-proof casserole, melt the butter with the oil and sauté the *mirepoix* until the onions are translucent and the carrots are soft. This is the bed of vegetables the artichokes will sit on during baking. Lay the artichokes on top of the *mirepoix*, add the thyme, bay leaf, and wine. Bring the liquid in the pan to a boil, cover, and place in a preheated oven for 45 to 55 minutes.

To serve, remove the artichokes from the pan, letting any liquid from the artichokes drain into the casserole. Take the string and fat off, and set artichokes on a heated serving platter. Skim off any fat in the cooking liquid and stir in the *glace de viande* or stock. Bring to a boil, reduce slightly, and pour over the artichokes. Serve immediately.

The Use of a Mirepoix in French Cooking

Mirepoix is thought of as an aromatic flavoring. It also functions to raise the vegetable a bit above the surface of the pan, allowing it to steam somewhat and not to toughen by taking the direct heat from the surface of the cooking vessel. Generally *mirepoix* is thought to have had the life cooked out of it and is not served. Sometimes, however, it can be prepared and served as a rather pretty decoration of the vegetable.

Note: The recipe for Braised Artichokes calls for a generous amount of butter mixed with oil, 8 tablespoons in all. I think that the recipe only needs enough oil to sauté the *mirepoix*, so use the butter to your own taste. It is also possible to use the full amount of butter and oil to sauté the *mirepoix*, and when the desired cooking is achieved, drain off the butter to lighten the dish. Draining off the excess butter and oil makes sense here, since the bacon adds fat and the dish needs further skimming. If the taste of fresh butter is desired in the final presentation, a small amount can be added just before serving.

Crumbled bacon in addition to that used for wrapping the vegetable during the cooking process could be used as a final flavoring. Josephine felt that if you made an *au gras* sauce for an artichoke and it accompanied a meat course, then the meat didn't need any sauce.

ARTICHOKE, CAULIFLOWER, AND BROCCOLI FRITTERS

Beignets d'Artichauts, de Choux-Fleurs, et de Brocoli

This recipe introduces another first class Breton vegetable, cauliflower. It is presented with a variety of vegetables making a good first course by itself, or as part of a composed salad on a bed of tiny baby lettuces for a luncheon. Serve with a crisp white wine from the Loire Valley, such as a Savennières or a Sancerre.

INGREDIENTS	SERVES 6

6 medium artichokes
6 to 8 broccoli flowerets
6 to 8 cauliflower flowerets

Fritter Batter
   1½ cups flour
   2 whole eggs

1 cup milk or white wine

Salt and pepper

Grapeseed or peanut oil for frying

METHOD

Prepare the artichokes for blanching as described in the recipe for Boiled Artichokes page 11. After they are cooked, remove all flesh from the leaves of the artichokes by scraping with a spoon; remove the chokes and quarter the hearts.

Blanch the broccoli in boiling salted water until tender and crisp. Remove the broccoli from the boiling water; refresh under cold water and drain on paper towels. Cook the cauliflower flowerets in the same water until tender and crisp; refresh under cold water and drain.

Fritter Batter: In a large bowl add the flour, and make a well in the center. Add the eggs, a third of the milk, salt, and pepper. Gradually whisk the flour into the egg mixture with a fork. Slowly whisk in the remaining liquid to make a batter free of lumps.

Bring frying oil to a low boil in a large pot that does not crowd the vegetables and allows them to be completely submerged. Make sure the vegetables are completely dry. If they retain water, they won't accept the batter. The water also causes the deep frying oil to spit.

Dip the broccoli, cauliflower, and the artichoke quarters in the batter. Fry in hot oil for 4 to 5 minutes, or until lightly browned. Remove them to drain on paper towels; keep warm, and continue with the next batch. When everything has been deep fried, arrange the vegetables on a platter. Garnish with the artichoke that was scraped from the leaves and tossed with a vinaigrette.

ARTICHOKES WITH CARROTS

Artichaut Crécy

This trio of tastes—artichokes, carrots, and herbs—provides a simple satisfaction that can be served as a first course or to accompany a roast of pork and a sauce made from cider.

INGREDIENTS	SERVES 6

12 small artichokes, trimmed and halved or quartered
Juice of 1 lemon or 2 tablespoons cider vinegar
4 tablespoons butter
1 tablespoon peanut oil
5 to 6 small young carrots, peeled and cut into 2-inch pieces, trimmed
   to resemble small French carrots
Pinch of sugar (optional)
¼ cup white wine
¼ cup stock, good homemade
4 tablespoons chopped parsley
Salt and freshly ground pepper

METHOD

Prepare the artichokes by trimming the root end of the vegetable; remove any flawed leaves and discard them. (See detailed explanation in Boiled Artichokes page 11.) Blanch the artichokes for 5 to 8 minutes in rapidly boiling salted water acidulated with lemon juice or vinegar. Drain the vegetables in a non-aluminum colander.

Preheat oven to 300 degrees. Select an oven-proof braising pan with a tight fitting lid, or use a skillet first, then change to a separate baking dish.

Heat the butter and oil, and then sauté the carrots and artichokes. Season with salt and add the sugar, if it is to be used. Add the wine and stock to the pan, and bring the liquid to a boil. Cover the pan and bake the vegetables in a preheated oven for 30 minutes. Remove from oven and sprinkle with chopped parsley, give a few grinds of pepper, and serve hot.

ARTICHOKE CRÊPES

Crêpes aux Artichauts

These crêpes are excellent when served with a roast of any meat. They lend a sense of simple luxury. This is the sort of recipe that uses the scrapings from artichoke leaves when the hearts have been used for other purposes. The artichokes get a deep flavor by being sautéed slowly until they brown.

INGREDIENTS	SERVES 6

2 tablespoons all-purpose flour
2 eggs
¼ teaspoon chopped fresh thyme
½ teaspoon chopped parsley
2 cups cooked artichoke flesh (all edible parts of 6 to 8 artichokes)
Salt and freshly ground pepper
4 to 5 tablespoons butter
4 to 6 tablespoons white wine

METHOD

In a medium-size mixing bowl, combine the flour and eggs with a fork. Add the thyme and parsley, and mix in the artichoke. Season the mixture with salt and freshly ground pepper. Mix everything well.

Melt the butter in a heavy-bottomed skillet that will not make the artichokes discolor. Sauté silver dollar-size rounds of the mixture on both sides until they are lightly browned. Add the wine and simmer the pancakes for about 15 minutes or until the wine has been absorbed. Correct the seasoning, add additional herbs if desired, and serve hot.

DEVILED ARTICHOKES

Artichauts au Diable

These could be finished with the flavor of walnut or hazelnut, using the nuts themselves, or drizzling a light amount of either oil directly onto the vegetable just before it is presented. This use of nuts lends a local taste; it's a *truc*, or trick, that brings out the luxurious nuttiness of the vegetable itself.

INGREDIENTS	SERVES 6

6 medium artichokes, trimmed
1 cup breadcrumbs
4 large cloves garlic, minced
1 tablespoon chopped parsley
1 tablespoon chopped sour pickle (cornichons)
4 tablespoons butter plus 1 tablespoon vegetable oil
Vegetable oil
Juice of 1 lemon
Salt and freshly ground pepper

METHOD

Prepare the artichokes as described in the recipe for Braised Stuffed Artichokes on page 14. Cool under running water. Drain and remove choke.

Combine breadcrumbs, garlic, parsley, and pickle. Season the mixture with salt and freshly ground pepper. Stuff the artichokes with the seasoned breadcrumb mixture.

Melt the butter and oil in a sauté pan. Tightly pack the artichokes in the pan, season with salt and pepper, and sprinkle generously with oil and lemon juice. Cover the artichokes and cook over medium heat, basting frequently. Continue cooking until the artichokes are tender but still retain a little crispness.

Arrange the vegetable in a heated dish and serve with the cooking juices.

ARTICHOKE FRITTERS

Beignets d'Artichauts

The artichokes are already cooked, so the beignets are only cooked in oil long enough to make the batter crisp. This technique allows the beignets to remain very light. However they are prepared, they would love the company of a white wine.

INGREDIENTS	SERVES 6

12 medium artichokes

1 recipe fritter batter (see Artichoke, Cauliflower, and Broccoli Fritters page 16)

9 tablespoons peanut oil for the marinade

6 tablespoons freshly squeezed lemon juice

1 tablespoon *fines herbes*: any combination of parsley, tarragon, and chives

Grapeseed oil for deep frying

Salt and freshly ground pepper

METHOD

Cook the artichokes in boiling salted water (see Boiled Artichokes page 11). Remove the choke and leaves; quarter the bottoms and set aside in a bowl.

Prepare the fritter batter as described on page 17. Season with salt and pepper and set aside until ready.

Prepare a marinade with the peanut oil, lemon juice, salt, pepper, and *fines herbes*. Add the artichoke quarters and marinate for at least an hour.

In a large pot, heat enough frying oil to completely submerge the vegetable. Wipe the excess marinade from the artichokes and save it.

Dip the artichoke quarters in the fritter batter. Deep fry in the hot oil; drain on paper towels and serve hot on a large platter. Put the remaining marinade in a small bowl for dipping the beignets.

ARTICHOKES AND MIXED VEGETABLES WITH OLIVES

Macédoine Bretonne

This recipe came from Josephine without a method. When I prepare it, I visualize artichokes and olives garnished with a confetti of mushrooms, celery root, and turnips prepared as a *mirepoix*. That is how the ingredients are styled for use in the restaurant where it would be served with a breast of duck roasted on the bone, accompanied by a wine from the Côtes du Rhône.

When blanching the turnips note that they like a long and slow cooking so that they don't become sulfurous and strong tasting. They provide a nutty sweet taste when they are slow cooked to tenderness.

INGREDIENTS	SERVES 6

¼ pound celery root, ¼-inch dice
½ pound turnips, ¼-inch dice
2 to 4 tablespoons butter
½ pound mushrooms, ¼-inch dice
1 clove garlic, finely minced
3 tablespoons chopped parsley
12 artichoke hearts, cooked and quartered (see Boiled Artichokes page 11)
¼ pound desalted green olives, pitted
Salt and freshly ground pepper

METHOD

Blanch the celery root and turnips in boiling, salted water for 4 to 6 minutes. Remove from the pan with a slotted spoon and drain in a strainer.

In a large skillet, melt the butter over medium-high heat. When the foam starts to subside, add the mushrooms and sauté them with a little salt for 3 to 4 minutes, until they begin to give up their liquid. Toss the mushrooms with the garlic and parsley.

Add the artichokes and all of the blanched vegetables to the mushrooms, and sauté gently until vegetables are cooked to desired doneness, 3 to 4 minutes. Add the olives. (Olives can be cut in spirals to remove their pits; rewind to reassemble the olive.) Season lightly with salt and give a generous grinding of pepper. Serve on a heated platter.

Asparagus

FROM JOSEPHINE'S NOTES

There are several different types of asparagus, but the green or common asparagus is the most widely used. This type resembles the wild asparagus that grows in the meadows and sandy soil in many parts of France, especially on the Atlantic coast. The principal kinds of asparagus grown and appreciated by the French are the Argenteuil, which is white with a purple head, and the purple Genoa. On any species of asparagus, the tips of the stalk, or *pointes d'asperges*, are the most tender and flavorful.

To prepare asparagus, one needn't use a knife. By holding both ends of the stalk between the thumb and index finger of each hand and then bending, the stalk will break at the point between tough and tender parts.

Whereas most Americans do not peel the asparagus, the French always do for two reasons: first, they claim that the asparagus cooks faster and more evenly; and second, because the entire stalk can be eaten to the end without waste. If you do not have an asparagus steamer, it is best to

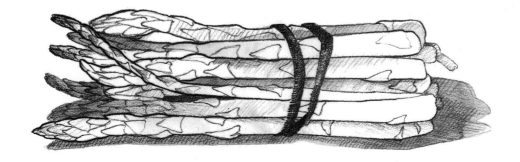

tie the asparagus in bunches and cook it standing up. If you do not wish to eat them whole, break as described above, wash and dry, then cut them as you wish.

Remember that asparagus can be eaten hot or cold, and is wonderful in salads. For example, you might steam or boil the asparagus in chicken stock until tender, drain and cool, and serve smothered in Green Mayonnaise (see page 13). No matter how it is served in the repertoire of Breton cooking, asparagus will always love a marriage with French cider.

VEGETABLE SOUP

Soupe aux Légumes Grandmère

This is a recipe for a don't-waste-anything soup of leftovers and trimmings; the things that Josephine never threw away. It can also be prepared without the noodles and puréed before adding the egg and cream liaison. Serve the soup with a crusty bread and a light red wine from the Côtes de Bordeaux.

INGREDIENTS	SERVES 6

6 tablespoons butter
1 cup chopped onion
2 tablespoons rice flour
4 cups vegetable stock
1 cup thin noodles
Cooked, chopped vegetable stems and discards: broccoli stems, cauliflower leaves, asparagus trimmings
1 egg yolk
½ cup crème fraîche
Salt and freshly ground pepper

METHOD

Melt the butter in a 2-quart pot, add the onion and a pinch of salt and sauté for a few minutes until limp. Add the flour and stir; add the liquid and whisk well. Stir the soup while bringing it to a boil, then simmer.

After 10 minutes, add the noodles and continue to cook for another 10 minutes. Add the cooked, chopped vegetables and continue the cooking to heat through, 3 to 4 minutes.

In a small bowl, mix the egg yolk into the cream; then whisk the mixture into the soup stirring well. Continue heating for another 1 to 2 minutes. Correct the seasonings and serve very hot.

The Use of Asparagus Trimmings: Asparagus is the sort of vegetable that Josephine loved to use to emphasize that nothing should be wasted. Indeed, the wonderful thing about asparagus is that nothing need be discarded. The stalks get trimmed, or even peeled, and these trimmings can be cooked and puréed and used as a complementary flavor to a dish, such as a purée of potatoes. The blanched stalks can be puréed, strained, and mixed into crème fraîche to make an asparagus sauce. Or the purée and eggs can be added to light cream, seasoned with salt and pepper, and made into a vegetable custard.

The Use of Asparagus Blanching Water: The blanching liquid can be made into a broth on its own: for example, a consommé flavored with leeks and finished with orange. Or the liquid can be used for cooking rice, and by obvious extension, for cooking risotto; it gives extra savor. Clearly asparagus comes with a built in gift. Josephine included a recipe for vegetable soup (see page 24), which is typical of this sort of economy.

ASPARAGUS WITH BREADCRUMBS

Asperges à la Polonaise

Crisp fresh vegetables, the soft richness of chopped egg, and the crunch of breadcrumbs flavored with butter make a simple and satisfying dish.

INGREDIENTS	SERVES 6

3 dozen asparagus
2 hard-boiled eggs, finely chopped
4 to 6 tablespoons butter
1 cup breadcrumbs
2 to 4 tablespoons chopped parsley
1 teaspoon salt
Freshly ground pepper

METHOD

Prepare the asparagus by snapping the stem at the weakest point. Reserve these pieces for another purpose as discussed above. With a paring knife, remove the fiber from the outside stalk of each asparagus. When all the asparagus are peeled, plunge into boiling, salted water and blanch until tender. The cooking time depends on the thickness of the asparagus, anywhere from 4 to 10 minutes. Remove them to a colander, and run under cold water to stop the cooking. The cold water also helps to retain their fresh green color. Then drain them to dry on a towel.

Arrange the asparagus with the tips in one direction on a heated serving platter and sprinkle the chopped egg across the root end. Melt some butter in a small pan or skillet, and fry the breadcrumbs until lightly browned. Sprinkle the parsley over the asparagus just above the eggs.

ASPARAGUS WITH BUTTER AND LEMON

Asperges Meunière

The simplest and most honest presentation of asparagus, this dish combines a trio of tastes that are sublime when all the ingredients are at their best.

INGREDIENTS	SERVES 6

3 dozen asparagus, cut diagonally in 1-inch pieces
Juice of 1 lemon
4 tablespoons butter
Salt and freshly ground pepper

METHOD

In a heavy-bottomed skillet, melt the butter and roll the asparagus in it to coat them. Add the lemon juice, a pinch of salt, stir, and cover the pot. On a medium-low flame, allow the asparagus to simmer, to sweat, for about 5 to 8 minutes, until tender. Correct the seasoning and finish with pepper to taste.

ASPARAGUS FRITTERS

Beignets d'Asperges

Serve these beignets as a first course on a plate with orange segments and finely diced shallots. Wring the shallots of their bitterness by placing them inside a kitchen towel and twisting until their juices are extracted. This permits the shallots to be eaten raw. If you would rather sauté the shallots, then cook them lightly in butter and finish with a bit of tarragon. Accompany the dish with a crisp Loire Valley white wine, such as a Sancerre.

INGREDIENTS	SERVES 6

2 pounds asparagus
½ cup peanut oil
3 tablespoons freshly squeezed lemon juice
2 tablespoons cider vinegar
1 tablespoon Dijon mustard
Fritter batter (see Artichoke, Cauliflower, and Broccoli Fritters page 17)
Grapeseed oil for deep frying
Salt and freshly ground pepper

METHOD

Break the asparagus just below the tips. (Reserve the stems for another use such as soup, see Vegetable Soup page 24). Blanch the tips in boiling salted water for 3 to 4 minutes so that they retain some crunch. Drain them in a colander, refresh under cold water, and allow to dry thoroughly.

Prepare a marinade with the oil, lemon juice, vinegar, and mustard. Mix well and add salt and pepper to taste. Marinate the asparagus for a minimum of 30 minutes.

In a large pan, heat enough grapeseed oil to completely submerge the asparagus. Drain the asparagus of any excess vinaigrette and dip them into the fritter batter. Deep fry until they are golden and drain on absorbent paper. Sprinkle with salt and serve hot.

ASPARAGUS IN SMALL CUTS

Pointes d'Asperges en Petits Pois

This dish can be prepared for a roast of lamb garnished simply with herbs and accompanied by a light red Burgundy.

| INGREDIENTS | SERVES 6 |

2 pounds asparagus
4 tablespoons butter
½ pound shelled fresh peas
Green part of 3 to 4 scallions, finely sliced
3 tablespoons heavy cream
Juice of ½ lemon
Salt, freshly ground pepper, and cayenne

METHOD

Prepare the asparagus by breaking the stalk at the weakest point. Use the bottom part of the stalk for other purposes (see page 25). With a paring knife, remove the fiber from the stalk of each asparagus. Cut the remaining tender part of the stalks into pea-size pieces.

Melt the butter in a heavy pan and add the asparagus. Season with salt and a dash of cayenne. Lower the heat and add the peas and scallions. Cook at a simmer for about 7 minutes. Then stir in the cream. Remove from the heat and add the lemon juice. Correct the seasonings, give a grinding of pepper, and serve very hot.

Variation: The pea-size pieces of asparagus can also be blanched in boiling salted water until tender. If you do that, sort out the tips from the stalks and blanch each separately. Then remix, toss in a dry skillet to evaporate the water, and finish with the peas, cream, lemon, seasonings, and garnish with scallions.

ASPARAGUS WITH SOURED CREAM

Asperges à la Sauce Aigre

When asparagus are young and tender, they should be served with the finest of creams, such as those in France from Isigny or Echiré. They can also be served on a bed of tender young lettuce as a composed salad, or with tiny steamed potatoes, the first of the season. However the idea is achieved for the asparagus, present them as a first course.

INGREDIENTS	SERVES 6

24 to 36 asparagus
1 tablespoon olive oil
1 tablespoon cider vinegar
2 tablespoons sugar
1 cup crème fraîche
3 scallions, finely sliced on the diagonal
Salt and freshly ground pepper

METHOD

Prepare the asparagus by breaking the stalk at the weakest point. With a paring knife, remove the fiber from the stalk of each asparagus. Blanch them in boiling salted water. Drain and refresh under cold water to stop the cooking. Set aside.

Mix the oil, vinegar, sugar, and crème fraîche to make a sauce. If the asparagus are to be served warm, toss the asparagus in a small skillet and heat on a low flame only long enough to rewarm the vegetable. Season with salt and freshly ground pepper.

Serve the asparagus on a platter garnished with sliced scallion and pass the sauce in a small pitcher.

Beans

GREEN BEANS FROM THE BRITTANY COAST

Haricots Verts Côte de Bretagne

This recipe calls for the same procedures as Green Beans with Cherries (page 32), with the exception of using small new potatoes instead of

cherries. Serve the green beans with braised rabbit and cornichon sauce, and accompany the dish with a French cider.

INGREDIENTS	SERVES 6

1½ pounds string beans, cut in ½-inch lengths
½ pound very small new potatoes, peeled
1 small bunch scallions or 2 shallots, chopped
2 cloves garlic, minced
4 tablespoons butter
¼ cup chopped parsley
Salt and freshly ground pepper

METHOD

Blanch vegetables in boiling salted water, first the green beans until tender, 4 to 6 minutes, then the potatoes until they can be pierced easily with a skewer. Drain the vegetables when they are cooked and reserve.

While the vegetables blanch, sauté the scallions and garlic in the butter until limp. Add the blanched vegetables to the scallion/garlic mixture. Stir to coat with butter, adding to taste. Toss in the parsley and season with salt and pepper. Serve very hot.

GREEN BEANS AND CELERY ROOT

Haricots Verts et Céleri-Rave

Serve the beans with a roasted pork loin and quartered potatoes sautéed in duck fat, and pour a French cider to drink.

INGREDIENTS   SERVES 6

1 pound green beans, cut in 1-inch lengths
½ pound celery root, cut in ¼-inch julienne
4 to 6 tablespoons butter
6 to 8 radishes, grated
2 to 3 tablespoons cider vinegar
Salt and freshly ground pepper

METHOD

Clean, trim, and prepare all the vegetables and keep ready in bowls. Blanch the green beans in a large pot of boiling salted water for 6 to 8 minutes, until tender, and remove to a colander. Blanch the celery root in the same water for 4 to 6 minutes, until tender. Drain in a colander.

Melt the butter in a skillet. Add the beans and celery root and toss to coat. When they are rewarmed, season with salt and pepper. Stir in the grated radishes and pour vinegar over in a thin stream; toss everything well and serve hot.

GREEN BEANS WITH CHERRIES

Haricots Verts Montmorency

This is a wonderful dish of the foraged foods of La Mère Jacquette. In Brittany the cherries would be from the woods, the beans and herbs from the garden. Serve it with a roast of chicken, along with a plain gratin of potato and a chilled bottle of French cider.

INGREDIENTS   SERVES 6

4 to 6 tablespoons butter
1 pound green beans
¼ pound cherries, pitted
Persillade: 2 tablespoons chopped parsley mixed with 1 clove mince
    garlic
1 tablespoon finely chopped fresh tarragon
Salt and freshly ground pepper

METHOD

Clean the green beans, trim the ends, and cut them on a steep diagonal
about ¼-inch wide (French cut). Melt the butter, add the green beans,
and gently toss to coat. Season with salt, and cover the pot and cook on
a medium-low flame so that they gently sweat (*étuver*) to doneness, 8 to
10 minutes.

Add the cherries, correct the seasoning, and give a fresh grind of
pepper. Make sure the cherries are heated through before serving. Sprinkle with parsley, garlic, and tarragon and serve.

Variation

½ pound green beans, in ¼-inch French cut
1 cup cherries, pitted
1 to 2 tablespoons butter, in pea-size pieces
2 tablespoons chopped parsley
½ clove garlic, minced
1 tablespoon chopped fresh tarragon
Salt and freshly ground pepper

METHOD

Blanch the beans in boiling salted water until tender, about 4 or 5
minutes. Drain them in a colander and refresh under cold water.

Put the green beans in a dry skillet and heat them until the surface
moisture evaporates. Add the cherries, herbs, garlic, and butter, tossing
to coat well; correct the seasonings and serve at once.

GREEN BEAN AND CHICKPEA SALAD

Salade d'Haricots Verts et de Pois Chiches

Prepare this dish with enough time to allow it to rest for an hour so the flavors can develop. Enjoy it with a good red table wine, such as those from Corbières, along with a crusty bread; and dream of France because this dish carries the tastes of France.

INGREDIENTS   SERVES 6 TO 8

1½ cups uncooked chickpeas

Vinaigrette
6 anchovy filets, soaked in water to desalt
1 tablespoon Dijon mustard
¾ cup olive oil
Freshly squeezed lemon juice
Pinch of nutmeg

½ cup green beans, cut in ¼-inch julienne
6 olives, green or black, pitted and finely chopped
¼ green pepper, finely chopped
5 to 6 radishes, grated and salted
4 scallions, sliced paper thin
1 clove garlic, minced
2 to 4 tablespoons chopped *fines herbes*: parsley, chives, and tarragon
Salt and freshly ground pepper

METHOD

Soak the chickpeas in water overnight. Drain, put in a large pot, and cover with cold water. Cook at a simmer 1 to 1½ hours, until tender. Drain in a colander.

Prepare the vinaigrette. Crush the anchovies in a mortar and mix with the mustard to make a smooth paste. Slowly add the olive oil drop by drop, whisking as you would in making mayonnaise. Season with salt and pepper. Lighten it with a few drops of lemon juice and add nutmeg.

Prepare all the vegetables; cut the green beans and blanch them in

boiling salted water for 4 to 6 minutes. Pit and chop the olives; julienne, peel, and dice the green pepper; grate the radishes; cut the scallions paper thin on the bias, and mince the garlic.

In a large bowl, mix the blanched green beans and the chickpeas with the vinaigrette. Add the olives, pepper, and radishes. Toss all the remaining ingredients and correct seasoning if necessary. Allow the dish to rest an hour before serving.

MIXED BEANS

Haricots Panachés

Present these beans in a vegetable dish to accompany a roast of chicken with prune sauce, and serve a red wine from Chinon.

INGREDIENTS   SERVES 6

1 cup dried white beans or flageolets
Bouquet garni: thyme and bay leaf tied in 2 celery stalks
1 pound green beans, cut in ½-inch pieces
4 tablespoons butter
1 medium onion, finely diced
1 tablespoon chopped chervil or parsley
Salt and freshly ground pepper

METHOD

Soak the dried beans in cold water overnight. Drain and put into a large pot, and cover with cold water 2 inches above the beans. Simmer at least 1 hour. The beans should be soft, keep their shape, and not split. Drain and return the beans to the pot.

Fifteen minutes before the dried beans are cooked, blanch the green beans in boiling water, adding salt after the water comes back to a boil. Blanch 6 to 8 minutes to desired doneness, then drain and add them to the pot of cooked beans.

In a small skillet, melt 1 tablespoon butter and sauté the onion until

very lightly browned. Add the onion to the beans. Mix in 3 tablespoons butter broken into small pieces, along with the chervil, and season with salt and pepper.

BEANS AND WATERCRESS

Haricots au Cresson

In different parts of France, watercress is used as a garnish, just like parsley. The tender peppery leaves of the watercress are a wonderful addition to the beans fattened in butter. The beans can be served with any roast meat and like the accompaniment of a light red wine from the Loire Valley, such as a wine from Sancerre.

INGREDIENTS	SERVES 6

½ pound dry white beans
Bouquet garni: parsley, thyme, bay leaf, tied in celery stalks
1 medium onion, whole, stuck with 1 clove
1 medium carrot, finely diced
6 tablespoons butter
1 bunch watercress, coarsely chopped
1 bunch scallions, coarsely chopped
Salt and freshly ground pepper

METHOD

Soak the beans in cold water overnight. Drain, put into a large pot, and cover with cold water. Add the bouquet garni tied with kitchen string, the onion, and carrot. Cook at a simmer for 1 to 1½ hours, until the beans are soft but haven't split. Strain the liquid and return the beans to the pot.

Toss the beans with the butter broken into pieces along with the chopped watercress and scallions. Season with salt and freshly ground pepper to taste. Serve very hot.

RED BEANS IN WINE

Haricots Secs au Vin Rouge

Serve in a large flat soup bowl and garnish with sautéed chard, some good crusty bread, and a friendly red wine from the Côtes du Rhône. This provides a satisfying lunch or light supper.

INGREDIENTS	SERVES 6

2 cups dried red beans
1 ham hock or ¼ pound lean salt pork
1 carrot, sliced
1 onion, whole, stuck with 3 cloves
2 tablespoons chopped shallots
2 tablespoons butter
2 tablespoons flour
1 cup red wine: Burgundy or Bordeaux
2 to 4 tablespoons chopped chervil
Salt and freshly ground pepper

METHOD

Soak the beans overnight in enough cold water to cover. Drain them in a colander and reserve.

In a 2-quart saucepan, boil the ham hock for 10 minutes to remove some salt. Follow the same procedure for the salt pork.

To a large pot, add the ham hock, beans, carrots, and onion. Cover with cold water 2 inches above the beans. Bring to a boil and simmer until the beans are tender but not split, about 1½ to 2 hours.

In a skillet, sauté the chopped shallots in 2 tablespoons butter until limp, not brown. Remove the ham hock from the beans and dice finely. Add the meat to shallots and cook until the meat is lightly browned. Add 2 tablespoons of flour and cook 3 to 4 minutes. Add the wine and simmer for 10 minutes.

Drain off any excess water from the beans and add the meat and wine

sauce to the beans. Season with salt and pepper if necessary, and sprinkle with chervil. Toss well and serve hot.

Beets

BEETS WITH FRESH BLACK CURRANTS

Betteraves au Cassis

This recipe comes from the repertoire of La Mère Jacquette. Serve it with braised rabbit. I have also taken the elements of this recipe—beets and currants—and used them in many fashions. For a very elegant first course at Le Trou restaurant, we make the beets into a vegetable custard. I use the same amount of cooked beets called for in this recipe. They are puréed, added to 3 eggs with a cup of light cream, and baked. The onions can be sautéed in a skillet until they are well caramelized and then flavored with vinegar; this yields a kind of *confiture*, or jam, which is used to garnish the custard along with the currants and herbs. As a first course, or to accompany poached medallions of salmon, the dish is accompanied by a flowery Gewürztraminer from the Alsace.

INGREDIENTS	SERVES 6

3 medium red beets
1 tablespoon butter
1 tablespoon peanut oil
2 scallions, sliced
1 clove garlic, finely minced
2 tablespoons cider vinegar
1 cup fresh black currants
2 to 4 tablespoons chopped parsley and tarragon
Salt and freshly ground pepper

Preheat oven to 400 degrees. Bake the beets until tender, about 45 minutes. Remove to a cutting board and when cool enough to handle, peel the beets and cut them into ¼-inch dice, about the size of the currants.

In a skillet, heat the butter with the oil and sauté the scallions and garlic for 2 to 3 minutes. Add the beets and vinegar, tossing to coat the vegetables, and continue to heat until they are well warmed. Roll the currants in with the beets, season everything with salt and some fresh grindings of pepper. Add the herbs and toss everything well. Serve at once.

Broccoli

BROCCOLI FRITTERS

Beignets de Brocoli

These little fritters can be used as a part of a very interesting assortment of first course tastes. They can be served with a garnish of tomatoes with a green grape and cognac dressing; accompany a vegetable like celery root, cut in julienne matchsticks and flavored with an apple mayonnaise; or be part of a composed salad of blanched vegetables and mussels in vinaigrette.

1 bunch broccoli
Juice of 1 lemon
2 tablespoons chopped parsley plus some parsley flowerets
Fritter batter (see page 17)
Grapeseed oil for deep frying
Salt and freshly ground pepper

METHOD

Trim broccoli into flowerets. Blanch in boiling salted water until lightly done, about 3 to 5 minutes. Refresh under cold water and dry completely.

Marinate the broccoli in the lemon juice, salt, pepper, and a tablespoon of parsley; allow to sit for at least 20 minutes.

When ready to serve, dip broccoli into the fritter batter and deep fry in hot grapeseed oil until golden. Drain the cooked vegetable on paper towels, and place on a heated platter.

Dip whole parsley flowerets into the hot oil and fry. Garnish the broccoli with the fried parsley and a sprinkling of fresh chopped parsley. Season with salt and pepper. Serve at once.

BROCCOLI WITH BROWNED BUTTER

Brocoli au Beurre Noir

This dish could be served with medallions of pork with hazelnuts, a ragout of sweet peppers and zucchini, and then accompanied by a fresh young Beaujolais or a light fruity Italian Chianti.

INGREDIENTS	SERVES 4 TO 6

1 bunch broccoli
4 tablespoons butter
Juice of ½ lemon
2 to 4 tablespoons chopped parsley
Salt and freshly ground pepper

METHOD

Trim the broccoli into flowerets. Cut the stems into 1 to 1½ inch lengths and peel the stems of the tough outer skin. Julienne the inner flesh in ¼-inch matchsticks. Blanch the flowerets and stems in boiling salted water until done, about 4 to 6 minutes. Flush under cold water to stop the cooking and set to drain in a non-aluminum colander.

Melt the butter in a skillet and heat gradually over medium flame until the butter particles brown first to a golden color and then a golden hazelnut. Be careful not to work too fast or the butter will burn.

Rewarm the vegetable in a dry skillet to rid it of any excess water. Sprinkle with the lemon juice and chopped parsley. Pour over the melted, browned butter; season with salt and freshly ground pepper and serve while still warm.

Cabbages

The cabbage family is one of the largest vegetable families; it includes a variety of vegetables that Americans think of in different ways. For example, we speak of both the green and red cabbage in this group, but it also includes cauliflower, broccoli, brussels sprouts, and kohlrabi. In this book, turnips, which are also in this group, have a section of their own. However, the same cooking methods apply to these different vegetables: they can be steamed, braised, and so forth. They are sulfurous vegetables and if they are cooked too hot their natural sulfur is activated. These vegetables need long, slow cooking. They also like to be fat, that is to say they like lots of butter.

Cabbage can be served raw marinated, with vinaigrette (see page 74) or mayonnaise (page 94). To serve cabbage this way, it is usually cut into

thin strips. Green cabbage is generally used for sauerkraut. *Choucroute garni*, which is based on cabbage, is the national dish of the Alsace and has the distinction of being a recipe both in the repertoire of haute cuisine and the cuisine of the countryside. Traditionally cabbage is one of the primary ingredients of the peasant soup of the southwest of France known as *garbure*.

BRUSSELS SPROUTS IN CREAM

Choux de Bruxelles à la Crème

It is important to remember when blanching cabbage family vegetables that the cooking should go slowly, because with slower cooking they develop a sweetness. "Cabbage loves to be fat," Josephine would say; it is a guideline for flavoring this dish.

Serve Brussels Sprouts in Cream with a sautéed leg of chicken stuffed with Roquefort and walnuts, garnished with sautéed apple quarters. Accompany the dish with a cold French cider.

INGREDIENTS	SERVES 6

1½ pounds brussels sprouts
2 tablespoons butter
¾ cup heavy cream
Salt and freshly ground pepper
2 to 4 tablespoons chopped parsley
Juice of ½ lemon

METHOD

Trim the root end of the brussels sprouts and score with an "X" ⅛-inch deep. Remove any flawed leaves. Blanch the vegetable in boiling salted water. Turn the heat to simmer and slowly cook the sprouts until tender, about 10 to 15 minutes. Drain them in a colander and chop coarsely.

In a skillet, melt 2 tablespoons butter and add the chopped sprouts, tossing to coat. When they are warm, add the cream and continue to simmer until the cream has almost evaporated.

Just before serving, add the lemon juice and parsley; toss well and serve hot.

GRATIN OF BRUSSELS SPROUTS

Choux de Bruxelles au Gratin

One technique for cooking certain vegetables calls for two blanchings. It is used to create a change of temperature—cold-hot, cold-hot—which breaks down fiber and eliminates elements that make digestion difficult.

This gratin can also be done by adding sautéed apples or ham to the sprouts and then baking as directed in the recipe.

INGREDIENTS	SERVES 6

1 pound brussels sprouts, washed, trimmed, and damaged leaves removed (see Brussels Sprouts in Cream page 43)
4 tablespoons butter
4 tablespoons flour
1½ cups milk, warmed
Nutmeg
½ cup Gruyère cheese, grated
1 egg yolk
½ cup crème fraîche
Salt and freshly ground pepper

METHOD

Preheat oven to 375 degrees. Blanch the brussels sprouts in boiling water for 1 minute. Drain and drop into a second pot of boiling water. Add salt and cook rapidly for 7 to 8 minutes. Drain well and dry. Season with salt and pepper and set aside.

To prepare a white sauce (page 80), melt 4 tablespoons butter in a small saucepan. Add the flour, stir, and gradually add milk. Season with salt, freshly ground pepper, and nutmeg. Simmer for at least 10 minutes, stirring to prevent scorching. Keep warm.

Remove the sauce from heat and stir in two thirds of the cheese. Combine the yolk and crème fraîche and stir into the sauce, mixing completely. Butter an oven-proof gratin dish and arrange the brussels sprouts inside. Pour the sauce over the sprouts and sprinkle with the remaining cheese. Bake for 10 minutes, until the cheese is melted.

BRUSSELS SPROUTS WITH MUSHROOMS AND HERBS

Choux de Bruxelles aux Champignons et à la Sarriette

Serve this dish with a pan-fried steak and a purée of potatoes, accompanied by a red wine from the Loire, such as Chinon.

INGREDIENTS	SERVES 6

2 tablespoons butter
¼ cup sliced onions
¼ pound mushrooms, sliced or quartered
1 pound brussels sprouts, blanched tender (see Brussel Sprouts in Cream page 43)
2 tablespoons chopped fresh summer savory or tarragon
Salt and freshly ground pepper

METHOD

Heat the butter in a skillet; when the foam subsides add the onions and sauté 1 minute. Add the mushrooms with a pinch of salt, tossing well to coat the mushrooms with butter and continue to sauté until they begin to give up their water.

Add the blanched brussels sprouts, tossing again to distribute the ingredients. Cover the pan and allow the vegetables to come to temperature, perhaps 5 minutes. Uncover and evaporate any liquid left in the

pan, add the chopped herbs, correct the seasoning, and serve hot with additional butter, if desired.

BRUSSELS SPROUTS WITH SPRING VEGETABLES

Choux de Bruxelles Printanière

The brussels sprouts are scored with an "X" on the bottom to allow the heat to penetrate the dense part of the root so that the vegetable cooks to the center.

This preparation goes well with a roast of lamb garnished with lentils or some other dry legume, such as white beans, and accompanied by a southern Rhône wine to drink.

INGREDIENTS	SERVES 6

2 tablespoons butter
2 tablespoons peanut oil
½ cup diced celery root, or celery stalk and leaves, diced
2 medium turnips, peeled and shredded
1 pound tomatoes, peeled, seeded, and chopped

½ cup fresh peas

1 pound brussels sprouts, blanched tender (see Brussels Sprouts in Cream page 43)

2 tablespoons mixed herbs: oregano, marjoram, parsley, or tarragon (any combination)

1 bunch of spring onions, finely sliced on the diagonal

Salt and freshly ground pepper

METHOD

Melt the butter and oil in a skillet and sauté the celery root and turnips until tender, about 5 to 7 minutes. Add the tomato and peas, season with a bit of salt and continue to cook covered until the peas are tender, another 5 minutes.

When the peas are almost cooked, add the brussels sprouts and herbs, and continue to heat long enough to rewarm the sprouts. Uncover the pot and allow any liquid that has accumulated to reduce or evaporate. Add the spring onions and toss everything well. Correct the seasonings, give a grinding of fresh pepper, and serve hot.

BRUSSELS SPROUTS AND SWEET PEPPERS

Choux de Bruxelles aux Poivrons

Serve this dish with sautéed lamb chops, and noodles tossed with garlic and parsley. Drizzle fresh olive oil, as though it were butter, on the noodles just before serving.

Herbs can be added to a dish at the beginning of the cooking to give flavor to the base of the dish, or they can be added at the end of the cooking where they greet the palate with the fresh tastes of the garden. Certain herbs used at the beginning can be added again just before serving to refresh them if their oils are volatile and fragile.

1 pound brussels sprouts, blanched tender (see Brussels Sprouts in
   Cream page 43)
2 tablespoons olive oil
½ cup finely chopped onions
1 red bell pepper, cut in ¼-inch strips and peeled (see page 228)
1 green bell pepper, cut in ¼-inch strips and peeled (see page 228)
½ cup finely diced celery root
3 cloves of garlic, chopped
2 tablespoons *fines herbes:* tarragon, chives, parsley, or chervil (any
   combination)
2 tablespoons butter
Salt and freshly ground pepper

METHOD

While the brussels sprouts blanch, heat the olive oil in a large skillet.
Sauté the onions and peeled sweet peppers with a pinch or two of salt
for 3 to 4 minutes, until they start to get limp. Add the celery root and
garlic and continue to cook for 5 more minutes, until tender. Add the
blanched brussels sprouts, cover, and cook for 5 minutes until everything
is well heated. Correct the seasonings, and give a grinding of pepper.
Add the chopped herbs and the butter broken into pea-size pieces; toss
everything well. Serve hot.

RED CABBAGE WITH APPLES AND RAISINS

Chou Rouge aux Pommes

This red cabbage can be served with poached salmon garnished with
bacon and chopped herbs, and steamed potatoes, and accompanied by a
Pinot Blanc from the Alsace.

4 tablespoons butter
1 tablespoon chicken or duck fat
½ cup chopped celery leaves
1 cup chopped onion
1 head red cabbage, coarsely shredded
1¼ cups red wine
2 apples, peeled and grated
⅓ to ½ cup raisins, soaked in ½ cup white wine
Butter for seasoning
2 to 4 tablespoons chopped parsley
Salt and freshly ground pepper

METHOD

Melt butter and chicken fat in a braising pot. Add celery and onion and sauté for a few minutes. Add the cabbage and season with salt. Cook for a few minutes to coat the cabbage with fats. Add the wine and apples; cover and cook until tender, about 20 to 25 minutes. Add the raisins during the last five minutes.

Most of the liquid should be absorbed by the time the cabbage is tender. If it needs more liquid during the cooking, don't hesitate to add more wine from soaking the raisins, or water. When it is ready to present, add a generous pat of butter and freshly chopped parsley, correct the seasonings, and serve.

RED CABBAGE WITH BLUEBERRIES

Chou Rouge Forestière

La Mère Jacquette would have used whatever wild berries she found in the woods. In California, I use any wild or blue berries.

The flavor of the mushrooms can be boosted by the addition of dried, wild mushrooms (see page 215). The water to revive them is also added, and reduced with the regular, white mushrooms and the revived, chopped wild mushrooms. Mushrooms always get a bit of garlic and parsley; as Josephine often commented, without those elements, *"Cela ne vaut pas le pet de lapin,"* (it's not worth the fart of a rabbit). This particular dish goes well with pork, lamb, sausage, or game, and is very delicious.

INGREDIENTS	SERVES 6

5 tablespoons butter
2 tablespoons bacon fat
1 onion thinly sliced
1 small head red cabbage, shredded
½ cup red wine
½ pound mushrooms, sliced
Persillade: 1 small clove garlic, minced, and 2 to 4 tablespoons chopped parsley
1 cup fresh blueberries
Salt and freshly ground pepper

METHOD

Heat 2 tablespoons of butter and the bacon fat in a heavy pot. Add the onion and sauté until they are lightly browned. Add the shredded cabbage and red wine; season with salt and cook over slow heat, covered, for 20 to 30 minutes, until the cabbage is tender.

While the cabbage is braising, sauté the mushrooms in 2 tablespoons butter in a hot skillet without letting them render their water. Season with salt and pepper; toss with the *persillade*.

On a low flame, add the mushrooms to the cabbage. When everything is warm, add the raw berries and toss with 1 additional tablespoon butter. Correct the seasonings and serve.

BRAISED CABBAGE

Chou Vert Braisé

The cabbage is blanched before it is set to bake in a braising pan in the oven. The blanching helps make the fibrous vegetable more digestible. Long, slow cooking results in a cabbage that is tender, digestible, and sweet. It could be served on its own as a vegetable, or with roasted duck and pear sauce accompanied by a fruity Beaujolais.

INGREDIENTS   SERVES 4 TO 6

¼ pound pancetta or bacon
1 large cabbage (approximately 2 pounds)
Mirepoix: tiny dice of 2 onions and 1 carrot
2 to 3 tablespoons butter
Bouquet garni: 1 bay leaf and a sprig of thyme tied in celery stalks
1 cup chicken or veal stock, good homemade (see page 331)
Salt, freshly ground pepper, and nutmeg

METHOD

If you are using fresh, uncured bacon, cut it into ¾-inch dice and simmer for 30 minutes in boiling water; rinse and refresh under cold water. Cut cured bacon or pancetta in ¾-inch dice; do not precook.

Cut the cabbage into quarters, remove and discard tough outer leaves. Blanch the quarters in boiling salted water for 5 minutes, refresh under cold water, and drain.

Preheat oven to 350 degrees. Sauté the *mirepoix* in butter for a few minutes. Arrange the vegetables in the bottom of an oven-proof casserole and place the bouquet garni and the cabbage on top. Season with salt, pepper, and nutmeg to taste. Scatter the bacon pieces throughout and pour the stock over all. Bring the liquid to a boil on top of the stove. Cover the pan and place it in a preheated oven for 1 to 1½ hours.

CABBAGE WITH AN ASSORTMENT OF VEGETABLES

Chou Panaché

This is a cabbage to be treated with *panache*, i.e., style. The vegetables should be prepared (cut, chopped, shredded) at one time and kept in separate containers. The work goes more smoothly if all this preparation is done before the cooking starts. Serve this dish with a roast duck and quarters of potatoes sautéed in butter. Accompany the dish with a southern Rhône wine.

INGREDIENTS	SERVES 6

2 to 3 whole beets
1 small head of cabbage, thinly sliced
½ to 1 cup white wine or French cider
1 small rutabaga, ½-inch dice
2 to 3 medium carrots, ⅛-inch julienne
12 dry apricots, revived in water
¼ cup pitted olives
10 coriander seeds
4 juniper berries
1 dry sage leaf
2 to 3 tablespoons butter
Persillade: 1 clove of garlic, finely minced, and 2 to 4 tablespoons chopped parsley
Salt and freshly ground pepper

METHOD

Bake the beets in a 375 degree oven for an hour, until a skewer can pierce them easily. While the beets are roasting, prepare the other vegetables. Keep them separate and ready on a tray.

Put the cabbage in a large skillet with a tight fitting lid, add ½ to 1 cup white wine or cider and a generous pinch of salt; simmer slowly until the cabbage is tender, about 45 minutes to an hour.

While the cabbage is cooking, bring a large pot of water to a boil, add a teaspoon of salt, and blanch the rutabaga 3 to 4 minutes; add the carrots and blanch 4 to 6 minutes more, until both vegetables are tender. Drain the carrots and rutabaga and keep them ready. Cube the cooked beets to the same size dice as the rutabaga.

When the cabbage is tender, mix in all the remaining vegetables, season with salt, and rewarm them. Add the apricots and olives. Taste again for seasoning and correct. Grind the coriander seeds, juniper berries, and sage in a mortar to a coarse powder. Finish the dish with butter, and the *persillade*, along with the ground spices and some grindings of pepper.

CABBAGE AND RUTABAGAS WITH ALMONDS

Chou en Macédoine

This cabbage can be served with a roast of pork, and noodles prepared with mustard and cream. Accompany this dish with a Pinot Noir from the Alsace.

The carcass of a goose or duck makes stock just as the carcass of the chicken does. The bonus is that when the stock is made from goose or duck and then refrigerated, the fat that solidifies on the surface is a flavorful cooking medium. Naturally, as with most fats, use it with discretion.

INGREDIENTS	SERVES 6

1 bunch small beets, with greens
2 tablespoons goose or duck fat
4 tablespoons butter
1 medium rutabaga, shredded
1 small cabbage, shredded
Juice of 1 lemon
⅓ cup slivered almonds
Salt and freshly ground pepper

Remove the greens from the beets; wash and set aside. Cook the whole beets in boiling salted water until tender, drain and when they are cool enough to handle, peel and cut them into ½-inch dice.

In a skillet, melt 2 tablespoons goose fat with 2 tablespoons butter. Add the rutabaga and shredded cabbage and toss to coat with the fat. Season with salt and lemon juice. Cover and cook over low heat until tender. Stir occasionally to keep the vegetables from sticking and scorching, adding more fat if necessary to keep the vegetables moist.

In a separate skillet, melt 2 tablespoons butter and sauté the beet greens until limp. Toss in the cubed beets and heat enough to rewarm the vegetables; season with salt and pepper.

When the cabbage is completely cooked tender, combine with the beet mixture. Add the almonds, correct the seasonings, and serve.

CABBAGE SOUP FROM THE VENDEE

Soupe au Chou Vert Vendéenne

The Vendée is the region along France's Atlantic coast just below Nantes, a city that once belonged in Brittany. Something called *Vendéenne* or *à la Vendée* would first make me think of classical French, or Parisian, cooking. I have included it in this section because it evokes a local style. This soup can also be puréed and finished with a garnish of parsley and a compound butter made with equal parts Roquefort and butter. In any case, serve with a good crusty French bread and a crisp white vin de Haut Poitou.

6 tablespoons butter
1 onion, finely chopped
1 large leek, white part only, finely sliced
1 large carrot, sliced
½ cup chopped celery or celery root

2 cups potatoes, ½-inch dice
1 green cabbage, finely sliced
¼ cup flour
6 cups chicken stock, good homemade (see page 331)
¼ cup chopped parsley
Salt and freshly ground pepper

METHOD

Melt the butter in a large pot; add the onion and leek, and give a pinch or two of salt; sauté 2 to 3 minutes. Add the carrot, celery, potatoes, and cabbage, tossing everything well to coat the vegetables with butter. Sprinkle lightly with salt and cook 3 to 5 minutes, until everything is warm.

Add the flour, tossing again to coat everything and allow the vegetables to cook another 3 to 5 minutes. Add the heated stock and bring the soup to a boil. Turn the heat to a simmer and cook, covered, until all the vegetables are tender. Do not hesitate to add more broth if necessary. Season to taste. Add the parsley and freshly ground pepper when the soup is served.

CAULIFLOWER AND SHRIMP SALAD

Chou-Fleur à la Bretonne

Serve this salad from Brittany with a good crusty bread and drink a French cider. The pancetta called for in this recipe is found in Italian delicatessens; it is a rolled bacon that is flavored with ground pepper. It is recommended where pork fatback is called for in Josephine's recipes. It is cut in ½-inch-thick slices from the roll. The resulting strip is laid out flat and then cut into ½-inch lengths; these pieces are called lardons. To render their fat, sauté slowly in a skillet to a golden brown, or drop into boiling water and simmer for 10 minutes. I find that when they are sautéed in a little butter after blanching, they turn golden rather quickly and have a creamy interior texture and very flavorful taste.

In France, dandelion greens are usually found at farmer's markets.

They are most often sold by someone who has the time to gather them, like grandpa or grandma. The best I have ever found were presented in a small basket, and whoever wanted to buy them had to take the whole lot. This kind of green is about the size of a silver dollar, and once cleaned it is quickly sautéed limp in the fat rendered from bacon, such as pancetta.

The type of dandelion greens found in U.S. markets is anywhere from 18 to 24 inches long, and while it is the same plant as the one found in France, it clearly requires a different cooking approach. Usually it is chopped into ½-inch lengths and blanched in boiling salted water until tender.

California markets have tender young lettuce available in the name of frisée, which can be used in place of dandelion greens. If someone is available to gather true dandelion greens, however, there is nothing like them.

INGREDIENTS   SERVES 4

1 head cauliflower, in flowerets
2 cups water with juice of 1 lemon

Vinaigrette
3 tablespoons cider vinegar
1 teaspoon Dijon mustard
Pinch of cayenne pepper
Salt and freshly ground pepper
½ cup peanut oil

¼ pound pancetta, cut in ¾-inch lardons (see above)
1 cup small bay shrimp, cooked
1 cup cooked navy beans
Chives or white of 2 to 3 scallions, finely sliced
2 to 3 tablespoons chopped chervil and/or parsley
1 shallot, minced
1 cup dandelion greens, chicory, or other tender salad greens
2 hard-boiled eggs

METHOD

Soak the cauliflower in the lemon water for 30 minutes and rinse. Make the vinaigrette by mixing the vinegar, mustard, and seasonings, then slowly whisk in the oil with a fork.

Dry the cauliflower and toss it with half the vinaigrette, allowing to marinate for an hour.

Blanch the lardons in boiling water for 10 minutes. The sauté them golden in butter and set aside. In a bowl, combine the lardons, shrimp, beans, chives, herbs, and shallot. Season with salt and give a few grindings of pepper.

In a salad bowl, add the dandelions or chicory cut in small pieces. If the greens are young and tender, use them as they are; if the leaves are large and tough, blanch for 2 to 3 minutes. Add the remaining vinaigrette, toss, and arrange on six individual salad plates. Garnish each in the center with the shrimp and bean mixture. Cut the eggs lengthwise in quarters and garnish each portion with two pieces.

COUNTRY-STYLE KOHLRABI

Chou-Rave Paysanne

Double cooking some vegetables makes them more digestible; this recipe is a case in point (see page 44). Serve the kohlrabi with pan-fried trout and a gratin of potatoes, accompanied by a Chardonnay from the Jura. Use pancetta in place of the pork breast for a variation. Cut it into lardons (see previous recipe) and slowly brown in a skillet. Reserve enough fat to sauté the onions. Then mix in the blanched kohlrabi with the onions, bacon, and flavorings. Alternatively, kohlrabi can be enriched with a bit of reduced cream and perhaps a garnish of chopped dill or chervil.

INGREDIENTS	SERVES 6

½ pound fresh breast of pork, or ½ pound pancetta in two ½-inch slices
Bouquet garni: parsley, thyme, and a bay leaf tied inside 2 celery
  stalks
2 onions, whole, each stuck with a clove
1 to 2 cups dry white wine
4 heads of kohlrabi
2 medium onions, thinly sliced
Pinch of cayenne
1 tablespoon chopped parsley
1 tablespoon butter
Salt and freshly ground pepper

METHOD

In a large pot, cover the breast of pork with cold water and bring to a boil. Add the bouquet garni, onions, and white wine; simmer for 45 minutes.

Peel the kohlrabi and cut into a julienne. Blanch in boiling salted water for 4 to 6 minutes.

Cut the cooked pork breast into cubes. In a large skillet, sauté the pork in its own fat. Remove the meat and set aside. Discard some of the fat, reserving enough to sauté the onions. Add the onions and sauté until soft but not brown. Add the kohlrabi and cook slowly until tender, approximately 20 to 25 minutes.

Add the browned pork to the cooked kohlrabi and season with salt and pepper to taste. Add a pinch of cayenne and the parsley. Toss in butter broken into pea-size pieces, mixing to coat well. Correct seasoning, give a grinding of pepper, and serve at once.

SAUERKRAUT SOUP

Soupe à la Choucroute

This is "comfort" food to be served with dark-grained bread and a bottle of beer. And so much the better if the sauerkraut is homemade. Before preparing, be sure to read Josephine's notes on preparing cabbage (page 42).

INGREDIENTS	SERVES 6

1½ pounds sauerkraut, fresh or canned
1 large onion, finely chopped
4 tablespoons butter, goose fat, or bacon fat
10 cups chicken or veal stock, good homemade (see page 331)
2 cups dry white wine
1 tablespoon caraway or anise seeds
¼ cup chopped parsley
Butter for garnish
Salt and freshly ground pepper

METHOD

If the sauerkraut is fresh, soak in cold water overnight to desalt completely. Rinse and then drain it. In a 4-quart soup pot, sauté the onion in the butter or fat. Chop the sauerkraut coarsely and add it to the onion, mixing well. Add the stock and the wine, and bring to a boil.

Tie the seeds in a little cloth, add to the soup, and allow to simmer for 1½ to 2 hours. The liquid reduces to about 2 quarts.

When ready to serve, remove the seed pouch and correct the seasoning. Serve the soup with a garnish of chopped parsley and a generous pat of butter for each portion.

Carrots

CARROTS WITH CREAM

Carottes à la Flamande

Serve this dish with rabbit braised in stock, along with steamed potatoes. One might drink a light red wine from Chinon for simple satisfaction.

I have seen Josephine reach for a bottle of cider and pour it into a pan whenever she needed liquid. Once a student asked her why she used cider and her natural response was, "Well, it tastes better than water, don't you agree?" This dish of carrots could be cooked like that, using cider for the liquid.

I also prepare carrot loaves at the restaurant using these flavors. When the carrots are cooked in liquid, I chop half of them very coarsely. I mix the coarse and whole carrots together. Then I add cream, eggs, and seasonings, and mix everything together. I place half of this mixture in a small glass loaf pan, cover it with loads of parsley (and sometimes a little grated Gruyère cheese), then spread the second half of the carrot mixture over the filling. It is set to bake in a water bath in a slow oven for about 20 to 30 minutes.

INGREDIENTS	SERVES 6

2 pounds carrots
2 tablespoons butter
1 teaspoon sugar
½ cup liquid: French cider, stock, or water
2 egg yolks
4 ounces heavy cream
Chopped parsley
Salt and freshly ground pepper

METHOD

Prepare the carrots by washing and scraping. Cut them crosswise on the diagonal into ½-inch slices. Melt the butter in a heavy pan, add the carrots, and toss. Season with a pinch of salt and the sugar. Add the liquid, cover and simmer for 15 to 20 minutes. The carrots should be caramelized slightly by the time they are cooked. Check them while cooking to be sure the liquid hasn't completely evaporated and that they don't burn. Ideally, the carrots should be done when the liquid evaporates.

In a small bowl, blend the egg yolks and cream thoroughly using a fork. Remove the carrots from the heat and stir in the yolk/cream mixture. Season with salt, place the carrots back on a heat diffuser over a slow flame to warm the sauce and to thicken it gently, so the eggs don't curdle. Sprinkle with chopped parsley, give a grinding of pepper, and serve hot.

CARROTS WITH GRAPES

Carottes aux Raisins

Serve these carrots with a small roasted bird and sautéed potatoes with herbs, accompanied by a rosé from Anjou.

It is possible that this recipe of Josephine's represents one of La Mère Jacquette's foraged dishes, although there are also dishes cooked with grapes in classic French cooking. I have the impression that the sugar is needed for the grapes rather than for the carrots, because they might be sour or wild.

INGREDIENTS	SERVES 6

3 tablespoons butter plus an extra tablespoon
2 bunches young carrots, cleaned
1 cup chicken stock, cider, or wine
½ pound seedless grapes
1 tablespoon sugar (optional)
1 tablespoon chopped mint
1 tablespoon chopped parsley
Salt and freshly ground pepper

METHOD

In a saucepan large enough to hold the carrots, melt 3 tablespoons butter. Add the carrots whole, tossing to coat with the butter, give a pinch of salt, and add the stock. Cover and cook on low heat for 15 minutes, until tender.

Peel the grapes while the carrots cook. Add the grapes and the sugar, if desired, and toss well to mix the ingredients. Add 1 tablespoon of butter broken into pea-size pieces; then add the mint and parsley. Mix again gently and serve immediately.

Blanching or steaming the carrots is an alternate method of preparing this dish.

CARROTS WITH MUSHROOMS

Carottes Forestière

Often in Josephine's recipes, sugar is added to carrots. I used to think it was an attempt to correct for the lack of sweetness in the young tender carrots she knew in France. However, old professional texts make use of the technique; the taste of sugar is a sought after one. If the carrots you use are young and tender and have a natural sweetness, then they don't need sugar. If they are giants, however, you may want to give them back some of the sweetness they lost having grown into horse fodder. For the most part, French vegetables are considered at their prime when they are small and tender and their flavor is concentrated.

Serve the carrots with a roasted leg of lamb and a red wine from the Loire, such as a Bourgueil.

INGREDIENTS	SERVES 6

1 or 2 bunches young carrots, or 2 cups larger carrots, cleaned and
   cut into 1- to 2-inch lengths
6 tablespoons butter
1 teaspoon sugar (optional)
¼ cup chicken stock, good homemade (see page 331)
¼ pound mushrooms, quartered
1 clove garlic, minced
½ to 1 teaspoon freshly squeezed lemon juice
1 tablespoon chopped fresh tarragon
Salt and freshly ground pepper

METHOD

Sauté the carrots in 2 to 3 tablespoons of butter and add sugar, if desired; turn the carrots to coat. Add the stock and a pinch of salt; simmer slowly for about 20 minutes, until tender.

Melt the remaining butter in a large saucepan over high heat. When the foam starts to subside, add the mushrooms and sauté for 2 to 3 minutes, until they start to give up their water. Add garlic and lemon juice, and continue to sauté until cooked.

Mix the carrots and their cooking juices with the mushrooms. Season with salt and pepper. Continue to heat for a minute or two, sprinkle with chopped tarragon, and serve.

GLAZED CARROTS WITH ONIONS

Carottes Glacées aux Oignons

This is a simple and straightforward preparation. The liquid called for to cook the carrots could just as well be French cider, stock, or water. While the carrots cook, Swiss chard and raisins could be prepared as a bed on which to set a poached chicken breast. You can prepare the entire menu in the time one vegetable cooks. *Voilà*, healthy simplicity.

INGREDIENTS	SERVES 6

4 tablespoons butter
1 tablespoon peanut oil
1 large onion, thinly sliced
2 bunches young carrots
½ cup dry white wine
¼ cup chopped parsley
Salt and freshly ground pepper

METHOD

Melt the butter and oil in a 2-quart saucepan; when hot, sauté the onion on a medium slow heat until golden.

Wash and scrape the carrots; cook them whole or cut into coarse chunks and add to the pan with the onion. Pour in the wine, salt lightly, and cover to cook on a low flame for about 20 minutes, until the carrots are tender.

Correct the seasoning, giving the carrots a grinding of pepper. Add the chopped parsley and toss well. Remove to a serving dish and serve hot.

CARROTS WITH PARSLEY

Carottes Persillées

These carrots can be served with a breast of chicken garnished with wild mushrooms, and lentils cooked with a *mirepoix*, a tiny dice of shallots, carrots, and celery root. The wine to accompany the dish could be a white Corbières from the southwest of France.

INGREDIENTS   SERVES 6

2 bunches young carrots
2 tablespoons butter
1 teaspoon sugar (optional)
¼ cup chopped parsley
Salt and freshly ground pepper

METHOD

Clean and scrape the carrots. Cut them in half lengthwise, then into ½-inch half moons. Blanch in boiling salted water for 5 minutes, so that they are still crisp and not completely cooked. Drain them in a colander.

Melt 2 tablespoons of butter in a 2-quart saucepan. Sweat the carrots in the butter (with the optional sugar) over a low flame for about 10 minutes. Stir occasionally to make sure that they don't scorch. Season with salt and freshly ground pepper. Add the chopped parsley and mix well. Serve hot.

CARROTS WITH PERSIMMONS

Carottes au Kaki

This recipe comes from Josephine's grandmother, from the foraged dishes that Josephine remembered. The persimmons are ready to eat when they have softened completely. There is also a Japanese variety of persimmon that can be sliced and eaten when it is firm; ask your greengrocer which variety is available. Either can be used. Serve this dish as an accompaniment to a daube of beef or a navarin of lamb. Pour a friendly southern Côtes-du-Rhône to go with the dish.

INGREDIENTS	SERVES 6

2 bunches young carrots
2 to 4 tablespoons butter
1 to 2 persimmons, completely ripe
2 tablespoons chopped parsley and tarragon
Salt and freshly ground pepper

METHOD

Clean and scrape the carrots and cook them until tender. If they are young carrots, sauté in butter; if larger, blanch in boiling salted water. Season with salt and pepper and sprinkle with herbs. Squeeze the completely ripened persimmons over the carrots, and toss to coat the vegetable with the fruit. Serve at once.

PICKLED CARROTS

Carottes en Conserve

Here is a recipe calling for the use of corn syrup. I have included it because the idea evokes countryside cooking even though corn syrup would not have been used in Brittany. This pickle, which will keep indefinitely, may be used to garnish salads, cold meats, and *pâtés*.

INGREDIENTS	SERVES 6

2 bunches carrots
1 cup cider vinegar
1 cup white corn syrup
1 to 2 sticks cinnamon

1 tablespoon whole cloves
½ teaspoon allspice
1 teaspoon mace

METHOD

Wash and scrape the carrots. Cut them in half lengthwise; then into ½-inch half moons. Blanch the carrots in boiling salted water until they are tender and crisp, about 5 to 7 minutes. Remove them to a colander to drain and then place in a metal bowl.

To make the conserve syrup, mix the vinegar and corn syrup in a pan. Tie the spices in a cloth bag and add to the pan. Heat the syrup to the boiling point. Pour the liquid over the carrots and allow to stand overnight.

The next day, strain the carrots, reserving syrup, and put into sterilized jars. Heat the syrup again to the boiling point and pour over the carrots to within 1 inch of the top, making sure the carrots are well covered by the liquid. Process the jars in a boiling water bath for 10 minutes, or in a water bath in a 275 degree oven for 30 minutes. Remove from the bath when the water has cooled.

CARROTS WITH FRUITS

Carottes du Verger

The *verger* takes care of the orchard that provides the fruit. La Mère Jacquette's garden provided carrots whose sweetness perhaps matched that of plums. Fruit, honey, mustard, and herbs give new meaning to root vegetables. Serve this dish with a roast of pork and a purée of potatoes accompanied by a French cider. You can't imagine that something so good was so easily made.

INGREDIENTS   SERVES 6

Grated rind of 1 orange
1 cup freshly squeezed orange juice
2 bunches young carrots
2 white turnips or parsnips
4 tablespoons butter
½ pound plums, pitted and halved
½ cup fresh or dried pitted prunes, diced
1 teaspoon Dijon mustard
1 tablespoon honey
2 to 4 tablespoons chopped parsley
1 tablespoon chopped fresh tarragon
Salt and freshly ground pepper

METHOD

Grate the rind of an orange and set aside. Squeeze and strain the orange juice. Julienne the carrots in 1-inch lengths, or grate them through the large holes of a grater. Prepare the turnips or parsnips in the same manner.

Melt 2 to 3 tablespoons of butter in a skillet large enough to hold the vegetables; add the orange rind and juice, and then the vegetables. Add a generous pinch of salt and simmer on a slow heat for about 15 minutes, or until the vegetables are cooked. They should be tender and most of the liquid absorbed.

Prepare the plums and prunes. In a skillet, melt the remaining 1 to 2 tablespoons of butter and toss the fruit in the butter to coat and warm to the same temperature as the vegetables. They should only be warmed, not cooked, or they will disintegrate. Add the fruit to the vegetables. Then add the mustard, honey, parsley, and tarragon; fold everything well. Correct the seasonings and serve immediately.

SPICED CARROTS

Carottes Epicées

Once the mustard has been added to this dish, it can be kept warm, but any further cooking causes the mustard to turn bitter. Serve these carrots with pork and prune sauce, accompanied by a gratin of potatoes baked in milk. Pour a dry and fruity rosé from Anjou to drink.

INGREDIENTS   SERVES 6

2 bunches young carrots
2 tablespoons butter
1 onion, finely sliced
1 tablespoon brown sugar
1 teaspoon Dijon mustard
Chopped parsley
Salt and freshly ground pepper

METHOD

Clean and scrape the carrots. Julienne the carrots in ¼-inch lengths or grate them through the large holes of a grater. Melt the butter in a 2-quart saucepan and sauté the onion with brown sugar until it is caramelized, about 10 to 15 minutes.

Put the carrots into the same saucepan and cover; simmer on low heat until tender, about 8 to 10 minutes. Flavor the vegetables with mustard, chopped parsley, salt and pepper. Mix everything well and serve hot.

Celery Root

CELERY ROOT WITH CHEESE AND ANCHOVY

Céleri-Rave au Gratin

These soufflé-like dishes that are prepared in low-sided gratin dishes are known as *zéphyrs,* because they are intended to be very light. This presentation would make a fine first course, or the main course for a vegetarian supper, when served with a crispy potato cake and accompanied by a Sauvignon Blanc.

Celery root is a milder vegetable than celery stalks, which can be very strong tasting. Celery root lends itself to use in soups, purées, and soufflés. The trick of salting the dish with fish gives a hint of its coastal origins.

INGREDIENTS	SERVES 6

4 tablespoons butter plus an additional 2 tablespoons
½ cup breadcrumbs
1 cup milk
2 to 3 shallots or 1 small onion, finely chopped
8 anchovies, chopped
1 large head celery root, cut into 2-inch pieces, poached in stock for
    12 to 15 minutes
½ cup grated Gruyère cheese
Additional grated cheese for the topping
2 egg yolks
2 egg whites
Salt, freshly ground pepper, and nutmeg

METHOD

Preheat oven to 375 degrees. Butter a gratin dish and set aside.

Melt 2 to 3 tablespoons of butter in the top of a double boiler. Add the breadcrumbs and stir together. Add the milk and heat the mixture through.

In a small skillet, melt 1 to 2 tablespoons of butter and sauté the shallots for 2 minutes. Add half of the anchovies and continue to sauté for a minute or two longer. Add to the breadcrumb mixture.

Coarsely chop the cooked celery root and add it to the rest of the ingredients in the double boiler. Season with salt, pepper, and nutmeg to taste, being generous with the pepper and the nutmeg. Pay attention to the salt because of the salty nature of the anchovies.

Remove the pan from the heat and stir in one-third cup of the cheese, mixing well. Then add the egg yolks one at a time, again mixing well. Beat the egg whites with a dash of salt until they are stiff. Gently fold in the whites; then spoon the celery mixture into the buttered gratin dish. Sprinkle the top first with the remaining grated cheese, then with the rest of the anchovies. Place the gratin in a preheated oven and bake for 20 to 25 minutes, or until mixture puffs and is slightly browned on top.

Chard

FROM JOSEPHINE'S NOTES

Swiss chard is a type of vegetable similar to beetroot and has spinach-like leaves with a broad white or red rib. In French it is called *bette* or *blette*.

Preparation of Swiss Chard: Wash the Swiss chard thoroughly in cold water. Lay each leaf flat, and remove the stem all the way into the middle of the leaf. Set the greens aside. Trim the coarse ends from the chard stalks. The outer layer of the stalk can be fibrous; it is desirable to remove it by slipping a knife under the surface and peeling it away, in the same way that tough fiber is removed from celery stalks. Cut these stalks in ½-inch slices; cut on the diagonal. Cook the ribs in boiling salted water for 5 to 10 minutes, until they are tender. Drain and prepare as indicated in the recipes.

The green part of Swiss chard can also be cooked in boiling salted water and prepared like spinach. The entire chard leaf is often prepared thus: cut into 1-inch-wide slices, boil in water, season with salt, pepper, and butter. You can also serve chard with herbs or spices, or in a sauce such as béchamel or reduced cream flavored with cheese.

SWISS CHARD IN CREAM

Bettes à la Crème

This recipe can be served with roasted duck and quartered potatoes that have been sautéed in duck fat; everything is accompanied by a crisp French cider.

Swiss chard is a vegetable that allows for no waste. The greens are used separately from the stems, in effect giving two vegetables in one. The water that is used to blanch the vegetable can be saved and used as a very flavorful stock, enriched with crème fraîche, some minced garlic and parsley, and served hot. It is a lifesaving soup.

INGREDIENTS	SERVES 6

1 cup heavy cream
1 or 2 bunches Swiss chard
2 to 4 tablespoons chopped parsley
Salt, freshly ground pepper, and nutmeg

METHOD

Put the heavy cream in a 1-quart saucepan and allow it to reduce by half. While the cream reduces, prepare the vegetable. Trim the ribs, saving the green. Remove all the stringy parts (see Josephine's notes on Swiss chard on page 71). Cut the ribs on the bias into ½- to 1-inch lengths.

Cook the chard greens until tender in boiling salted water. The cooking time and method depend on the size of the greens. Young greens are so tender that they can also be sautéed in a little butter; they are cooked as soon as they collapse. Older greens are denser and require a longer cooking time by blanching. When they are blanched, remove the greens to a non-aluminum colander and run under cold water. Chop the greens coarsely.

In the same water used to blanch the greens, blanch the stems for 4 to 6 minutes until tender. Remove to a non-aluminum colander and refresh under cold water.

When they are ready to serve, put the stems and greens in a dry skillet and heat until the water has completely evaporated. When the greens are dry, they more readily accept the reduced cream. Add the cream, tossing the chard to coat well. Season with salt and pepper, and finish the dish with several gratings of nutmeg.

SWISS CHARD WITH FRENCH DRESSING

Bettes à la Vinaigrette

This is a simple and delicious way to use the part of a vegetable that might otherwise be discarded. It lends great flavor and color to a composed salad, and has good flavor on its own. The vinaigrette can be made a little stronger in flavor with the addition of mustard, or it can have a hint of the Arabic spices found in *quatre épices* (see page 184), i.e., cinnamon, clove, coriander, and the like.

INGREDIENTS	SERVES 6

1 or 2 bunches Swiss chard stalks
1 recipe vinaigrette (your personal favorite, or see page 74)
1 teaspoon salt

Wash the Swiss chard; separate the stems from the greens. Reserve the greens for another use (see previous recipe). Peel the stems and cut them in 1-inch pieces. Blanch in boiling salted water for 4 to 6 minutes or until tender. Drain and toss in the vinaigrette. Serve either hot or cold.

Basic Vinaigrette
½ cup vinegar (cider or wine preferred)
¾ teaspoon salt
½ teaspoon freshly ground pepper
1 tablespoon prepared mustard (Dijon preferred)
1 teaspoon Worcestershire sauce
1 clove garlic, minced
1½ cups olive or vegetable oil

Place the vinegar into a small bowl and stir in the salt, pepper, mustard, and Worcestershire sauce until the flavorings are dissolved. Add the garlic and then whisk in the oil.

The Uses of Salt in the Cooking of Vegetables

The procedure for blanching vegetables that Josephine always used calls for adding salt after the vegetable has been put into boiling water and the water has returned to a boil. You want to avoid throwing salt into a pan of cold water, bringing it to a boil, and making a chemical soup by the time the vegetables are ready to be tossed in.

Salt is used in blanching to help draw water from the vegetable; this extraction of water partly causes the vegetable to cook. Therefore, you want the vegetables in boiling salted water only long enough to do the job. Bring cold water to a boil, add the vegetable, and when the water returns to a boil, add the salt. Blanch the vegetable to the desired tenderness and remove from the water. At this point, you can either run it under cold water to stop the cooking, which also helps green vegetables retain their greenness, or, you can take the hot vegetables and continue cooking them by sautéeing, baking in a gratin, puréeing, and so on.

SWISS CHARD GRATIN

Bettes au Gratin

This gratin goes well with a roast of pork accompanied by sautéed apples and a white wine from the Savoie, an Apremont or a Crépy.

INGREDIENTS	SERVES 4 TO 6

1 or 2 bunches Swiss chard with ribs
1 cup white sauce (see recipe page 80)
¼ cup grated Gruyère cheese
4 tablespoons melted butter
Salt and freshly ground pepper

METHOD

Preheat oven to 400 degrees. Remove the Swiss chard stems from the greens and save the greens for another use. Remove the tough outer fiber of the stalks by slipping a knife under the cut end of the stalk and peeling it away. Cut the stalks into ½-inch pieces on the diagonal. Blanch the stalks in boiling salted water until done, about 4 to 6 minutes. Drain in a non-aluminum colander and flush in cold water. The vegetable water from cooking can be saved and used for a flavorful stock.

In a bowl, season the chard stalks with salt and pepper, and then mix in the white sauce; set in an oven-proof casserole. Sprinkle the surface with the cheese. Dribble the melted butter over the top and brown the gratin in a preheated oven. The gratin can also be placed under the broiler provided the mixture has been warmed before being put into the gratin dish.

SWISS CHARD AND RHUBARB

Bettes et Rhubarbe Scorvienne

Here is another recipe from the repertoire of La Mère Jacquette. On the surface we can see that chard and rhubarb have color and shape in common. At the simplest level we can understand how Josephine's grandmother might have combined these ingredients. She learned how to make these things work, how to marry the earthy taste of the chard to the tart taste of the rhubarb. She might have seen the opposite in each element, that is, she might have opposed the chard by lending it a little lemon; and conversely, she might have opposed the rhubarb by giving it garlic, parsley, and herbs.

Spinach or beet greens can be substituted for the Swiss chard. For a good balance, use 1 cup of rhubarb to 2 cups of chopped greens. This dish goes particularly well as an accompaniment to baked salmon. It also would go well with pork or veal roasts, and a white wine from the Alsace, a Pinot Blanc or a Riesling.

INGREDIENTS	SERVES 6

1 bunch Swiss chard
3 to 4 rhubarb stalks
1 tablespoon sugar
4 tablespoons butter

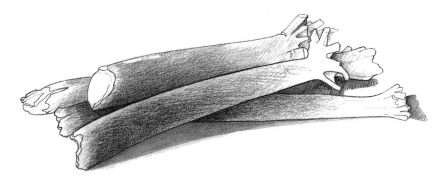

¼ cup chopped parsley
Salt and freshly ground pepper

METHOD

Wash the Swiss chard well in cold water. Remove the stems and save for another use (see previous recipe). Bring a large pot of water to a boil, add the greens and some salt, and blanch 3 to 5 minutes, until cooked tender.

Remove the coarse outer fiber and string from the rhubarb and cut the stalks into 1½-inch pieces. Place the rhubarb in a 2-quart saucepan along with the sugar and a tablespoon of water. Cover and sweat the vegetable over a slow heat until it cooks through and collapses, about 6 to 8 minutes. Taste the rhubarb to make sure that it is not too acid for your taste, and, if necessary, correct with more sugar or butter.

Put the Swiss chard in a dry skillet over medium heat to rid it of any excess water. When the chard is dry, stir in the rhubarb and mix well. When everything is well warmed, add the butter broken into pea-size pieces and toss to coat. Season to taste with salt and pepper, add the parsley, and toss again. Serve at once.

Chestnuts

FROM JOSEPHINE'S NOTES

Chestnuts are a basic element in the provincial cooking of Brittany, where they are cultivated. One variety of chestnut is known as *châtaigne*, and another variety is called *marron*. They can be boiled, steamed, or grilled. They are also used for sweets, particularly for cakes that go well with chocolate.

To Peel Chestnuts: Preheat oven to 400 degrees. With a sharp knife, cut an "X" on the flat surface of the nuts and place in a baking pan with a little water. Roast for 8 to 10 minutes. Peel them while they are still hot or rub them in a coarse, heavy towel to remove skins.

Another peeling method is to slit them as described above and boil

5 to 10 minutes. Both outer and inner skins should be peeled off while the nuts are hot.

BOILED CHESTNUTS

Châtaignes Bouillies

Josephine's notes say that the chestnuts can be used with any sauce after they are sautéed in butter. Serve them as an accompaniment to a roasted bird, ranging from turkey to quail. Prepare a nice green vegetable and serve with a Côtes de Bordeaux.

INGREDIENTS	SERVES 6

2 pounds chestnuts, peeled (see page 77)
1 or 2 whole star anise pods
4 tablespoons butter
2 to 4 tablespoons chopped parsley
Salt and freshly ground pepper

METHOD

Put the chestnuts in cold water, season with a pinch of salt, and add the star anise. Bring to a boil, cover, and simmer until tender, about 45 minutes; then drain.

Sauté the chestnuts in 4 tablespoons butter so that they are coated. Season to taste with salt and pepper. Add parsley and serve.

BRAISED CHESTNUTS

Châtaignes Braisées

Serve these chestnuts with roasted beef, veal, or pork with wild mushrooms, accompanied by a wine from the southwest, a vin de Cahors for example.

INGREDIENTS   SERVES 6

2 pounds chestnuts, peeled (see page 77)
4 tablespoons butter
Bouquet garni: parsley, thyme, and bay leaf tied in celery stalks (see
    page 332)
Veal or chicken stock for braising (see page 331)
Salt and freshly ground pepper

METHOD

Preheat oven to 250 degrees. In a large braising pan, sauté the peeled chestnuts in butter for 8 to 10 minutes. Stir carefully so as not to break them. Add the bouquet garni and season to taste with salt and pepper. Barely cover the chestnuts with the stock and bring to a boil. Cover the pan and cook over a heat diffuser on a slow flame, or in a preheated oven, for 1 hour. Do not stir; this will break the chestnuts.

CHESTNUTS AND BRUSSELS SPROUTS

Marrons et Choux de Bruxelles

These make a good appetizer. They also make a good entrée garnished with additional chopped sprouts, a whole chestnut, or even a third, complementary vegetable. Serve with an Alsatian Pinot Blanc.

INGREDIENTS	SERVES 6

White Sauce

   3 tablespoons butter

   3 tablespoons flour

   1 cup hot milk

   ½ cup heavy cream

   Nutmeg and paprika

   Salt and freshly ground pepper

   ½ pound whole chestnuts, peeled and cooked (see Boiled
     Chestnuts page 78)

   ½ pound blanched brussels sprouts (see Brussels Sprouts in Cream
     page 43)

   1 tablespoon butter

   2 whole eggs

   Salt and freshly ground pepper

METHOD

Preheat oven to 375 degrees. Make the white sauce by melting the butter in a small saucepan. Whisk in the flour and allow to cook for 3 to 4 minutes. Slowly whisk in the hot milk and then the heavy cream. Season with salt and pepper. Flavor with paprika and nutmeg to taste. Allow the sauce to simmer 20 minutes; reserve and keep warm.

Make a purée of the whole chestnuts. Season them with salt and freshly ground pepper, and whisk in one whole egg. Spread the mixture in a lightly buttered gratin dish, or in individual 2-ounce ramekins. Leave enough room to put the chopped brussels sprouts on top.

Coarsely chop the blanched brussels sprouts; season with salt, and set in a dry skillet over medium heat to rewarm them and evaporate any water. When they are dry, toss with 1 tablespoon butter broken into pea-size pieces to coat the vegetable. Season with salt and give a grinding of fresh pepper. In a small bowl, lightly beat the second egg with a fork; pour it over the brussels sprouts and toss well to coat. Set the brussels sprouts in a layer on top of the purée of chestnut.

Put the molded dish in a water bath and set it to bake in a preheated oven (25 minutes for a large mold; 10 to 15 minutes for small ramekins).

When they are cooked, remove from the oven. Invert the mold onto a plate and nap with the white sauce and serve hot.

CHESTNUTS WITH CELERY ROOT

Marrons au Céleri-Rave

Serve this chestnut purée with roast of turkey or other fowl and pour a Pinot Noir from Burgundy.

INGREDIENTS	SERVES 6

1 pound whole chestnuts, peeled and cooked (see page 77)
1 cup blanched celery root
2 to 4 tablespoons butter
¼ cup crème fraîche (optional)
Salt and freshly ground pepper

METHOD

Put the cooked chestnuts and the blanched celery root through a ricer to make a purée. Add the butter and mix until it is completely blended. Season the mixture with salt and freshly ground pepper. If the purée is too thick, thin with a small amount of crème fraîche. Serve hot.

PEAS AND CHESTNUTS IN THE FRENCH MANNER

Petits Pois et Marrons à la Française

The combination of these tastes is delicious, and satisfying. The dish can be used to accompany roast beef for which you might like to pour a Pinot Noir.

The flavors in this recipe have been used at Le Trou restaurant to

make chestnut soup as well as chestnut custards garnished with peas and lettuce.

INGREDIENTS	SERVES 6

½ pound small whole onions
2 tablespoons butter
1 tablespoon peanut oil
5 ounces chestnuts, peeled, cooked, and broken into pieces (see page 77)
½ cup chicken stock, good homemade (see page 331)
1 cup shelled fresh peas
4 to 6 leaves bibb lettuce, cut in a chiffonnade
Salt and freshly ground pepper

METHOD

Prepare the onions by trimming the root end and lightly scoring an "X" ⅛-inch deep with a knife. Remove the papery outer layers and discard.

Melt the butter and oil in a skillet and sauté the onions lightly for 3 to 4 minutes. Add the pieces of cooked chestnuts and cover with stock. Add the peas, season with a bit of salt, and simmer until the peas are tender, about 5 to 7 minutes. Add the lettuce chiffonnade, correct seasonings to taste, and serve.

Cucumbers

Cucumbers belong to the family of squashes or gourds and have been cultivated for over three-thousand years. They can be white or green, smooth or rough skinned, and grow in a variety of sizes and forms.

The very small cucumbers with rough skin that are cultivated in France for pickling are called *cornichons.* They are the same size as gherkins.

The watery overgrown variety of cucumber, which is laden with seeds and seems unattractive and coarse, has a good texture. They can be shaped into lozenges, cooked, and served with cream flavored with tarragon; this is especially good with fish. In France, cucumbers are a traditional part of salmon dishes, served either hot or cold. With hot salmon, cut them into cubes or lozenges, then simmer in butter and flavor with fresh herbs. For cold salmon, slice them paper thin and serve with a piquant vinaigrette; sprinkle with tarragon and dill, or green fennel, and chopped green onions, and you will have an unsurpassed treat.

Another variety of cucumber is about the size of a large lemon. It has a yellow skin and a good, fresh lemon taste; you want to eat them like you would eat a fruit.

There is a long slender variety called the English hothouse cucumber, which has hardly any seeds. They are very crisp, making them perfect for salads and sandwiches when sliced paper thin and given a grind of fresh pepper and a light spread of mayonnaise.

Cucumber and tomato make a favorite cooling salad in summer. To create another summer salad, cut a cucumber into long thin shreds and mix with yogurt or sour cream, flavor with ground pepper, very little salt, and lemon juice, and finish with a sprinkle of chopped mint and parsley. Cucumbers, anchovies, and a good vinaigrette are yet another favorite in France.

CUCUMBERS AND BRUSSELS SPROUTS WITH LIME

Concombres et Choux de Bruxelles au Citron Vert

This vegetable dish can be served with game, fish, or white meats. It lends life to ordinary vegetables that are often staples in winter climates.

INGREDIENTS	SERVES 6 TO 8

½ to 1 pound brussels sprouts
4 tablespoons butter
1 medium onion, coarsely chopped or sliced
2 cucumbers, peeled and coarsely chopped
1 tablespoon chopped fresh dill weed or dill seed
1 tablespoon (6 to 7) juniper berries, crushed, or 2 to 3 tablespoons
    gin
Juice of 1 lime (preferred) or lemon
1 teaspoon sugar
1 tablespoon chopped fresh tarragon
2 tablespoons coarsely chopped parsley
Salt and freshly ground pepper

METHOD

Prepare the brussels sprouts as described in Brussels Sprouts in Cream (see page 43) and blanch for 5 minutes. Drain and refresh under cold water.

Melt 2 tablespoons butter in a large skillet; add the onion and sauté until golden. Add the cucumber, brussels sprouts, dill, juniper berries, lime juice, and sugar. Season with salt and pepper to taste. Toss everything well to coat all the ingredients with the butter. Cover and heat the vegetables until they are cooked tender. Correct the seasoning, give a grinding of fresh pepper, and add more butter to taste. Finish with tarragon and parsley. Serve at once.

Dandelion Greens

SAUTEED DANDELION

Pissenlits Minute

Serve the dandelions with a pork roast and apples accompanied by a French cider.

At the market in Niort in France, where I go each year to teach American students, I find tiny greens that I like to sauté in the rendered fat of pancetta and use as a filling for a memorable omelette.

Josephine remembered some cultivated varieties such as the *Pissenlit Plein-Coeur* (full heart) and the *Très Hatif* (very young). Tender leaves are eaten raw like any salad green; larger leaves are cooked by sautéeing or blanching.

INGREDIENTS	SERVES 6

1 pound young dandelion greens
2 tablespoons oil
2 tablespoons butter
2 cloves garlic, minced
Juice of 1 lemon or 2 tablespoons cider vinegar
Salt and freshly ground pepper

METHOD

Wash and drain the dandelion leaves. Depending on their tenderness, cut up the greens or leave them whole as desired. Heat the butter and oil in a skillet. Add the dandelion and garlic, and season with salt and pepper. Sauté for a few minutes before adding the lemon juice. Serve hot.

Eggplant

Eggplant is often difficult to sauté because it drinks the oil. If you put more oil in the pan, it drinks that as well. Then when it is cooked the eggplant collapses and vast amounts of oil leach out, making the dish unpleasant.

To avoid this problem, cut the eggplant in thick slices, salt them on both sides, and set to rest for about 30 minutes. This serves two purposes: It draws the acids and water to the surface where they are rinsed away with the salt, which makes the eggplant less bitter and leaves the surface of the eggplant oil resistant.

When it is time to cook the eggplant, a small amount of oil, enough to cover the bottom, is added to the skillet. When the oil is hot, the eggplant is put in and tossed well so that every surface is coated with oil. Sauté so that the surfaces brown nicely on medium heat, then turn down the heat so that it cooks through. This way, the eggplant holds its shape and doesn't turn to mush.

EGGPLANT WITH ANCHOVY

Aubergines aux Anchois

This is a simple idea, easy to execute, and deliciously flavorful. While the eggplant is salting and baking, you can prepare the remainder of a menu. This dish can be served hot or cold and finished with a drizzling of superior quality olive oil. Serve it hot with a sweet whitefish, such as baked cod garnished with tomatoes. For a wine, choose a Pouilly Fumé.

INGREDIENTS	SERVES 6

1 large firm eggplant
4 tablespoons butter melted with 1 tablespoon olive oil
3 cloves garlic, minced
¼ cup finely chopped parsley
10 small anchovy fillets, finely chopped
¼ cup breadcrumbs
Salt and freshly ground pepper

METHOD

Preheat oven to 400 degrees. Slice the eggplant in ½-inch-thick slices. Sprinkle both sides generously with salt and allow to rest 30 minutes, until the salt draws beads of water to the surface. Rinse the eggplant under cold running water to rid it of any trace of salt and pat completely dry. Brush each piece of eggplant with the butter/oil mixture. Add any leftover oil to the skillet. Heat the oil, and sauté the slices to brown on each side. The eggplant is not cooked at this point. It is only browned and will finish cooking in the oven to give it deeper flavor.

Arrange the browned eggplant slices in an oiled gratin dish. Sauté the garlic and parsley in a little oil until browned. Mix the anchovy fillets with the breadcrumbs, and then stir into the browned garlic and parsley. Sprinkle the breadcrumb mixture over the eggplant and bake in a pre-heated oven for 30 minutes. Serve piping hot.

EGGPLANT SAUTEED IN BUTTER

Aubergines Sautées au Beurre

Salting eggplant is the key to ridding it of its bitterness. Sautéeing it until brown develops a nuttiness. The deep cooking creates a very flavorful result; it's what Josephine referred to when she spoke of cooking certain vegetables "to the bone."

INGREDIENTS   SERVES 6

1 large firm eggplant
4 tablespoons butter
1 large onion, sliced
1 tablespoon peanut oil
Salt and freshly ground pepper

METHOD

Remove the skin from the eggplant; slice into 2-inch-thick slices. Salt and rinse as described in the previous recipe. Cut into 1-inch dice, and keep ready.

In a skillet, sauté the onion in 1 tablespoon butter until golden; remove with a slotted spoon and set aside. In the same pan, heat the remaining 3 tablespoons butter and the oil, add the eggplant, and toss to coat well. Cook on medium heat until the vegetable browns. The eggplant should hold its shape during the cooking; don't allow it to become mushy. Add the onion, cover, and continue cooking until the vegetable is completely cooked yet retains its shape. Season with salt and pepper, and serve immediately.

EGGPLANT FRITTERS WITH HERBS

Beignets d'Aubergines aux Fines Herbes

Sometimes at the restaurant these fritters are made in the shape of french fries and served as *faux fries,* with lamb chops and a tomato sauce, accompanied by a red Rhône wine, and followed by a green salad.

INGREDIENTS	SERVES 6

1 large or 2 small eggplants

Fritter batter
- 1½ cups flour
- 2 whole eggs
- 1 cup milk
- 1 tablespoon chopped *fines herbes*: tarragon, chives, sweet basil, and chervil (any combination)
- ½ teaspoon or 1 sprig chopped thyme
- A few leaves oregano
- Salt and freshly ground pepper

Grapeseed oil for deep frying

METHOD

Peel the eggplant and cut into ½-inch-thick slices. Salt and rinse as described in Eggplant with Anchovy (see page 87). Pat completely dry.

To make the fritter batter, put the flour in a mixing bowl. Make a well in the flour and add the eggs. Whisking with a fork, work in 1 cup of cold milk to make a smooth batter. Add the herbs and season with some salt and pepper.

In a large skillet, heat the grapeseed oil. Make sure there is enough room to completely submerge the eggplant slices in the hot oil. Do not bring the oil to a rolling boil because the slices will brown faster than they can cook.

Dip each slice of eggplant in the batter. Deep fry the slices in hot oil until the vegetable is tender and golden. Remove to paper towels and drain. Serve hot.

Endive

The curly leaved salad plant that the French call *chicorée,* Americans call French or curly endive. However, in the context of this book, *endive* refers to what is called Belgian endive. It has a flavor that is entirely different from that of chicory. Endive is usually pale white with tightly packed leaves and has a bullet shape. It is a little on the bitter side, yet delicate. Endive can be served raw, cooked, or combined with other foods to add texture and flavor. It can be stuffed like celery for an appetizer or even used for a first course. Endive is usually available from September to April.

ENDIVE GRATIN

Gratin d'Endives

This dish makes a wonderful supper: serve with a dish of buttered noodles garnished with applesauce and mixed with whole grain mustard, a crusty bread, and a French beer, and follow with a green salad.

INGREDIENTS	SERVES 6

¾ pound potatoes
6 large endives
2 onions, chopped
2 tablespoons butter
1 tablespoon dill
5 tablespoons clarified butter (see page 112)
1 to 2 tablespoons chopped *fines herbes:* parsley, chervil, and tarragon (any combination)
2 to 4 tablespoons breadcrumbs
Salt and freshly ground pepper

METHOD

Preheat oven to 350 degrees. Steam the potatoes in their jackets until they are soft; when they are cool enough to handle, remove skins and keep ready.

Double blanch the endives in boiling salted water; this process helps eliminate some of the vegetable's bitterness. Blanch them 2 to 3 minutes and strain. Then put them in another pot of boiling water, add salt and gently boil for 15 to 20 minutes; drain in a colander and keep ready.

While blanching the endive, sauté the onion in the 2 tablespoons butter until lightly browned. Season with salt, fresh grindings of pepper, and dill. Put the onions in a layer at the bottom of an oven-proof gratin dish. Cut the potatoes and endives into large chunks and arrange them on top of the bed of onions. Drizzle the surface of the vegetables with the clarified butter, half of the chopped herbs, and all of the breadcrumbs.

Bake in a preheated oven for 15 to 20 minutes. Just before serving, sprinkle the dish with the remaining herbs and serve at once.

Fennel

GRILLED FENNEL

Fenouil Grillé

This is delicious with grilled fish and sweet peppers.

INGREDIENTS	SERVES 6

6 small fennel bulbs
Extra virgin olive oil
Salt and freshly ground pepper

METHOD

Trim the fennel at the root, remove the stalks down to the bulb. Blanch the bulbs whole for 10 minutes in a large pot of boiling salted water. Drain in a colander and allow to dry. Cut the bulbs in half lengthwise, then into ½-inch-thick slices. Brush the slices with oil, arrange on a grill or broiler, and cook until tender enough to be pierced with a skewer. Season with salt and pepper and drizzle on a little olive oil as a last minute flavoring.

FENNEL SALAD

Fenouil Sauce Rémoulade

Use the fennel branches to flavor soups, stocks, or potato cooking water. Do something resourceful with them because they are flavorful. The feathery leaves can be chopped and added as an herb garnish.

Enjoy this salad at a luncheon. Follow it with poached fish and steamed potatoes, accompanied by a good white wine from Cassis, and end with cheese and fruit.

INGREDIENTS	SERVES 6

1 large fennel bulb
1 celery root or heart of celery

Vinaigrette
1 tablespoon wine vinegar
1 teaspoon Dijon mustard
Salt and freshly ground pepper
3 tablespoons peanut oil
Chopped *fines herbes*: parsley, chives, chervil, and tarragon (any combination)

Handmade mayonnaise (see following recipe)
Finely chopped chives or scallions for garnish
2 to 4 tablespoons finely chopped parsley
1 clove of garlic, minced

METHOD

Prepare the fennel by trimming the root end of any dried flesh; then trim the top branches to the top of the bulb. Save the fine feathery leaves to add to the herb mixture. Place the bulb with the root end on the cutting board so that it won't wobble and cut vertically in half. From each half, thinly slice the vegetable in ¼-inch slices, retaining a portion of the dense root end in each slice so that the vegetable holds its shape.

Cut the celery root into matchsticks (⅛-inch julienne), or cut the heart of celery into julienne. To make the vinaigrette, put the vinegar, mustard, salt, and pepper in a bowl; whisk in the oil with a fork and add the herbs of choice. Marinate all the julienned vegetables for several hours or overnight. Just before serving, mix in the mayonnaise to taste. Season with salt and pepper and sprinkle with chives, parsley, and garlic. Toss everything together.

Variation: This dish can also be made using lemon juice for the dressing and adding a fine julienne of blanched lemon rind along with the herbs.

MAYONNAISE

Sauce Mayonnaise

I think it is a good idea to know how to make mayonnaise by hand before making it in a blender or food processor. Making it by hand allows you to feel what it takes to make this sauce work. There are many recipes for blender mayonnaise; I offer only a recipe for making it by hand.

INGREDIENTS	YIELDS 1½ CUPS

2 egg yolks
Generous pinch of salt, to taste
Freshly ground white pepper
2 tablespoons freshly squeezed lemon juice or vinegar
1 cup salad oil (¼ cup can be olive oil)

METHOD

Put the egg yolks in a 2-quart bowl; add the salt and 1 tablespoon lemon juice; whisk everything to incorporate well. Working slowly, whisk ½ teaspoon of oil at a time into the egg base, mixing in each addition completely before adding the next few drops, until ¼ cup oil has been used. Don't go too fast. You whisk to create an emulsion in which the fat of the egg yolks accepts the fat of the oil; it does this reluctantly unless the addition of oil is very slow. After the ¼ cup oil has been worked into an emulsion, work in the remainder of the oil. Again it must go slowly, but not as slowly as the first quarter cup; now the base can accept 1 to 2 tablespoons of oil at a time. Again, make sure the oil is well incorporated before adding more. Beat in the remaining tablespoon of lemon juice at the end. Put the mayonnaise into a small container, cover it with plastic, and allow it to rest and chill in the refrigerator until you are ready to use it.

Jerusalem Artichokes

Jerusalem artichokes are also known in France as *artichauts du Canada*. When real artichokes are not in season at the beginning of winter and in the early spring, they are a substitute. Jerusalem artichokes have a firm consistency, cook in only 5 to 10 minutes, and taste, to some extent, like real artichokes. They are excellent when substituted for potato in potato salad, or added to flavor a gratin of potato. They can be cooked whole with their skins and then peeled easily. If peeled before cooking, keep them in acidulated water before cooking to prevent discoloration.

JERUSALEM ARTICHOKES IN BUTTER

Topinambours au Beurre

Serve these Jerusalem artichokes with a pan-fried rabbit garnished with whole onions and bacon, and drink a young Beaujolais.

INGREDIENTS   SERVES 6

1 pound Jerusalem artichokes
4 tablespoons butter
2 to 4 tablespoons chopped parsley
Salt and freshly ground pepper

METHOD

Peel the artichokes, wash, and cook whole in butter on a low flame for 10 minutes, until done. You can also cut them in any shape desired.

Season to taste with the salt and pepper. Serve in a vegetable dish. Sprinkle with parsley.

JERUSALEM ARTICHOKES IN CREAM

Topinambours à la Crème

Serve these Jerusalem artichokes with roast chicken, a purée of carrots, and a Savennières or another white wine from the Loire valley.

INGREDIENTS	SERVES 6

1½ pounds Jerusalem artichokes, peeled and washed
4 tablespoons butter
8 ounces crème fraîche or heavy cream
Salt, freshly ground pepper, and nutmeg

METHOD

Cut artichokes into pieces about the size of a pigeon's egg. In a skillet, melt the butter and add the artichokes. Stir to coat each piece with butter. Cook on medium-low heat for 5 minutes. Add enough cream to cover the artichokes. Season with salt, pepper, and nutmeg. Continue to cook over the very lowest heat until artichokes have cooked through. They can also be baked, covered, in a 300-degree oven until cooked tender and to desired doneness. Just before serving, stir in another tablespoon of cream.

JERUSALEM ARTICHOKE FRITTERS

Beignets de Topinambours

Serve these beignets as a garnish to a first course salad of mixed greens, and pour a French cider.

INGREDIENTS	SERVES 4 TO 6

4 tablespoons butter
⅓ cup water
1½ pounds Jerusalem artichokes, peeled and thickly sliced
Fritter batter (see page 17)
Grapeseed oil for deep frying
Salt and freshly ground pepper

METHOD

In a skillet, melt the butter and add ⅓ cup water. Add the artichokes and simmer until barely tender. Drain well. Season with salt and pepper. Just before serving, dip them in the fritter batter and fry in the hot oil. Drain on a paper towel and serve warm.

JERUSALEM ARTICHOKE PUREE

Purée de Topinambours

Serve these artichokes with sautéed veal and green beans with walnuts. This purée can also be used for a soufflé just like potato or celery root (see pages 243 and 306) so that it would be presented as a vegetable accompaniment to a main course, or as a first course. Serve with a Pinot Noir from the Alsace.

INGREDIENTS	SERVES 6

4 tablespoons butter plus a piece the size of a walnut
⅓ cup water
2 pounds Jerusalem artichokes, peeled and thinly sliced
1 potato, peeled and thinly sliced
⅓ cup cream, boiled until thickened slightly
Salt, freshly ground pepper, and nutmeg

METHOD

Melt the 4 tablespoons butter and add ⅓ cup water. Add the artichokes and potatoes and simmer until tender. Purée or rub through a sieve. Place back onto the heat and season with salt, pepper, and nutmeg to taste. Stir in the cream, adding enough until you reach a consistency that is not too firm or too runny. Stir in the walnut-size piece of butter. Serve warm.

Leeks

FROM JOSEPHINE'S NOTES

Leeks are a member of the onion family, and in France they are called the "asparagus of the poor" because they are so plentiful. Leeks are

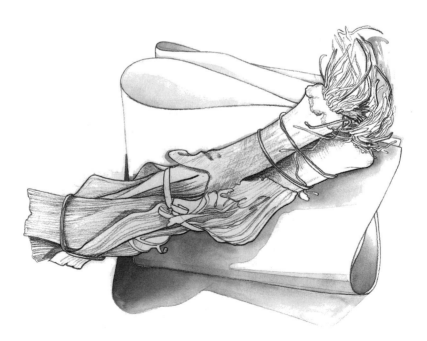

indispensable for the flavor they give and are used primarily in soups because their delicate flavor blends easily. Leeks are especially good when cooked as a vegetable and served cold with a well-seasoned vinaigrette dressing. Mother and grandmother served them with marinated beets, tomatoes, and many other vegetables.

LEEKS WITH SHRIMP

Poireaux aux Crevettes

Serve hot or cold as an appetizer with a chilled white wine from Entre-Deux-Mers.

INGREDIENTS	SERVES 6

4 large leeks, white parts only
¼ pound cooked shrimp
2 yolks from hard-boiled eggs
½ cup handmade mayonnaise (see page 94)
Fines herbes: parsley, chives, tarragon, and chervil (any combination)
Salt and freshly ground pepper

METHOD

Trim the root of the leeks, and remove the stalk at the point where the color turns green. Lay the leek flat and cut all the way through, but only half-way along its length. Fan the leek layers under cold running water, with the root end facing up, so that no sand or grit gets trapped inside. Set aside to drain.

Bring a large pot of water to a boil and blanch the leeks at a simmer with 1 teaspoon salt for 15 to 20 minutes. Remove from the water and allow them to drain and cool.

Purée the shrimp and egg yolks in a food processor. Season with salt and pepper. Arrange the leeks on a plate with the cut surface placed so that the leek layers can be fanned out. Garnish each leek with puréed shrimp and mayonnaise and sprinkle with herbs.

Lettuce

LETTUCE CUSTARD

Pain de Laitue

INGREDIENTS   **SERVES 6 TO 8**

6 heads lettuce, any tender variety: Boston, escarole, or romaine
1 cup thick white sauce (see Chestnuts and Brussels Sprouts page 79)
4 tablespoons butter plus butter for the baking dish
3 eggs, beaten slightly
Salt, freshly ground pepper, and nutmeg

METHOD

Preheat oven to 325 degrees. Butter individual 3- to 4-ounce custard cups or a 1-quart oven-proof dish. Coarsely chop the lettuce greens and simmer in a little water until cooked, about 4 to 6 minutes. Purée in a food processor. This should yield about 2 to 2¼ cups of lettuce purée.

Prepare the white sauce. Melt 4 tablespoons butter in a saucepan and stir in the lettuce purée. Sauté for a few minutes before adding the white sauce; cook until the mixture thickens. Season with salt, pepper, and nutmeg to taste. Remove from the heat and stir in the eggs. Pour into custard cups or oven-proof dish. Cover with foil and bake in a preheated oven for 30 to 35 minutes (20 to 25 minutes if using custard cups), or until a knife inserted into the middle of the custard comes out clean. Serve warm or cold.

CREAMED ESCAROLE

Chicorée à la Crème

This dish could be topped with poached eggs and a hollandaise sauce (see page 165) for a luncheon. Serve with veal chops and a good Burgundy for an excellent dinner.

INGREDIENTS	SERVES 6

2 heads escarole
1 cup heavy cream reduced by half or ½ cup white sauce (see Chestnuts and Brussels Sprouts page 79)
2 to 4 tablespoons butter
Salt, freshly ground pepper, and nutmeg

METHOD

Blanch the whole heads of escarole in boiling salted water. Or, take any outside green leaves from various salads (lettuce, escarole, chicory, romaine) and blanch until wilted. The cooking time depends on the density of the lettuces used. Drain the greens, and run them under cold water to stop the cooking. Press as much water out of the vegetable as you can, and then chop coarsely.

In a dry saucepan, rewarm the greens to evaporate any water left in them before adding enough reduced cream or white sauce to coat the leaves. Add salt and pepper to taste, a few gratings of nutmeg, and a few pea-size pieces of butter, and mix well.

Onions

FROM JOSEPHINE'S NOTES

Onions can be divided into four culinary categories by color: the white onion, most esteemed in cooking; the yellow onion, noted for its keeping ability; the pale red onion; and the red-black or Spanish onion. Of all the vegetables used in cooking, onions are about the most important. French chefs consider them indispensable because they produce flavor that nothing else can equal. They are often combined with carrots, celery, herbs, and parsley to make a *mirepoix*. Onions are the vegetables you should never be without.

American varieties are more pungent, stronger in flavor, and contain more juice than the European varieties. Italian onions are mild in flavor, and are long and pointed at one end and flat at the other. There are also small silvery-yellow Egyptian onions. Breton onions are a variety of the all-purpose onion found in this country. All varieties can be used in any kind of cooking.

Spanish onions are the favorite onions for eating raw, and also for frying and baking; they tend to become hard and indigestible when boiled. They are good when they are large, round, and glossy skinned because then they are very mild. The best time for these onions is after the late autumn harvest.

Scallions are eaten raw in salads, but they can also be cooked. Look for those that have long stems and not a bulbous shape. They are available almost all of the year, but especially from February to July.

Silverskin onions are usually available fresh. They are small, white-fleshed onions that are favored for pickling, but have other uses. They are particularly good cooked whole, braised in stock.

Shallots are sweet, delicate-flavored onions that grow in cloves. They are small and have purple-brown skin. These onions are used particularly

for fish and meat sauces. They are also served with pâtés and as vegetables on their own.

Welsh onions are milk flavored and are available year round. They look like small leeks, and both the stalk and bulb are used in cooking. They can be cooked whole or sliced for use in different casserole dishes, or used raw when finely minced in salads or for sandwiches.

APRICOT AND KIDNEY STUFFED ONIONS

Oignons Farcis aux Abricots

These are excellent when served with tomato sauce. They are a wonderful accompaniment to lamb prepared almost any way, or served with Beans with Lemon Butter (see page 172) along with a robust red wine from the southern end of the Rhône, such as a Coteaux du Tricastin.

INGREDIENTS	SERVES 1-2

12 small white or yellow onions
1 veal, lamb, or beef kidney
12 tablespoons butter
⅓ cup uncooked rice
½ cup coarse breadcrumbs
⅓ cup grated Gruyère or Parmesan cheese
¼ cup chopped parsley
2 tablespoons basil
1 tablespoon tarragon
1 teaspoon thyme
¼ cup heavy cream
¼ cup sherry
¼ pound apricots, peeled, stoned, and chopped
½ cup stock
Salt and freshly ground pepper

METHOD

Preheat the oven to 375 degrees. Prepare the onions by peeling the outer papery layers; trim the root end and cut out the core to make a shell. Save the cores to sauté for the onion filling. Place onions in a 3-quart saucepan and cover with water. Bring the water to a boil, add a teaspoon of salt, and let the onions simmer for 7 minutes. Remove the onions to a rack and set aside.

If using a lamb or beef kidney, it is necessary to parboil it gently for 5 minutes before using. Cut the kidney into a small dice.

Melt 4 tablespoons butter in a large skillet and sauté the chopped onion cores until translucent. Add the rice and continue to sauté until the surface of the grains turns opaque white. Add the chopped kidney and sauté a few minutes longer.

Mix the breadcrumbs and cheese. Reserve a little of the breadcrumb mixture to garnish the top. Mix the remainder into the rice mixture along with all the herbs, cream, and sherry. Mix in the apricots.

Season the inside of the onion shells with salt and pepper. Fill each shell with the kidney mixture. Set the filled shells in a buttered, oven-proof baking dish. Sprinkle the top with the reserved cheese and bread-crumbs. Dot the top surface with little pieces of butter. Pour the stock into the dish and set the onions to bake in a preheated oven for 1 hour.

BAKED STUFFED ONIONS

Oignons Farcis

These baked onions are excellent hot or cold, and can be served as a first course for a luncheon or dinner, as an accompaniment to roasted meats or fowl, or as the principal part of a vegetarian supper, accompanied by herbed noodles and sautéed spinach. If they are served with a white meat and white sauce, they would enjoy the company of a crisp white wine such as a Savennières.

INGREDIENTS   SERVES 6

6 large yellow onions
2 slices bread
1 tablespoon of mixed *fines herbes*: tarragon, parsley, chives, or chervil
   (any combination)
Grated rind of 1 lemon
¼ cup grated Gruyère or Parmesan cheese
2 slices ham, diced
4 tablespoons butter
1 tablespoon mustard
½ cup white wine for braising
Salt and freshly ground pepper

METHOD

Preheat oven to 400 degrees. Trim the root end of the onion and score it with an "X" ⅙-inch deep. Remove and discard the first few papery layers from the onions. Bring a large pot of water to a boil, and then submerge the onions, adding a teaspoon of salt, and allow to blanch for about 10 minutes. Drain the onions on a rack and cool.

When the onions are cool enough to handle, slice the top off each one and scoop out the center with a spoon. Finely chop the scooped out onion and set aside in a bowl. Put the onion "shells" on a work surface.

Remove the bread crusts and cut the bread in a dice. Add to the chopped onion and then add the remainder of the ingredients except the wine.

Carefully pack the filling into the onion "shells" and arrange in a lightly buttered oven-proof dish that has a tight-fitting lid. Dot the surface with butter broken into pea-size pieces. Pour a little wine into the vessel to keep the bottom moist; replenish as needed to prevent the dish from drying out. Bake at the center of a preheated oven for 30 to 40 minutes, or until the onions are soft but still whole.

ONIONS BAKED WITH CHEESE

Oignons au Gratin

This gratin can be served with a roast of lamb and sweet peppers and artichokes, accompanied by a white Côtes-du-Rhône from Lirac.

INGREDIENTS   SERVES 6

1½ pounds small whole onions
2 eggs, beaten lightly with a fork
¼ cup milk
1 clove garlic, minced
⅓ cup grated Gruyère cheese
Salt, freshly ground pepper, and nutmeg

METHOD

Preheat oven to 425 degrees. Cook the onions in a large pot of boiling salted water for 7 to 10 minutes. Remove to a colander and drain until cool enough to handle. Peel the cooled onions and chop coarsely. Reserve in a bowl.

Mix the beaten eggs and the milk; add the garlic, salt, pepper, and nutmeg. Pour over the onions, tossing to coat completely.

Pour the onion mixture into a 9-inch buttered glass pie plate, or into individual buttered ramekins. Top with grated cheese and bake in a preheated oven until set, 15 to 20 minutes for the 9-inch plate, 10 to 12 minutes for the small ramekins.

FRIED ONIONS

Oignons Frits

INGREDIENTS   SERVES 6 ·

2 to 4 large onions cut in ½-inch slices
Milk for dipping
Flour seasoned with salt
Grapeseed oil for deep frying

METHOD

Peel the onions whole, set them on their sides and cut into ½-inch slices. Separate the onion slices into rings in a large bowl. Dip each ring in the milk, drain and dip into the seasoned flour. Shake off the excess flour.

In a pot or deep skillet, bring the frying oil to a low boil. Drop the coated slices into the hot oil and cook until golden brown. Drain on paper towels; season with salt and serve immediately.

ONIONS GLAZED WITH HONEY

Oignons Glacés au Miel

This is a garnish for roasted meats or birds, served with sautéed potatoes and a comforting red wine from a sunny place, a Châteauneuf-du-Pape, for example.

INGREDIENTS	SERVES 6

3 tablespoons butter, melted
⅓ cup honey
3 tablespoons French cider or dry white wine
½ teaspoon freshly grated nutmeg
1 pound small white onions

METHOD

In a saucepan, mix the butter, honey, cider or wine, and nutmeg together and bring to a boil; simmer for a few minutes and reserve.

Score an "X" at the bottom of the onions; then peel the papery layers completely. Blanch the onions in a pot of boiling salted water for 7 to 8 minutes. They should not lose their shape or become mushy; they should retain some resistance when pierced by a cake tester.

Drain the onions and add to the honey mixture. Simmer very slowly until they are well glazed, shaking the pan frequently so that they do not stick. Continue cooking until the onions are completely cooked.

ONIONS WITH SAUSAGE

Saucisses à l'Oignon

These "sausages" can be served as they are, garnished with another vegetable such as sautéed chard, or accompanied by a brown meat sauce and served on their own as a first course.

INGREDIENTS	SERVES 6

1 to 2 large yellow onions

Roux
1 tablespoon flour
1 tablespoon butter
3 tablespoons warm cream

½ cup mashed potatoes or 2 slices bread soaked in ¼ cup milk and
squeezed dry

½ pound leftover cooked meat, ground: lamb, pork, chicken, veal,
or beef (if using fresh meat, sauté ¼ pound ground beef and ¼
pound ground pork)

2 to 4 tablespoons chopped parsley

2 eggs

¼ cup breadcrumbs

Butter for frying

Salt, freshly ground pepper, and allspice

METHOD

Place the whole onions in a pot with 2 to 3 quarts water. Bring the
water to a boil, lower the heat, and let simmer for 20 to 25 minutes.
Remove the onions to a colander to drain and let them cool.

While the onions cook, prepare the meat stuffing. Make the roux in
a 1-quart saucepan. Melt 1 tablespoon butter and 1 tablespoon of flour,
and cook over low heat for 2 to 3 minutes. Add the cream, whisking to
make a smooth paste; then add potatoes (or bread) and mix well. Cook
for a few minutes until thoroughly warmed. Remove the pan from the
heat and add the meat, parsley, salt, pepper, allspice (to taste), and 1 egg,
mixing everything well.

To make the sausages, slice the root end off each onion. Gently pull
off each onion layer separately, so that it remains whole. It should slide
off easily. Save the center part of the onion for another use. Use a heaping
teaspoon of the meat mixture to fill each onion layer; set them upright
on a buttered dish.

In a small bowl, beat the remaining egg. When the sausages are ready
to be cooked, dip them in the beaten egg, and roll in the breadcrumbs.
Heat some butter in a skillet and when hot, sauté the onion "sausages"
on all sides. Salt them lightly each time you turn them for the first few
turns and cook until nicely browned. Turn down the heat and cover until
they are cooked through, about 10 to 15 minutes.

Variation: This dish can also be cooked in a buttered shallow baking
dish in the oven. Place the onion "sausages" side by side; pour a little
melted butter over each one, sprinkle the top with breadcrumbs, and

bake in a preheated 400 degree oven for 15 minutes, or until the sausages are lightly browned.

Potatoes

The potato is a marvelous vegetable suitable to all palates and stomachs. I know at least two hundred ways of preparing them. The potato is as important as bread to the average Frenchman.

POTATO CAKE

Gâteau de Pommes de Terre

Sometimes at Le Trou restaurant I prepare this recipe without the milk. I use duck fat for the cooking, arrange the potatoes as explained in the recipe, and sauté them until brown on one side. Then I turn the cake over and brown the other side. Then the heat is turned down and the cake is cooked until it is tender. However they are prepared, potato cakes are a deliciously satisfying accompaniment to roasted birds, and I often pour a light red Loire wine, such as a Chinon.

INGREDIENTS   SERVES 6 TO 8

8 tablespoons clarified butter (see page 112)
2 pounds baking potatoes
1 small white turnip
1 to 2 cups milk
2 to 4 tablespoons chopped parsley
Salt and freshly ground pepper

METHOD

Preheat oven to 375 degrees. Peel the potatoes and cut into ⅙-inch slices. Rinse the slices in cold water to rid them of some of their starch; allow to dry out. Season the potatoes with salt and pepper, tossing to ensure their proper seasoning. Peel the turnip, slice into ⅙-inch slices, and add to potatoes.

Generously butter a round, straight-sided oven-proof dish. Place a layer of vegetable slices in concentric circles, each slice slightly overlapping the next one. With a pastry brush, spread the clarified butter over the layer, and then over each successive layer.

Pour enough milk over the layers of potatoes to cover them.

Place the dish in a preheated oven. Cook for 45 minutes, or until a golden crust has formed and the potatoes are tender.

GRATIN OF POTATOES

Gratin de Pommes de Terre Grandmère

This is good comforting food to go with a roast of lamb and currant sauce, accompanied by a Beaujolais.

INGREDIENTS   SERVES 6

8 tablespoons clarified butter, melted (see page 112)
2 pounds potatoes
1 cup cream or milk
Salt and freshly ground pepper
2 to 4 tablespoons chopped parsley

METHOD

Peel and cut the potatoes into ⅙-inch slices; rinse them in cold water and lay them out on toweling to dry. Generously butter a 9-inch round baking dish. Lay the potato slices in concentric circles with each slice slightly overlapping. With a brush, spread the butter over the layer and season lightly with salt and pepper. Keep making layers until there are no more potatoes. Pour on enough cream to cover the potatoes. Bake in a preheated oven at 375 degrees for 45 minutes, or until cooked to a golden crusty finish. Garnish with chopped parsley and serve.

Note on Clarifying Butter

There are a number of reasons for clarifying butter. First, the solid particles that rise to the top and fall to the bottom when butter is melted make it subject to invasion by microbes that turn the butter rancid. If these particles are removed, the butter lasts longer. Second, these solids also cause the butter to brown and burn at certain temperatures; so if they are removed, the butter can cook at a higher temperature.

One method of clarifying butter is to melt it and carefully skim off the particles that rise to the top with a spoon. These solids can be used to flavor soups or cooked vegetables. When every trace of these particles has been removed, the butter can then be carefully poured off to separate it from the liquid whey at the bottom of the pan. The liquid whey can be discarded.

Another method is to melt the butter and carefully remove all the solids that rise to the top. Pour off the melted butter into a container and refrigerate to set the butter. All the liquid will settle at the bottom of the container. Remove the solid butter, scrape away any liquid, and discard the liquid and scrapings.

MASHED POTATOES WITH EGGS

Pommes de Terre au Four

This is the favorite way to prepare mashed potatoes at Le Trou restaurant. If kept in a bowl and set into a water bath to keep their heat, they will soufflé lightly.

INGREDIENTS	SERVES 6

2 pounds boiling potatoes
4 tablespoons butter
⅓ cup milk or half-and-half
2 eggs, separated
Salt, freshly ground pepper, and nutmeg

METHOD

Preheat the oven to 375 degrees. Boil the potatoes until tender. Drain and peel. Mash with the butter until free of lumps and creamy. Then add the salt, pepper, and nutmeg to taste. Add the milk, little by little, making the purée a little thicker than ordinary mashed potatoes; then add the yolks, one at a time. About 15 minutes before serving, beat the egg whites stiff and fold thoroughly into the purée. Bake in a preheated oven in an oven-proof dish 10 to 15 minutes. They should be slightly puffed. Serve hot.

POTATOES WITH HERBS

Pommes de Terre aux Herbes

Serve these potatoes with a plain roasted chicken and a good Pinot Noir from the Alsace. While the chicken roasts, prepare the potatoes and the pleasures of the table are yours when everything is ready at the same time.

INGREDIENTS	SERVES 6

¼ pound pancetta, ½-inch dice, or 3 bacon strips, cut up
2 to 4 tablespoons butter
½ medium onion, chopped
4 to 5 medium potatoes, trimmed to olive shapes
1½ cups chicken stock, good homemade (see page 331)
Bouquet garni: bay leaf, thyme, fennel and parsley tied in celery stalks
Salt and freshly ground pepper

METHOD

In a skillet, slowly sauté the bacon until it renders its fat and starts to brown; remove to a bowl and keep ready. Discard all but 1 tablespoon of the bacon fat; add 1 to 2 tablespoons butter and sauté the onion until limp. Season with salt and pepper and remove to the bowl with the bacon. Add more butter to the skillet if necessary, and sauté the potatoes brown.

Mix the onions and bacon back into the potatoes. Pour in enough stock to barely cover the potatoes. Season with salt and pepper. Tie the bouquet garni with a string to facilitate removal and add it to the potatoes. Cover and simmer for 20 minutes, or until liquid is absorbed. Remove the bouquet garni and serve.

POTATOES BAKED IN MILK

Pommes de Terre au Lait

This is a simple and direct way of preparing a gratin of potatoes; its origins have to be in the countryside.

INGREDIENTS	SERVES 6

6 medium potatoes
2 to 4 tablespoons butter
1 cup warm milk

¼ cup chopped parsley
Salt, freshly ground pepper, and nutmeg

METHOD

Preheat oven to 350 degrees. Boil the potatoes for 15 minutes to cook them three quarters of the way through. Drain, then peel and slice. Place the sliced potatoes in a buttered casserole that has a tight-fitting lid. Season with the salt, pepper, and nutmeg. Place the butter broken into pieces on top and pour the milk into the dish to fill it halfway. Sprinkle with half the chopped parsley. Cover and place in a preheated oven until milk and butter are absorbed, about 15 to 20 minutes. Uncover and bake for 5 to 10 minutes to help the liquids evaporate. Remove from oven and pour off any excess liquid; then place under the broiler to brown. Sprinkle with fresh parsley and a light seasoning of salt before serving.

POTATOES WITH MINT

Pommes de Terre à la Menthe

Potatoes prepared this way with any single herb, or a combination of certain herbs, makes a marriage of flavors; it is a better marriage if the potatoes have a character of their own. Sometimes I toss a little lavender in the cooking water of small spring potatoes; it creates the illusion that they grew together in the same soil, and that the herb perfumed the potato while still in the ground.

INGREDIENTS   SERVES 6

1 pound small potatoes
4 tablespoons butter
1 tablespoon finely chopped mint
Salt and freshly ground pepper

Peel and boil the potatoes whole for 10 to 15 minutes. Drain. In a skillet, melt the butter and toss in the mint. Add the potatoes and stir to coat well. If the potatoes are not cooked enough, cover and continue to cook the potatoes until tender. Season with salt and a few grindings of pepper. Serve hot.

POTATOES WITH MUSTARD

Pommes de Terre à la Moutarde

Serve these potatoes with a plain roast of pork accompanied by Red Cabbage with Blueberries (see page 49). Pour a Pinot Noir from the Alsace. Both the amount of butter and mustard in this recipe are to taste. This combination of flavors, butter, mustard, and herbs, works well on noodles also.

INGREDIENTS   SERVES 6

2 pounds small boiling potatoes
4 tablespoons butter, softened
1 to 3 tablespoons Dijon mustard
¼ cup chopped parsley, chervil or chives
Salt and freshly ground pepper

METHOD

Parboil the potatoes whole until cooked through. While the potatoes cook, mix the softened butter in a bowl with a fork; add the mustard, mixing well. Peel the potatoes, toss in the butter, and coat. Add the chopped herbs and season with salt and pepper.

Pumpkin

PUMPKIN WITH A SMALL MELON

Potiron et Melon de Cavaillon

Josephine remembered these dishes from her grandmother. One memory triggers another. She asked me the name of the melon in French and we searched and searched for it. One day when Phanette, a French friend from Marseilles, was visiting, Josephine asked if Cavaillon wasn't the source of a melon from the south of France and the friend agreed. With that bit of information in place, Josephine then recalled that La Mère Jacquette served her melon with pumpkin and flavored the dish with lots of *fines herbes*.

This dish has much more flavor if it is allowed to marinate for a day. It can be served warm or cold to accompany sautéed scallops with tangerine sauce. Drink an Entre-Deux-Mers to accompany the dish.

INGREDIENTS	SERVES 6 TO 8

1 small sugar pumpkin
1 small ripe melon
4 tablespoons *fines herbes*: tarragon, parsley, chives, and chervil (any combination)
2 to 4 tablespoons olive oil
Salt and freshly ground pepper

METHOD

Slice the pumpkin in half. Lay the half flat and slice again in ¾-inch strips. From each slice, scrape away the soft and stringy interior with a paring knife; then carefully peel away the tough outer surface. Cut these slices into cubes. Blanch them in boiling salted water until tender, not more than 5 to 6 minutes. Watch them closely because they overcook easily and lose their shape. When they are cooked, remove to a colander and drain; then put them in a bowl.

Prepare the melon by cutting the same size and shape pieces as the pumpkin. Mix the melon with the pumpkin along with a generous amount of herbs. Toss with olive oil and serve warm.

Radishes

RADISHES WITH LADY APPLES

Radis aux Pommes

This is a dish Josephine remembered her grandmother making. The radishes should be peeled but the apples have their skins left on. Cooked radishes have the peppery flavor of turnips. French cider lends them a fruity sweetness that is further enhanced by the tiny apples. Serve with duck roasted on the bone and accompanied by a potato gratin. Pour a Beaujolais to drink.

Use the radish greens to make a soup with leeks, potatoes, and water, and finish with crème fraîche.

INGREDIENTS   SERVES 6

2 to 3 bunches of tender young radishes
2 tablespoons cider vinegar
12 lady apples, tiny sweet apples
2 to 4 tablespoons butter
1 cup French cider
Rind of 1 lemon, grated
3 tablespoons chopped chives
4 tablespoons chopped parsley
Salt and freshly ground pepper

METHOD

Prepare the radishes. Remove the stems and leaves and reserve for another use. Poach, unpeeled, in boiling salted water to which a little vinegar has been added. The vinegar helps them retain their color. Or, peel the radishes and sauté slowly in butter until tender.

While the radishes cook, prepare the lady apples. Cook whole in the French cider over a slow flame, until they can be easily pierced with a cake tester. Don't hesitate to add more cider if necessary. When the apples are cooked, remove with a slotted spoon.

Put the pan with the cider back on the burner, turn it to high, and reduce to a syrup, being careful not to burn it. When it has reduced, whisk in 2 tablespoons butter and remove from heat. Add the radishes, lady apples, lemon rind, chives, and parsley. Season with salt and pepper; toss everything to coat it well. Serve hot.

Rutabagas

RUTABAGAS AND QUINCES

Rutabagas et Coings

This dish calls for two techniques—blanching the vegetables and sautéing the fruit. The result is that both elements have the same color and you can't tell which is which until their flavor is released on the palate. Serve this dish with a pan-sautéed breast of duck and a fruity red Sancerre from the Loire.

INGREDIENTS	SERVES 6

3 to 4 medium rutabagas (yellow turnips)
2 quinces
2 to 4 tablespoons butter
Persillade: 2 tablespoons chopped parsley and 1 clove minced garlic
1 tablespoon chopped fresh tarragon
Salt and freshly ground pepper

METHOD

Peel the rutabagas and cut in ½-inch dice. Blanch the rutabagas in boiling salted water until tender, about 4 to 6 minutes. They should retain their shape. Drain in a colander and reserve.

Peel, slice, and core the quinces; cube them the same size as the rutabagas. In a heavy-bottomed skillet, melt 2 tablespoons butter on medium heat, add the quinces and toss to coat. Cover the skillet with a tight-fitting lid and cook on medium-low heat until tender, about 4 to 6 minutes. They should retain their shape.

Add the rutabagas to the quinces and rewarm completely. Add pieces of the remaining butter to taste. Mix in the *persillade* and tarragon; season with salt and pepper. Toss well and serve hot.

Sorrel

SORREL JELLY

Gelée d'Oseille

Josephine said that this is a jelly she learned to make in Brittany. Use it to make a sauce for whitefish, accompanied by noodles flavored with lemon rind, parsley, and butter, and pour a French cider to drink.

INGREDIENTS

2 pounds fresh sorrel
4 cups mineral water
2 teaspoons freshly squeezed lime juice
1-inch piece fresh ginger root, peeled and thinly sliced
2 pounds sugar

METHOD

Place the sorrel in a large pot with the mineral water. Add the lime juice and ginger root; bring the water to a boil. Cover and allow it to simmer for about 30 minutes.

Strain off the water and, for every 2 cups of liquid, add 1 pound of sugar and stir until the sugar dissolves. Quickly bring the mixture to a boil and continue cooking until it is at a soft-ball temperature on a thermometer (242 degrees), i.e., until a drop of it thickens in cold water and keeps its shape.

Pour it into sterilized jars and process in a water bath for 10 minutes, until it is sealed.

Spinach

The several varieties of spinach share the same important characteristics: they are all high in food value, very healthful, delicate in flavor, and adaptable to a number of uses.

Spinach has been called "the broom of the stomach" due to its digestibility. It has always been recommended for its rich nutritive value.

Spinach is one of the most versatile vegetables since it complements practically everything: roasts of all kinds, steaks, chops, eggs, fish, or game, and especially ham and sweetbreads. Serve spinach as a base for eggs prepared in different ways, or combine it with other items in a soufflé or quiche.

Due to its delicate nature, use Pyrex, enamel, or stainless steel cookware for spinach. Otherwise, it can pick up a metallic taste and will react with iron or aluminum.

When cooking spinach, boil or steam for only a few minutes, until it is limp. Drain and plunge into cold water to retain the color.

THE VERSATILE SPINACH

Epinards en Branches

This cooking technique calls for washing the spinach in lots of water and using the water that clings to the leaves to steam the vegetable. The spinach is tossed wet into a skillet, given a light sprinkle of salt, and cooked covered. After a minute, the steam builds up in the pan and the spinach collapses. Once it has collapsed, it is cooked.

INGREDIENTS	SERVES 6

½ pound mushrooms, minced
Persillade: 4 tablespoons coarsely chopped parsley and 1 clove garlic, minced
1 tablespoon coarsely chopped fresh marjoram
2 tablespoons butter
1 additional clove garlic, minced
1 pound fresh spinach, washed and stems removed
½ cup grated Gruyère or Parmesan cheese
Salt and freshly ground pepper

METHOD

In a dry skillet, cook the mushrooms with a generous pinch of salt over medium-high heat until they give up their water. Continue to cook until the water evaporates. Remove from heat. Add the *persillade*, marjoram, and 1 tablespoon butter to the mushrooms. Season with salt and pepper; keep ready.

Melt the remaining butter in a large saucepan. Roll the additional garlic in the butter and cook gently for a minute, without browning.

Raise the heat to medium high and add the spinach leaves and a sprinkling of salt. Toss the spinach well and cover the pot. Cook until the spinach wilts, shaking the pan back and forth a few times to prevent sticking and burning; it will not take long. Add the sautéed mushrooms, tossing everything well. Remove to a serving dish and top with the grated cheese and serve at once as an accompaniment to any meat or fowl.

SPINACH IN A CRUST

Epinards en Croûte

This makes a good first course served with any garnish of blanched vegetables, or sautéed apples or pears, and accompanied by a dry crisp white Burgundy, such as a Mâcon Chardonnay.

INGREDIENTS	SERVES 6

1 double pastry crust (see Alsatian Onion Tart page 224)
1½ pounds spinach
2 to 3 tablespoons butter
2 eggs, lightly beaten
1 cup heavy cream
⅓ cup grated Gruyère or Parmesan cheese
Egg glaze: Whisk 1 egg yolk with 1 tablespoon water or milk
Salt, freshly ground pepper, and nutmeg

METHOD

Preheat oven to 375 degrees. Roll out the pastry and line a *tourtière*, pie dish, or bread-loaf pan. (You must reserve a little less than half of the dough for the cover.) Keep it ready.

Clean the spinach in lots of cold water, leaving the stems attached. Plunge the spinach into a large pot of boiling water and bring back to a boil before adding 1 teaspoon salt. Blanch the spinach for a few minutes, until it is limp. Remove to a non-aluminum colander and allow to drain. On a cutting board chop the spinach very coarsely and squeeze out as much excess water as possible. Put the chopped spinach into a 2-quart bowl. (The spinach can also be put into a dry skillet on a low flame and tossed until its water evaporates, and then chopped and put into a bowl.)

Break the butter in small pieces and toss it with the warm spinach. Add the half-beaten eggs, cream, and generous amounts of freshly ground pepper and nutmeg. Mix everything well.

Put the spinach filling into the uncooked shell and spinkle with the cheese. Set the pastry cover made from the reserved dough onto the tart; pierce the top with a knife several times for steam to escape, and crimp the edges with a fork to seal. Brush the top with egg glaze.

Bake the tart in a preheated oven for 25 minutes, until a knife inserted into the center comes out clean.

If you have any dough trimmings left over, they can be rolled and used for decoration such as leaves. Apply any decoration to the glazed surface of the tart and then glaze the decoration, and set to bake.

SPINACH LOAF

Pain d'Epinards

This is excellent when served with chicken livers that have been quickly sautéed in butter and shallots. Unmold the spinach loaf and surround it with the chicken livers.

INGREDIENTS	SERVES 6

2 bunches fresh spinach
1 tablespoon butter
1 small onion, finely chopped
2 whole eggs plus 1 yolk
⅛ cup sherry
½ cup breadcrumbs
Salt, freshly ground pepper, and nutmeg

METHOD

Preheat oven to 375 degrees. Wash the spinach thoroughly in cold water. Put the spinach with a generous pinch of salt in a large non-oxidizing pan with a tight fitting lid; turn the heat to medium high. Put on the lid and allow the spinach to collapse. Remove the lid to evaporate the liquid. Remove the spinach to a cutting board and chop coarsely, squeezing any excess moisture from the cooked spinach.

In the same pan, heat 1 tablespoon butter and sauté the onion until limp. Put the onion and spinach in a blender, add the eggs and sherry. Pulse a few times to blend the ingredients. Season to taste with the salt, pepper, and nutmeg. Remove from the blender and stir in the breadcrumbs.

Pour the mixture into a buttered loaf pan or individual molds. Set in a pan of water and bake in a preheated oven for 25 to 30 minutes for the loaf, 10 to 15 minutes for the small molds, or until set.

SPINACH WITH GREEN PLUMS

Epinards aux Reines Claudes

This is one of the recipes Josephine recalled that her grandmother cooked in Brittany. This is not nouvelle cuisine, but rather a dish well thought out by an old woman who lived close to the earth. She knew better than most what she wanted for her table from the harmony of the garden and the woods.

Serve the spinach with sautéed fillet of sole, herbed mayonnaise, and steamed potatoes; then pour a white wine from the Loire Valley, a Savennières, to drink.

INGREDIENTS	SERVES 6

2 bunches fresh spinach
2 to 4 tablespoons butter
4 to 6 ripe green plums, quartered

Fines herbes: parsley, chervil, chives, and tarragon (any combination)
Salt and freshly ground pepper

METHOD

Clean the spinach, flushing it in several waters until it is completely clean and free of sand or grit; remove the stems (and save them for a soup; see Vegetable Soup page 24). Put the spinach in a non-aluminum colander but don't let it dry completely. The water left on the spinach will be used to steam it.

Place a large bunch of the wet spinach in a large non-oxidizing skillet on medium-high heat. Give it a pinch of salt and cover with a tight lid. Allow heat and steam to build up in the pot for a few minutes. Check to see if the spinach has collapsed and wilted. Stop the cooking before the spinach gives up its water. Set the cooked spinach aside and keep it warm; repeat the same process until all the spinach has been steamed. Remove the spinach to a bowl and keep warm.

Melt 2 tablespoons butter in the same skillet and toss the plums to coat, but be careful not to cook them because they will disintegrate. Add the spinach, then add the herbs, and season the dish with salt and pepper. Toss everything well to coat with butter and give the flavors time to blend. If it appears that the spinach needs more butter, add it in pea-size pieces. Serve the spinach hot.

SPINACH AND RICE WITH HERBS

Epinards au Verts-Prés

Serve this dish as a main course with steamed potatoes for a vegetarian supper, accompanied by a crisp white wine, a Chardonnay from Mâcon, or a French cider.

INGREDIENTS	SERVES 6

1 small onion, chopped
4 whole eggs
1 cup crème fraîche
4 tablespoons chopped parsely
2 teaspoons fresh tarragon
1 teaspoon fresh oregano
1 teaspoon fresh thyme
Freshly grated nutmeg
1½ pounds spinach, blanched and chopped
2 cups cooked rice
2 cups grated Gruyère cheese
Salt and freshly ground pepper

METHOD

Preheat oven to 350 degrees.

In a small skillet sauté the onion in a little butter until lightly browned. In a medium-size bowl, beat the eggs with salt and then add the crème fraîche, mixing well. Add the sautéed onions, herbs, and nutmeg and mix well.

Fold in the spinach and remaining ingredients, reserving ½ cup of the grated cheese. Pour the mixture into a buttered baking dish and place in a preheated oven and bake for 15 minutes. Turn down the oven to 325 degrees and bake another 30 minutes, until cooked through.

Sprinkle the remaining ½ cup cheese over the top and put it in the oven until the cheese is melted, or put under the broiler for a few minutes, until it browns and bubbles.

Turnips

The French grow a very delicate variety of turnip called *Les Navets*. They grow in about 4 or 5 weeks and become tender and meaty like potatoes. White turnips are eaten when just ripe; the yellow turnip, known as rutabaga, is stored for the winter. The smaller turnips are highly aromatic, have a sweet delicate flavor, and are easily digested. The larger ones are not as easily digested and absorb large quantities of fat; therefore, they are usually served with fatty meats such as pork, mutton, duck, or goose. They can be used in *pot-au-feu*, thick or cream soups, or cooked and served around a roast.

The white turnip goes well with figs (see recipe below); the yellow turnip, or rutabaga, goes well with quinces (see page 120).

TURNIPS AND FIGS

Navets et Figues

This is another foraged dish. It particularly likes roast duck with a sauce lightly flavored with raspberry; any first class wine, a Pomerol for example, could accompany it.

INGREDIENTS   SERVES 6

4 firm figs, peeled
4 to 8 tablespoons cognac
4 medium turnips
1 cup veal or chicken stock (see page 331)
4 tablespoons butter
Persillade: 1 clove garlic, minced and 4 tablespoons coarsely chopped
    parsley
Salt and freshly ground pepper

Quarter the figs and place them in a bowl. Pour the cognac over them and allow to marinate an hour or so.

Peel the turnips, cut into a ½-inch dice, and cook in boiling stock 5 to 7 minutes, until tender. Drain in a colander.

Toss the turnips in a dry skillet to rid them of any excess water, toss in pea-size pieces of butter, enough to coat and rewarm the turnips. When the turnips are warmed through, add the figs and the cognac. Raise the heat under the skillet to high and flambé the cognac *carefully*: tip the skillet away from your face when you ignite it. After the cognac ignites, set the pan back down on the burner and shake it well to give the flame lots of oxygen to make it burn. When the flame dies, add the *persillade* and toss everything. Correct the seasonings and serve at once.

GLAZED TURNIPS

Navets Glacés

The turnips prepared this way, sweated in butter and orange juice, are sometimes puréed and thinned with chicken stock to make a very elegant soup at Le Trou. We use 1½ quarts of stock for the amount of turnips called for here.

4 tablespoons butter
5 medium turnips, ½-inch dice
1 to 2 tablespoons sugar
1 cup freshly squeezed orange juice
¼ cup chopped parsley
Salt and freshly ground pepper

In a skillet, melt the butter. Add the turnips, making sure they get completely coated with the butter. Add the sugar and orange juice. Season with salt and pepper to taste. Cover and cook to desired doneness, 10 to 15 minutes. Add the chopped parsley before serving.

Zucchini

ZUCCHINI WITH APPLES

Courgettes aux Pommes

This zucchini can be served with a roast of veal and walnut sauce, and a purée of potatoes, accompanied by a Côtes-du-Rhône.

| INGREDIENTS | SERVES 6 |

6 tablespoons butter
3 onions, thinly sliced
2 apples, peeled, cored, and cut in quarters
1 large tomato, peeled, seeded, and chopped
2 pounds zucchini, julienned and blanched
1 tablespoon chopped parsley
Salt and freshly ground pepper

METHOD

Melt 4 tablespoons butter in a skillet and sauté the onions until they are limp. Add the apples and stir to coat with the butter. Add the tomato and set aside.

In another skillet, melt the remaining 2 tablespoons butter and sauté the zucchini with a sprinkling of salt until it gives up its water; raise the heat to high and evaporate all the liquid.

Add the apple and onion mixture to the zucchini, then the chopped parsley, and combine well. Simmer over low heat for a few minutes to mingle tastes. Correct seasonings, giving a grind of pepper, and serve well heated.

ZUCCHINI WITH BUTTER

Courgettes au Beurre

Serve with sautéed breast of chicken in a tomato sauce and roasted potatoes, accompanied by a Beaujolais.

| INGREDIENTS | SERVES 6 |

1½ pounds zucchini
Flour for dusting vegetables
2 tablespoons butter

2 tablespoons peanut oil
2 to 4 tablespoons coarsely chopped parsley
Salt and freshly ground pepper

METHOD

Preheat oven to 250 degrees. Cut zucchini lengthwise in flat, ¼-inch slices. Salt and let stand for 20 minutes, or until they give up water and it is beaded on the surface of each slice. Rinse well under cold water to rid them of all traces of salt; dry completely and dredge each slice in the flour, shaking off excess.

Heat the butter and the oil in a large skillet and sauté the slices until golden brown on both sides. Remove to a wire rack and keep warm in the oven while the remaining slices are sautéed. Season with salt and pepper, and garnish with parsley and serve hot.

Notes on Persillade

A *persillade* is a trick for flavoring many dishes. It is a simple mixture of chopped parsley and finely minced garlic. The proportions of one to the other are always changing depending on personal tastes; sometimes you may want just the slightest hint of garlic and use a small clove of garlic to ¼ cup chopped parsley. At other times you might want the taste of garlic to dominate. The thing to know about garlic is that the finer it is mashed the less bite it has. The acid is in the juice, so if the juices are mashed out, the garlic has less meanness. A *persillade* can also be worked into butter which is then used to flavor vegetables or soups; the prototype of this butter is escargot butter served with snails.

ZUCCHINI WITH CREAM

Courgettes à la Crème

This dish of zucchini can be served with roast pork, buttered noodles, and a light red wine such as a Borgueil.

INGREDIENTS	SERVES 6

4 tablespoons butter
1 pound zucchini, coarsely shredded
1½ cucumbers, peeled, shredded and drained
½ pound mushrooms, sliced
Persillade: 3 tablespoons finely chopped parsley and 2 cloves of garlic,
   finely minced
½ cup heavy cream
1 teaspoon juniper berries, crushed
Salt and freshly ground pepper

METHOD

Melt 2 tablespoons butter in a skillet; when it is hot add the zucchini
and toss in the cucumber. Give a seasoning of salt and cook on medium
heat until the vegetables begin to give up their water. Raise the heat to
high to evaporate the water. Keep the pan warm.

In a 2-quart saucepan, heat the remaining butter. When the butter is
very hot, it will foam and then the foam will subside. At this point,
quickly toss in the mushrooms with a pinch of salt and sauté the mushrooms until they begin to give up their liquid. Add the *persillade* and
season with salt and a grinding of pepper. Add the cream and cook for
3 to 4 minutes over medium-high heat to evaporate the liquid so there
is just enough to coat the mushrooms.

Add the mushrooms to the zucchini mixture and flavor with the
juniper and additional parsley if desired. Bring the vegetable to temperature, correct the seasonings, and serve very hot.

ZUCCHINI PUREE WITH HERBS

Purée des Courgettes aux Fines Herbes

These vegetable purées are always made individually and by feel; they
are given body with a thickener of choice, but the amount of thickener

always depends on the consistency of the cooked vegetable. This purée would be a wonderful garnish to a veal roast and a first class Bordeaux such as a Pomerol.

| INGREDIENTS | SERVES 6 |

4 tablespoons butter
1 tablespoon peanut oil
1 onion, fine dice
2 pounds zucchini, grated or chopped
Thickening agent: corn starch or potato starch, a *beurre manié*, or a whole potato
⅓ cup heavy cream
2 tablespoons chopped fresh *fines herbes*
1 tablespoon chopped chives
Salt, freshly ground pepper, and nutmeg

| METHOD |

Heat 1 to 2 tablespoons of butter with the oil in a large skillet. Add the onion and sauté until translucent. Add the zucchini with a light sprinkling of salt, and stir to coat the vegetables. Cover the skillet and cook over low heat for 5 to 7 minutes, or until the vegetables give up their water. Remove the lid, raise the temperature, and evaporate the liquid, being careful not to scorch.

When the vegetables are cooked through, remove from the heat and purée them coarsely with a potato masher. Season the purée with salt and freshly grated nutmeg to taste. Return purée to the skillet.

In a bowl, stir the cornstarch into the cold cream. Then warm it in a saucepan. If using other thickeners, heat the cream in a saucepan and then add the thickener, mixing until smooth. Then add it to the squash. Place the skillet back on the heat and cook until mixture develops some stoutness, which takes a minute or two. Correct the seasonings, add the herbs, and give a grind of pepper. Dot with 1 or 2 tablespoons of butter broken into pea-size pieces. Mix everything well and serve the purée piping hot.

About Beurre Manié

Beurre manié is made from equal parts of flour and butter mixed smooth. The butter must be soft (room temperature). It is quickly whisked into hot liquid, and as soon as it is incorporated it must be removed from the heat; otherwise it leaves the taste of raw flour in the dish.

GRANDMOTHER'S JARDINIERE

Ratatouille de Grandmère

This dish has its origin in Brittany. I have found variations on the theme from other Breton cooking sources, which lend authenticity to the dish. Josephine's grandmother would have called it a *jardinière*.

INGREDIENTS	SERVES 6

2 scallions, thinly sliced
2 small red or green peppers, julienned
1 pound zucchini
1 small bunch broccoli or cauliflower, in flowerets
1 small rutabaga, ½-inch dice
1 cup cooked dry beans
2 tablespoons butter
¼ cup olive oil
Juice of 1 lemon
2 tomatoes, sliced
¼ cup chopped parsley
1 clove of garlic, minced
Salt and freshly ground pepper

METHOD

Preheat oven to 350 degrees. Prepare all the vegetables first and have them ready on a tray. Cut the zucchini in half lengthwise, and then cut into ½-inch half-moon slices. In a heavy skillet, heat the butter and oil.

Sauté the scallions and then the peppers; reserve in a buttered oven-proof casserole. Sauté the zucchini in the same skillet as the scallions and peppers and reserve in the casserole.

Blanch the broccoli or cauliflower in boiling salted water 4 to 5 minutes, and then blanch the rutabaga in the same water for the same amount of time; add to reserved vegetables in the casserole. Add the cooked beans and toss all the ingredients. Flavor with lemon juice, salt, and pepper.

Place a layer of tomatoes on the top and garnish with parsley and garlic. Cover and bake in a preheated oven for 20 to 25 minutes and serve.

Notes on Butter

Despite the fact that Brittany is one of the few places in France where people traditionally use salted butter, any reference made to butter in this book calls for unsalted butter. In the United States, salted butter is much saltier than one would find in France. Unsalted butter to which salt has been added yields a more savory result.

Certain place names in France represent the highest quality. Isigny in Normandy or Echiré in the Deux-Sèvres are such places when the subject is butter. In the summer when the cows are in the pasture and eat grass and flowers, the butter they produce is sweet and has some of the yellow color of the carotene found in the flowers. In the fall and winter when the animals are on a diet of hay, the color of the butter becomes whiter almost overnight.

The best butter has a waxy quality; when you work with it in your hands it doesn't readily melt and feel greasy, rather it softens and is pliable like soft wax. A good test for determining the quality of butter is to clarify it (see page 112) and see the exact proportions of solids to liquids in it.

There are several ways to approach the use of fat. You can use a lot of butter to cook a vegetable, and then discard the butter when you add braising liquid. If richness is desired, fresh butter can be reintroduced just prior to serving. This reintroduction adds butter that isn't fatigued by cooking, the idea being that if you use it for flavoring, you use less of it.

PART II

Paris, France

Josephine at the Cordon Bleu

It was in the 1870s that the French built the rail line from Paris to Brest, located at the end of the Breton peninsula. This is the department of the *Finistère*, Land's End, and Josephine's *pays*, her place of origin. La Mère Jacquette would have been in her fifties at this point, and Josephine was not yet born. Paris chefs celebrated the advent of this train by naming a dessert the Paris-Brest. It is classic and remains popular. You can still find the Paris-Brest served in French pâtisseries and recipes for it in modern cookbooks.

Between the advent of the Paris-Brest train and the end of the first World War, French cuisine became a heavenly body. The grand chefs of Paris wove celestial designs. The existence of the train didn't signal mere convenience; it was the manifestation of a time of revolutionary change. France was launching itself into a series of wars that destroyed generation after generation of its youth. The farming culture of the countryside was shifting to a factory culture of the city. France was reaching out from Paris to its scattered regions to gather in the soldiers and workers it needed.

Over a period of decades, along the train route from Brest to Lorient—the connecting point to Pont-Scorff—the trains gathered Breton youth seeking wider horizons in the capital. The temperament of these youths underlined the generosity that is the temperament of Brittany itself. Many of them had training in cooking, and the possession of these qualities and skills often meant the chance to work. Restaurants were a natural point of gravitation. If city cooking was jaded or flat, country cooks knew improvisation. The Bretons, fresh and unfettered, joined those from other regions in the kitchens of Paris, and Paris noticed. Bretons also were commonly hired to cook in Parisian homes. When the

Loucher family in Paris, who had hired Josephine to cook for them, agreed to send Josephine to Henri-Paul Pellaprat at the Cordon Bleu to further her skills in the kitchen, she joined the history of French cuisine. She wove her native talent into the fabric of classic cuisine.

Cuisine is a tapestry full of vibrant color and texture. In one direction, it provides a look at the past that emerges from our ancestral cooking. It offers to us a glimpse of a way of life and a way of doing things that has all but disappeared. Regional cuisine, standing at the threshold of classic cuisine, provides us a look toward the future. Chefs built their techniques on its earth-bound knowledge and practical expression. It continues to inspire us in our own kitchens where modern food evolves.

Paris profited from the exchange with Brittany and the other provinces. The French love solutions and ask, "What is the best?" It is this commitment to the best that allows France to give the world Camembert, Brie, and Roquefort, the best cheeses; Sauternes, Cognac, and Châteauneuf-du-Pape, the best wines; Normandy creams, the prunes of Agen, the lentils of Puy, and butter from the Charentais. Bretons gave Paris vegetable dishes *à la Bretonne* and the fresh vegetables that France still calls *primeurs*—the best. Brittany also contributed butters, cream, crêpes, cakes, and *pur jus cidres*. Brittany offered seafood unsurpassed and dishes like *cotriade*, a celebrated fish chowder. The revered belon oyster comes from the Gulf of Morbihan, Brittany's Little Sea. The list goes on and on.

When Josephine's teacher, Pellaprat, wanted to praise his favored student, he would say to her that she was a natural cook. But Josephine would defer, giving La Mère Jacquette the credit for her own basic culinary outlook. Josephine knew she had the kernel of something pure because Monsieur Pellaprat, sitting at the height of the profession, acknowledged it. When Pellaprat informed her that he was "crowning" her with a toque, she replied, "I don't see any jewels in this crown, Henri." To which Pellaprat responded, "You are the jewel." She was irrepressible; from the start, a queen among chefs. Like Anne, a queen from Brittany who married a French king, Josephine married a Paris royal house, the Cordon Bleu. She brought Brittany and its cuisine as her dowry. She never lost sight of her Breton inheritance, the spirit of which she dispensed with joy, and without personal profit. How much she valued her Brittany and its people all of her life can only be judged by how brightly she kept alive their memory in her stories.

"A good teacher must have patience," Pellaprat would say. Josephine had a series of these sayings. It was her way of keeping him and the Cordon Bleu present. She had been the student of this man whose name is a household word in France just as Fannie Farmer's name is in this country. She spent seven years with Pellaprat; they addressed each other by their first names. She remained in contact with him until his death in the late 1940s.

The qualities that came to color her own culinary outlook were hers alone. Self-possession and faith imbued her work. She later imparted them to her students, as though these qualities were the air they breathed. She had a way of focusing on those around her; and she made students feel that they were all that mattered—that each one was the favorite. Her manner was underlined by the warmth of her Breton spirit, and she expressed it in the mirthful way Breton is spoken. When Josephine shined, she illuminated. "Sing," she would say, "it will improve your cooking."

One day at Josephine's we were sitting by the window overlooking the garden; we were lost in conversations about food. I pulled a small composition book from the shelf. I handled it very carefully because it seemed frail. The contents were written neatly in a consistent hand that I recognized was not her own. I asked about the book. She said it was a record of everything she did at the Cordon Bleu. It had been compiled by a friend who studied with her. As I turned the pages, she spoke on in her special way.

"There are ten fundamentals Pellaprat taught me," she said, raising her hand and spreading her fingers to test one by one their correspondence with her memory. "You must know the omelette, the pastes, the *pochage*, . . ." ticking off each to ten. She then launched into a litany of favorite expressions, many of them from Pellaprat and others. She loved repeating homilies like, "Don't let anything dampen your spirit." This was one of Pellaprat's favorites. Any magician has a litany of chants; Josephine was not without hers. Over and over she would repeat them. A gourmet dish is not an elaborate dish, nor one made with only fancy or expensive ingredients, nor is it swell-headed. "A gourmet dish is a well-prepared dish." Period. It follows, however, that well-prepared food must be made with good ingredients. A dish is the achievement of ingredients chosen for their distinctive qualities and then respectfully treated by the cook.

Josephine learned from her grandmother to seek the finest, freshest, seasonal ingredients and how to combine them. There simply was no other way to cook. From Pellaprat, she learned the techniques of *haute cuisine*. To these lessons, Josephine added her own spirit and personality to create her very own identity as a cook. A good cook is taught to know the fundamentals and to be capable with information. A great cook learns those things as well as how to be patient and completely self-possessed. A knife, to cut, needs to be surely held. The slightest detail of one's work in the kitchen needs to be done this way. An onion needs to be chopped with sureness. A sauce needs a deft eye, hand, and mind. "Texture and taste, *Robeirt*, are what you need to pay attention to." You finish a sauce with sureness, just the way you sign your name.

Classic French Recipes

This section introduces Josephine's recipes that use the ingredients of Paris society. These recipes have classic sauces—béchamel, mornay, and hollandaise. We see *foie gras* and other deluxe ingredients. Paris provided things that aren't found in the provinces, especially in a poor one like Brittany. This was not, however, a cuisine that had meaning only for the jaded. We see dishes here that are named for their origins, with national and international names: *Portugaise, Italienne, Provençale, Alsacienne*. These titles are in contrast to those of Breton dishes, for which a local name, such as Saint-Nazaire or Montmorency, is used to celebrate the dish.

These dishes have infinite merit. They inspire us to make use of their flavors, their combinations, and their esthetics. They were designed by brilliant men and women, chefs devoted to building a grander, richer cuisine from a strong regional foundation. Their efforts ensured that a developing body of culinary knowledge would be built on the best.

Artichokes

ARTICHOKES WITH STUFFING

Artichauts à la Barigoule

These artichokes can be served hot or cold as a first course, accompanied by a crisp white Pinot Blanc from Burgundy.

This recipe offers a mélange of flavorings that can take many forms; it is rich for reinterpretation, which is often what happens at the restaurant (see Cream of Artichoke Soup with Mushrooms and Ham page 281).

145

INGREDIENTS	SERVES 6

6 medium artichokes
3 to 4 tablespoons butter
¼ pound mushrooms
1 shallot or scallion, chopped
1 tablespoon chopped parsley
Juice of 1 lemon
1 tablespoon tomato paste
½ cup cooked ham, chopped
6 slices bacon or pork fatback
   ½ cup white wine
2 tablespoons tomato purée
¼ cup *glace de viande,* veal stock, or meat juices
Bouquet garni: parsley stems, thyme, bay, and marjoram tied in celery
   stalks
Salt and freshly ground pepper

METHOD

Preheat oven to 350 degrees. Prepare and blanch the artichokes as described in Braised Stuffed Artichokes (page 14).

Clean and trim the mushrooms, chop coarsely, and sauté in a little oil or butter. Add salt, pepper, shallot, parsley, lemon juice, and tomato paste. Allow this mixture to cook about 5 minutes, until the liquid has almost evaporated. Add the chopped ham. Fill each artichoke cavity with this mixture and wrap the outside of each one with a strip of bacon, and fasten with kitchen string.

Put the artichokes side by side in an oiled oven-proof casserole. Add the wine, tomato purée and *glace de viande*, veal stock, or juice of any roast. Then season with salt and a few grindings of pepper, and add the bouquet garni.

Cover the artichokes with a piece of buttered wax paper and bake in a preheated oven for 30 to 45 minutes. Test for doneness by plucking a leaf and tasting for tenderness. Remove the artichokes from the pan and remove the strings. Pour the pan juices into a small saucepan and reduce to concentrate their flavor. Serve a teaspoon or so of the juice with each artichoke.

QUARTERED ARTICHOKES WITH PEAS

Quartiers d'Artichauts Clamart

Artichokes and peas is a dish of many themes. It is one that lends itself to many styles of presentation from simple, humble fare to the most elegant. This is a generous version that would be content to accompany a roast chicken with tarragon sauce and a glass of a Sauvignon Blanc from the region around Bordeaux.

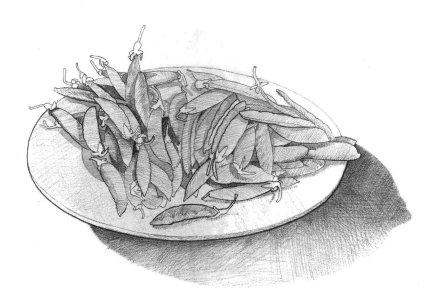

| INGREDIENTS | SERVES 6 |

12 small artichokes, blanched (see Boiled Artichokes page 11)
3 tablespoons clarified butter (see page 112) or 3 tablespoons butter
    and 1 tablespoon of peanut oil
1 onion, chopped
1 cup of shelled fresh peas
1 cup lettuce greens: escarole, romaine, etc., shredded
Pinch of sugar
1 cup chicken stock, good homemade (see page 331)
1 to 2 tablespoons butter
Salt and freshly ground pepper

METHOD

Trim the blanched artichokes, cut in quarters, and remove the choke.
Select a heavy skillet that will not react with the artichokes (i.e., not iron
or aluminum). Heat enough clarified butter to sauté the onion; cook until

it starts to turn golden. Remove and set aside. To the same pan, add additional butter and the artichokes and sauté until they begin to turn golden brown.

Add the onion, peas, and shredded lettuce greens. Season with sugar, salt, and pepper. Add the chicken stock, cover with a tight-fitting lid, and simmer gently for about 10 minutes or until tender. (It can also be cooked in an oven-proof dish in a 300-degree oven for about 45 minutes.) At the last moment, add a piece of butter the size of a walnut and whisk well to incorporate it with the juices. Remove to a vegetable dish and serve very hot.

ARTICHOKE BOTTOMS WITH CARROTS

Fonds d'Artichauts Crécy

This is a much more elegant presentation of a dish that we included in Part I, Pont-Scorff, Brittany. Here a regional taste for artichokes and carrots is presented "like a horse on parade," as Josephine would say. The tastes that were originally worked out in country kitchens found their way to the big city.

Serve as a garnish around a roast, for example, pork with hazelnut sauce accompanied by a white Côtes-du-Rhône.

INGREDIENTS	SERVES 6

6 medium to large artichokes
Juice of 1 lemon or 2 tablespoons wine vinegar
5 to 6 carrots, grated
2 tablespoons butter
1 tablespoon peanut oil
1 teaspoon sugar (optional)
Persillade: 2 to 4 tablespoons chopped parsley and 1 small clove garlic, minced
1 tablespoon chopped parsley
1 tablespoon chopped fresh tarragon
Salt and freshly ground pepper

METHOD

Trim the coarse leaves from around the artichoke, cut off the stem, and save for other purposes. Cut off the tip of the artichoke 1 inch from the top. Cook in boiling salted water with the lemon juice or 2 tablespoons vinegar until the leaves come off easily. Remove to a colander, flush under cold water to stop the cooking, and set aside.

Grate the carrots on the widest hole of the grater. In a large skillet, heat 2 tablespoons butter with the peanut oil, add the carrots, season with salt (and sugar, if desired), and cook on medium heat until soft; stir often to avoid sticking. Remove the carrots to a food processor and purée. Correct the seasoning and add the *persillade* mixing well. Spoon the puréed carrots into a pastry bag with a fluted tip and keep ready.

Remove the leaves and choke from the cooked artichokes and reserve for another use. Sauté the artichoke bottoms on low heat in the same butter as the carrots until they begin to color; don't hesitate to add more butter if necessary. Remove to a warm serving dish.

Season each artichoke bottom with a bit of salt and a grinding of pepper.

Pipe the purée of carrots onto the artichoke bottoms. Garnish with herbs and serve.

ARTICHOKES WITH CURRY AND EGGS

Artichauts au Cari et aux Oeufs

Serve these artichokes as the first course of an elegant dinner or as the principal course of a supper or lunch, accompanied by a white wine from the Loire, such as a Savennières.

This dish belongs in Paris, although a couple of things make me think it has ties to Brittany. The use of curry in local cuisine came from the sailing trade. The sailors from Brittany weren't directly involved in the spice trade, as were the Bordelais, but being port-to-port sailors were in contact with long-distance spice traders. For example, in La Rochelle, a city just south of the former Breton port of Nantes, local dishes, such as *mouclade* are based on saffron and curry, which are thoroughly exotic but still local.

Though this dish has moved away from its local roots, it nevertheless carries the aromas of a local dish in a new home; such was the evolution of French cuisine.

INGREDIENTS

4 to 6 medium artichokes, blanched (see Boiled Artichokes page 11)
Juice of 1 lemon
4 tablespoons butter
1 scallion, finely chopped
1 tablespoon curry powder
6 eggs, lightly beaten
¾ cup milk
1 tablespoon chopped fresh tarragon
¼ cup grated Gruyère or Emmenthaler cheese
3 to 4 tomatoes, peeled, seeded, and quartered
Salt and freshly ground pepper

METHOD

Blanch the artichokes in boiling salted water with the lemon juice, and drain completely. Scrape the edible part of the leaves with a teaspoon and discard the remainder of the leaves. Remove the chokes, chop the bottoms coarsely and add to the scraped artichoke meat.

In a skillet, heat 1 tablespoon butter and sauté the scallion. When limp, add the curry and cook for a minute to develop the flavor. In a bowl, combine the eggs, milk, curried scallion, and tarragon; beat well and season with salt and pepper to taste. Mix in the artichoke meat and grated cheese.

Melt the remaining butter in a double boiler. Have the heat at a steady simmer; it should not go to a galloping boil. Add the egg mixture and artichokes to the double boiler; stirring gently and constantly cook to a consistency slightly thicker than heavy cream, a soft curd. Serve with a garnish of tomatoes.

ARTICHOKE HEARTS WITH FOIE GRAS

Coeurs d'Artichauts Pompadour

This is ravishing first class food of extraordinary singularity; serve it with a Sauternes.

This dish inspires me at the restaurant where I prepare custards of bird livers such as duck, pheasant, or chicken—garnished with artichokes. Or, conversely, I make artichoke custards garnished with liver pâté on toast.

INGREDIENTS   SERVES 6

6 artichoke hearts, cooked (see Boiled Artichokes page 11)
6 slices cooked foie gras, each ¼-inch thick and the diameter of the
    artichoke hearts
6 baked pastry crust rounds, toasted brioche, or plain toast, the size
    of the artichoke hearts
6 tablespoons breadcrumbs
6 tablespoons grated Swiss or Gruyère cheese

METHOD

Fill artichoke hearts with the foie gras and set onto the crusts. Top with breadcrumbs and grated cheese. Broil very quickly so the cheese melts and serve.

QUARTERED ARTICHOKES WITH HERBS

Quartiers d'Artichauts aux Fines Herbes

Some of Josephine's recipes require the use of pan juices. She would save them from roasted meats and store them in a jar in the refrigerator. This dish can be prepared without the juices; they give flavor, but are not essential. The artichokes can be made with good homemade stock, wine, cider or even water.

Blanching artichokes and then slowly sweating them in butter until they brown lightly gives a profound depth of flavor. Serve the dish with a simple white meat roast, such as veal or pork, accompanied by a white Burgundy.

INGREDIENTS — SERVES 6

6 medium artichokes
1 lemon, cut in half
2 tablespoons butter
½ cup stock, good homemade, or pan juices from roasted meats, or white wine
2 to 4 tablespoons chopped *fines herbes*: tarragon, parsley, chervil, and chives (any combination)
1 teaspoon chopped thyme
1 teaspoon chopped sage
2 to 3 tablespoons freshly squeezed lemon juice
2 to 4 tablespoons chopped parsley
2 to 4 tablespoons butter in pea-size pieces
Salt and freshly ground pepper

METHOD

Trim and quarter the artichokes and remove the chokes. Rub the exposed flesh with the lemon. If the artichokes are small, sauté in butter; otherwise, blanch until tender in boiling salted water with the juice of the lemon used to rub the artichoke.

Melt butter in a heavy frying pan, add the blanched artichokes, and lightly brown. Season with salt and pepper. Pour the liquid—stock, meat juices, or wine—over the artichokes and bring to a boil. Reduce heat and simmer gently for 10 minutes to reduce the liquid by half. Remove the artichokes to a heated dish.

Add the *fines herbes*, thyme, and sage to the liquid in the skillet along with lemon juice and allow to steep on low heat 4 to 5 minutes. Bring the liquid to a rapid boil and quickly whisk in the pieces of butter. Strain the sauce through a fine strainer and pour over the artichokes. Sprinkle with parsley and serve.

ARTICHOKES WITH HERBS, WINE, AND TOMATOES

Artichauts Merveille

This kind of dish is best served with a plain presentation of meat, that is to say, properly seasoned but not sauced. Note the use of oil. Some cooks are spare with oil, others are generous.

INGREDIENTS   SERVES 6

2 to 3 tablespoons extra virgin olive oil
12 small boiling onions, whole, or 3 large onions, quartered
1 clove garlic, minced
1 cup veal, beef, or chicken stock (see page 331)
1 cup white wine
2 large tomatoes, peeled, seeded, and quartered
1 sprig fresh thyme, oregano, or marjoram
Juice and rind of 1 lemon
2 to 3 small artichokes without chokes
2 to 4 tablespoons chopped parsley
Salt and freshly ground pepper

METHOD

Very small artichokes have no chokes and are almost entirely edible. Trim the root end first, and then remove the top by slicing with a knife or snipping with a scissors. Select a large pot in which the artichokes can stand side by side. Heat the olive oil and sauté the onion and garlic for a few minutes. Add the stock, wine, tomatoes, herb, lemon juice, rind, and salt. Let the mixture come to a boil and put in the artichokes side by side. Reduce the heat and cook covered slowly for 30 minutes, until the artichokes are tender.

Serve with the tomato mixture on a heated platter. Sprinkle with chopped parsley and a grinding of pepper.

ARTICHOKE DUMPLINGS ITALIAN STYLE

Gnocchi d'Artichauts à l'Italienne

Serve as a first course, a main course supper with a salad of greens or spinach, or as an accompaniment to roasted meat or fowl. Pour a lovely white Provençal wine, a Bandol Blanc, or a Northern Italian wine, a Cinque Terre. Artichokes have too much tannin to complement a red wine.

INGREDIENTS   SERVES 6

6 medium artichokes, blanched (see Boiled Artichokes page 11)

Fresh tomato sauce
2 to 4 tablespoons olive oil
2 medium onions, small dice
2 pounds fresh tomatoes, coarsely chopped
Sprig of thyme
1 bay leaf

Pâte à Chou
4 tablespoons cold butter
1 cup cold water
1 cup flour
4 whole eggs

¼ to ½ cup freshly grated Parmesan cheese
Salt and freshly ground pepper

METHOD

Blanch the artichokes until tender, 20 to 25 minutes, and drain completely.

To make the tomato sauce, sauté the onions in olive oil and season lightly with salt. Add the tomatoes, thyme, and bay leaf, and simmer only long enough for the water in them to evaporate, so that they hold their shape, about 8 to 10 minutes. Correct seasonings.

While the artichokes cook, prepare the *pâte à chou*. Cut the cold butter in ½-inch cubes. Put the butter in a saucepan with the water and bring to a boil; try to have the butter melted before the water boils. If there are still pieces of butter, lower the heat and let it melt.

Remove the saucepan from the heat, add all the flour at once, stirring with a wooden spoon to incorporate; season with salt and pepper. Place the pan back on the burner over medium heat; spread the paste across the bottom of the pan, pushing it against the sides; then spread it back in the opposite direction. Work the paste across the pan in about three strokes. You want to expose as much surface of the paste to the heat as possible to evaporate the water and make the paste dry. This makes the final gnocchi lighter. When the paste is compact enough, there will be a film of cooked flour on the bottom of the pan indicating that the water has evaporated. As a further guide to determine doneness, there may also be a sheen of butter which works its way to the surface of the paste.

Remove the pan from the heat. Add the whole eggs one at a time, mixing with a wooden spoon. As the paste comes apart with the addition of each egg, work quickly to bring it back together. Season with salt and pepper and set aside.

Strip the leaves from the cooked artichokes and scrape the meat from them. Remove the chokes, mash the flesh, and mix with scrapings. This should yield about 2 cups of artichoke meat. Mix the artichokes into the gnocchi paste. Using two soup spoons, shape the paste into dumplings, *gnocchi*, about the size of a walnut.

Preheat oven to 350 degrees. Fill a large pot with 6 inches of water and bring to a boil. Make sure the pot is wide enough to hold several gnocchi at one time and deep enough so that they can cook in about 4 inches of water. When the water boils, reduce to a simmer and add 1 to 2 teaspoons salt. Drop the gnocchi into the heated water. They will sink to the bottom of the pot and then come to the surface when they are cooked. Remove the cooked gnocchi with a slotted spoon and place in a buttered, shallow gratin dish.

Cover the gnocchi with the fresh tomato sauce flavored with additional fresh thyme. Cover with the grated cheese and bake in a preheated oven until the cheese browns.

QUARTERED ARTICHOKES ITALIAN STYLE

Quartiers d'Artichauts à l'Italienne

This dish would love to be served with fresh noodles as a main course for a lunch or a vegetarian supper, followed by a green salad. It is also a wonderful first course for a dinner. If you simmer the artichokes in a lovely white wine, you can have the pleasure of the rest of the bottle to drink with the dish.

INGREDIENTS	SERVES 6

6 large artichokes
Juice of 1 lemon
2 to 4 tablespoons olive oil
1 medium onion, small dice
½ cup white wine
¼ cup stock, good homemade (see page 331)
1 pound fresh tomatoes, peeled, seeded, and coarsely chopped
Sprig of thyme
¼ cup shredded fresh basil
Salt and freshly ground pepper

METHOD

Trim and quarter the artichokes and remove the choke. Rub the exposed flesh with a lemon. Blanch the artichokes until tender and drain (see Boiled Artichokes page 11).

Heat the olive oil in a saucepan and sauté the onion with a little salt until translucent. Pour in the wine, stock, tomatoes, and thyme. Add the artichokes and simmer about 15 minutes, until the sauce has thickened and the vegetables are tender. The liquids evaporate to a sauce-like texture. Correct the seasoning; give a grinding of fresh pepper, finish the dish with the addition of basil shredded at the last moment, and serve.

LUGANO-STYLE STUFFED ARTICHOKES

Artichauts Farcis Lugano

Serve the artichokes as a course by themselves, accompanied by an Italian white wine, a Cinque Terre.

INGREDIENTS	SERVES 6

6 medium artichokes, boiled (see Boiled Artichokes page 11)
Juice of 2 lemons or ⅛ cup cider vinegar
⅓ cup breadcrumbs
1 clove garlic, minced
3 tablespoons freshly grated Parmesan cheese
Vinaigrette (see page 74)
Olive oil for baking dish
Compound butter: 4 tablespoons butter mixed with 2 tablespoons
   chopped parsley and 1 clove minced garlic

METHOD

Preheat oven to 350 degrees. Remove the outer leaves of the artichoke and trim off the tops of the remaining leaves; blanch in boiling salted water acidulated with lemon juice for 25 to 30 minutes.

Remove enough of the center leaves to be able to stuff the artichoke. Scrape the meat from these leaves and set aside to use with the filling. Remove the choke with a teaspoon.

Mix the breadcrumbs, garlic, and scraped artichoke meat; then moisten this mixture with 3 or 4 tablespoons of the vinaigrette. Finally, add the Parmesan cheese. Fill the artichoke centers with this mixture.

Lightly oil an oven-proof dish and set the artichokes to bake in a preheated oven for 10 minutes, or until well heated. To make the compound butter, first coarsely chop the parsley and finely mince the garlic. Using the flat side of a knife or metal spatula, mash the garlic and parsley into the butter until it is well mixed. Shape it back into a cube and keep it ready on a small plate. Serve the artichokes with additional vinaigrette and dot the top with compound butter.

ARTICHOKES STUFFED WITH ONIONS AND MEAT

Artichauts à la Lyonnaise

The tastes found in this recipe can be found in a different dish, Noodles with Sausage, Artichokes, and Herbs, page 280.

INGREDIENTS   SERVES 6

6 medium artichokes, blanched for stuffing (see Braised Stuffed Artichokes page 14)
1 cup cooked sausage or leftover meat for stuffing
1 large onion, chopped
¼ cup chopped parsley
¼ cup white wine
¼ cup stock, good homemade (see page 331)
1 tablespoon olive oil
2 tablespoons butter, in pieces
Juice of 1 lemon
Salt and freshly ground pepper

METHOD

Preheat oven to 350 degrees.
Blanch the artichokes, drain, and prepare for stuffing.
Sauté the sausage and onion until translucent, but not brown, and let cool. Mix in the parsley, and season with salt and pepper. Fill the cavity of the artichoke with the meat mixture.
Arrange the stuffed artichokes in an oven-proof casserole, side by side and bottom down. Pour the wine and stock over them and drizzle

the tops with a little olive oil and lemon juice. Add a piece of butter to each. Bake in a preheated oven for 35 to 40 minutes.

Drain the juices into a small saucepan; skim off any fat and reduce to make a sauce.

MARINATED ARTICHOKE BOTTOMS

Fonds d'Artichauts à la Grecque

The marinade can be used for any other cooked vegetable. This sort of recipe makes great use of artichoke scrapings; they make good marinated garnishes.

Serve these marinated artichokes as an element for a composed salad, accompanied by another vegetable such as steamed potatoes or string beans, and you have the makings of an *al fresco* lunch. Offer a good crusty bread and a sheep's milk cheese from Corsica or Provence, and pour a white Côtes-du-Rhône or Corbières.

INGREDIENTS	SERVES 1-2

2 cups dry white wine
Juice of 1 lemon
1 teaspoon Worcestershire sauce
2 tablespoons tomato coulis (see page 252)
Sprig of fresh thyme
1 bay leaf, broken in half
⅛ teaspoon ground coriander seeds
12 freshly cooked artichoke bottoms (see Boiled Artichokes
    page 11)

METHOD

Combine all of the ingredients except the artichoke bottoms and mix thoroughly. Add the artichokes and marinate for at least 2 hours.

ARTICHOKES WITH ONIONS, LARDONS, AND PORT

Artichauts Marseillaise

This is an excellent dish to accompany a pork roast with a fruit brandy-flavored sauce. Serve with a rosé from Corbières.

INGREDIENTS	SERVES 6

½ pound fresh bacon or pancetta
4 tablespoons butter
2 pounds onions, sliced
2 to 4 tablespoons extra virgin olive oil
12 cooked artichoke bottoms (see Boiled Artichokes page 11)
¼ cup port
Salt and freshly ground pepper

METHOD

Preheat oven to 350 degrees. Cut the bacon into ½-inch lardons and blanch in simmering water about 15 to 20 minutes. Put them in a skillet and sauté slowly in 2 tablespoons butter to crisp. Remove to a dish, reserving 1 tablespoon of the bacon fat.

In the same skillet, sauté the onions lightly in the bacon fat and the olive oil until limp but not brown. Season with salt and pepper to taste.

Blanch the artichokes, drain, and cool. Remove the chokes. Trim the artichoke bottoms so that they are rounded and smooth. Melt 2 tablespoons butter in a clean skillet and sauté the artichoke bottoms for a few minutes on each side until they start to brown. Season with salt and pepper.

Lightly oil an oven-proof dish. Moisten two thirds of the onion mixture with the port and place in the bottom of the baking dish. Set the artichoke bottoms on the onion mixture. Mix the bacon with the remaining onions, moisten it with a little more port if desired, and top each artichoke bottom with it. Place in a preheated oven for 15 minutes.

ARTICHOKES WITH ONIONS AND TOMATOES

Artichauts Lessieur

Serve with a roast of white meat with noodles garnished with the artichokes and a bottle of crisp white wine from the Loire, such as a Sancerre.

INGREDIENTS	SERVES 6

12 small artichokes, without chokes
Juice of 1 lemon
12 small boiling onions
¼ cup olive oil
½ cup stock, good homemade (see page 331)
2 tomatoes, peeled, seeded, and chopped
¼ cup chopped parsley
Salt and freshly ground pepper

METHOD

Remove any tough, bruised outer leaves of artichokes and discard. Trim the root end and any prickly ends of remaining leaves. In a large pot, blanch artichokes in boiling salted water with the lemon juice for 5 to 7 minutes. Drain in a colander and let dry.

Trim the root end of the small onions, score with an "X" about ⅛-inch deep, and peel away any papery silver skin.

In a heavy-bottomed pot, warm 2 to 4 tablespoons olive oil. Add the onions and a pinch of salt and sauté for a few minutes until they start to brown; then add the artichokes, broth, and tomato. Simmer covered for 20 to 25 minutes, until the artichokes are tender. Correct the seasoning and give a grinding of pepper. Cool the mixture in the cooking juices. Serve either warm or at room temperature; sprinkle with chopped parsley. Drizzle 1 to 2 tablespoons of fresh olive oil for flavoring.

ARTICHOKES WITH TOMATOES AND OLIVES

Artichauts Provençale

These are a wonderful accompaniment to roast leg of lamb and tiny dumplings known as gnocchi (see page 235). Drink a white wine from the southern regions, such as a Bandol, Cassis, or Corbières.

INGREDIENTS	SERVES 6

1 pound small artichokes, quartered and hearts removed
1 quart water acidulated with 2 tablespoons lemon or white wine vinegar in a bowl
4 to 6 tablespoons extra virgin olive oil
1 tablespoon butter
½ pound mushrooms, sliced
1 large tomato, peeled, seeded, and diced
2 cloves garlic, chopped
½ cup black olives, pitted
2 tablespoons chopped fresh tarragon
2 tablespoons chopped fresh parsley
Salt and freshly ground pepper

METHOD

Trim and quarter the artichokes; remove the chokes. Toss them in the bowl of acidulated water to keep their color. In a skillet, heat 2 to 3 tablespoons olive oil mixed with a bit of butter, if desired. Add the artichokes, season lightly with salt, and sauté slowly for about 10 minutes, until tender and beginning to color slightly. Remove the vegetable from the skillet, and reserve. Discard the cooking oil.

In the same skillet, heat 2 tablespoons olive oil, add the mushrooms and a pinch of salt, and sauté until they give up their liquid; add the tomato and cook for another minute. Add the garlic, olives, and chopped herbs. Add the artichokes and simmer for 5 minutes. Correct the sea-

soning, give a grinding of pepper, and serve with additional herbs sprinkled on top.

PUREED ARTICHOKES

Timbales d'Artichauts

Serve these as a first course with an elegant sauce such as a hollandaise
or mousseline (see following recipes). Or serve as a vegetable garnish
for a roast veal with noodles and a hazelnut butter, accompanied by a
mountain wine from the Savoie, such as an Apremont or Crépy.

INGREDIENTS	SERVES 8 TO 12

¾ cup breadcrumbs
⅓ cup milk
4 tablespoons butter, melted
2 to 3 shallots, minced
3 cups cooked artichoke flesh (about 9 medium artichokes)
¼ cup heavy cream
3 egg yolks
10 ounces spinach, blanched and squeezed dry
5 egg whites
Salt, freshly ground pepper, and nutmeg

METHOD

Preheat oven to 325 degrees. Butter twelve 3-ounce timbale molds
or use a 6-cup soufflé dish.

Soak the breadcrumbs in the milk. In a skillet, melt 1 tablespoon
butter and sauté the shallots for 2 to 3 minutes, until limp. Purée all the
ingredients in a food processor, except the egg whites. Season with salt,
pepper, and nutmeg to taste. Remove the purée to a 3-quart bowl.

In a clean copper bowl, beat the whites stiff with a pinch of salt. Fold
one quarter of the egg whites into the vegetable base, and then fold in
the remaining whites. Pour the filling into buttered molds. Place the

molds in a water bath, and bake in a preheated oven 15 to 20 minutes for smaller molds, 35 to 40 minutes for a large mold, until set. Unmold and serve, garnished with hollandaise sauce or mousseline sauce.

Note: You can also make a cream sauce by boiling 1 cup heavy cream with 3 tablespoons chopped fresh tarragon. Season with salt, pepper, and nutmeg and pour over artichokes.

HOLLANDAISE SAUCE

Sauce Hollandaise

INGREDIENTS

4 egg yolks
3 tablespoons freshly squeezed lemon juice
8 tablespoons butter, at room temperature
Salt and freshly ground pepper

METHOD

In a double boiler, beat the yolks, lemon juice, salt, and pepper over hot but not boiling water. Beat until mixture thickens slightly. Remove from heat and stir in the butter, one tablespoon at a time. The butter may not melt immediately, but will soften from the heat. After all the butter has been added, return the pan to the heat and keep stirring until sauce has thickened and the butter is thoroughly incorporated. Remove from heat and serve.

MOUSSELINE SAUCE

Sauce Mousseline

Mousseline sauce is nothing more than a hollandaise sauce with the addition of egg whites or whipped cream to make a lighter, more delicate sauce. Whipped cream is not as desirable as egg whites because it can thin out the sauce. Stiffly whip the egg whites (from the eggs used in making the hollandaise) and fold them into the sauce. If you are using the sauce for fish, add 2 to 3 tablespoons of fish stock to the sauce.

BRAISED ARTICHOKES WITH VEGETABLES

Artichauts Braisés à la Mirepoix

When using onions and carrots to flavor a dish, use twice as many onions as carrots; otherwise the sweetness of the carrots tends to take over. If you add celery root to make the *mirepoix*, use the same amount of celery root as carrots, but if you use celery stalks, use half the amount of celery as carrot. Celery root is a milder tasting vegetable than celery. Serve these braised artichokes as a first course, or as a garnish for roast rabbit with tarragon cream and serve a cold French cider.

INGREDIENTS	SERVES 6

6 medium artichokes, blanched (see Braised Stuffed Artichokes page 14)
1 carrot, ¼-inch dice
2 small onions, ¼-inch dice
½ small celery root, ¼-inch dice
3 tablespoons butter
  ½ pound ham, diced
Juice of 1 lemon
2 tablespoons butter, melted
¼ cup white wine
¼ cup chicken stock, good homemade (see page 331)
1 bay leaf
Thyme
Olive oil for drizzling
2 to 4 tablespoons chopped parsley
Salt and freshly ground pepper

METHOD

Preheat oven to 350 degrees.

Prepare the artichokes for stuffing. Prepare a *mirepoix* of the carrots, onion, and celery root (see page 15), and keep everything ready on a tray.

Heat 3 tablespoons butter in a skillet and sauté the *mirepoix*. Add half the diced ham and continue to cook for 3 to 4 minutes until the vegetables have softened. Season with salt and pepper. Make a bed of the *mirepoix* in an oven-proof casserole.

Cool the artichokes under running water when they are done. Scrape the meat off the leaves and set aside in a separate bowl. Sprinkle the scrapings with a bit of lemon juice and 2 tablespoons melted butter, and then mix in the remaining ham.

Sprinkle the cavity of the artichoke with more lemon juice and pack with the artichoke scrapings.

Lay artichokes side by side stem side down on the *mirepoix*. Add the white wine, stock, bay leaf, thyme, salt, and pepper. Bring to a gentle boil on a medium flame; sprinkle a few drops of olive oil over the top of the artichokes, cover with a tight-fitting lid, and braise in a preheated oven 30 to 35 minutes. Serve in a vegetable dish with the *mirepoix* over it. Sprinkle with parsley.

Asparagus

ASPARAGUS WITH CORN

Asperges au Maïs

Serve the asparagus as a first course with a Loire white wine, such as a Savennières, a Vouvray, or Sancerre, along with a crusty bread.

INGREDIENTS   SERVES 6

2 pounds fresh asparagus, tips only
3 cups French cider or white wine
3 ears corn
2 scallions or shallots, finely chopped
1 tablespoon butter
3 whole eggs
1 teaspoon sugar
Dash of cayenne
Salt and freshly ground pepper

METHOD

Remove the head tips of the asparagus, about 1 inch. Reserve the stems for other purposes, such as soups (see Vegetable Soup page 24). Blanch the asparagus tips in the French cider or white wine with a pinch of salt until they are just tender, 3 to 4 minutes. With a slotted spoon, remove the asparagus to a warmed serving dish. Do not discard the liquid; keep it hot. It will be used for a sauce.

In a skillet, sauté the scallions in the butter until limp. Add the asparagus, season with salt and pepper, and toss to coat; keep ready.

Cook the corn in boiling salted water; shuck the corn from the cob, and add to the asparagus; keep everything warm.

In a 2-quart saucepan, beat the eggs with the sugar. Slowly whisk in

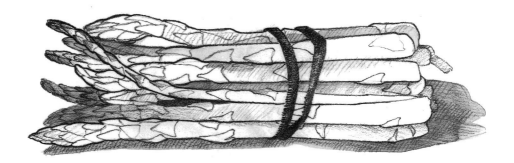

1 cup of the hot liquid used to blanch the asparagus. Keep over medium heat and whisk continuously until the eggs double in volume like a *sabayon*. They will begin to show the tracks of the whisk and achieve a consistency like soft whipped cream. Be careful not to let the eggs hard cook. Remove the pan from heat; continue whisking for a full minute and season with salt, pepper, and cayenne.

Pour this sauce over the warmed asparagus and corn.

ASPARAGUS SOUFFLE

Soufflé d'Asperges

Read about the preparation of soufflés on page 215. Serve this soufflé as the first course of an important dinner, with a garnish of orange segments and minced shallots, accompanied by a crisp white wine from the Alsace, such as a Pinot Blanc.

INGREDIENTS	SERVES 6

Butter and freshly grated Parmesan cheese or breadcrumbs for soufflé dish
½ cup stiff béchamel (see page 208)
1½ pounds asparagus or enough to make 2 cups when cut into ½-inch pieces
4 egg yolks
6 egg whites, beaten stiff
4 tablespoons butter for *beurre noisette*
Salt, freshly ground pepper, and nutmeg

METHOD

Preheat oven to 375 degrees. Prepare a 6-cup soufflé dish or other deep oven-proof dish with straight sides. Butter generously and sprinkle the sides with grated Parmesan cheese or breadcrumbs.

Prepare the béchamel and reserve. Wash, peel, and cut the asparagus into small pieces, separating the tips. Blanch the tips first; drop them into boiling water. When water returns to a boil, add salt and cook until tender. Remove from the water with a slotted spoon and drain. Reserve some cooked tips for a garnish. Then blanch the stalks until tender, 5 to 7 minutes. Purée the vegetables in a food processor; season the purée with salt, pepper, and nutmeg. You should have at least 1 cup of purée; a little more does not make any difference.

In a bowl, stir the asparagus purée into ½ cup of béchamel and mix well. Then add the egg yolks, one at a time, again mixing well. In a copper bowl, beat the whites stiff with a pinch of salt. Fold one third of the whites into the vegetable base mixture to lighten it. Fold in the rest of the whites. Pour into the soufflé dish and set in a water bath. Bake in a preheated oven for 25 minutes.

Beurre noisette: Melt the butter and let it brown slightly. Add the reserved asparagus and rewarm. Spoon some of this noisette butter over each serving of soufflé, and garnish with asparagus.

ASPARAGUS IN WHITE WINE

Asperges au Vin Blanc

Serve the asparagus warm as a first course, or as a vegetable accompaniment to a baked salmon with cucumbers and dill. Offer a Chardonnay from the Jura to drink.

INGREDIENTS	SERVES 6

2 pounds asparagus, peeled
4 tablespoons butter
1 cup dry white wine
¼ cup chopped parsley
⅓ cup grated Swiss or Gruyère cheese
Salt and freshly ground pepper

Preheat oven to 425 degrees. Prepare the asparagus by snapping the root end at the weakest point; trim the stalks from the bottom with a paring knife. Tie the asparagus in a bundle with kitchen string.

Melt 2 tablespoons butter in a large flat oven-proof pan with a tight-fitting lid. Place the asparagus in the pan and season with salt and pepper to taste. Pour in the wine and cover; simmer until done. The cooking time varies depending on the size of the asparagus. When tender, remove the string, allowing the spears to spread out.

Drain off the liquid into a small saucepan. Bring it to a boil, reduce the heat, and whisk in 2 tablespoons butter. Correct the seasonings and finish with a sprinkling of parsley and set aside.

Sprinkle the entire surface of the asparagus with cheese. Place the pan on the middle rack of a preheated oven or under the broiler; heat until the cheese has browned. Pour the butter sauce over the vegetable and serve very hot.

Beans

GREEN BEANS WITH BACON AND TOMATOES

Haricots Verts Portugaise

Serve these beans with braised rabbit and crisp sautéed potatoes, along with a red wine from Corbières.

INGREDIENTS	SERVES 6

¼ pound fresh lean salt pork or pancetta
1 tablespoon butter
1 pound string beans, trimmed and julienned
2 large tomatoes, peeled, seeded, and chopped
1 cup chicken or veal stock, good homemade (see page 331)
½ teaspoon finely chopped chervil or parsley
Salt and freshly ground pepper

METHOD

Cut the pork into lardons, ½-inch thick. Desalt the pork or bacon by placing it in slowly boiling water for 10 minutes. Sauté slowly in a little butter until it turns a nice golden color; remove from the pan, drain off the fat, and return the pork to it.

Clean the beans and trim the ends; cut on the diagonal and place in the pan with the pork.

Add the tomatoes to pork and green beans; add the stock, season with a little salt, and bring the liquid to a boil. Turn the heat to a simmer, cover, and cook until tender, about 15 to 20 minutes. Correct the seasoning, give a few grindings of pepper, sprinkle with chervil or parsley, and serve hot.

BEANS WITH LEMON BUTTER

Haricots Secs Maître d'Hôtel

If you have no time to soak the beans overnight, cover them with cold water, bring to a boil, and simmer for 15 minutes. Drain and cover with cold water again and proceed as described. Never put salt into the cooking water with the beans; this will make the beans burst.

INGREDIENTS	SERVES 6 TO 8

1 pound dry green beans (*haricots verts secs*)
Beurre manié: 4 tablespoons butter and 1 tablespoon flour (see
    page 136)
¼ cup coarsely chopped parsley
Juice of 1 lemon
Salt and freshly ground pepper

METHOD

Soak the beans overnight. Drain them, put in a 4-quart pot with a
heavy bottom. Refresh with cold water and cover with at least 1 inch of
water. Bring to a boil and simmer for 1 to 1½ hours, adding no salt
during cooking. Simmer until they are tender to the touch, but have not
split. Replenish the water during the cooking as needed. When the beans
are done, drain into a colander over a bowl to save the cooking water.
Reserve the beans.

Prepare a *beurre manié* by working the butter soft under the flat edge
of a knife and then adding the flour. Fold it into the butter until evenly
mixed. Put the *beurre manié* into the pot in which the beans were cooked;
slowly add the hot bean water and whisk so that it is well integrated.
Return the beans to the pot to reheat and thicken the sauce. Season with
salt and pepper. Add the parsley and lemon juice. Mix everything well
and serve warm.

LITTLE BEANS

Haricots Mausallon, Sauce Sauternes

Serve with sautéed medallions of pork and a tomato sauce, accompanied by a fruity Côtes-du-Rhône.

INGREDIENTS	SERVES 6

1 cup béchamel (see page 208)
½ cup Sauternes
1 pound green beans
½ pound white onions, sliced in ½-inch rings
Fritter batter (see page 17)
Grapeseed oil for deep frying
Salt and freshly ground pepper

METHOD

Preheat oven to 350 degrees. Prepare the béchamel in a 2-quart pan and add the Sauternes; cook slowly until the sauce thickens.

Blanch the whole green beans in boiling salted water, drain, and set aside.

Slice the onions, dip in batter, and deep fry. You don't want the oil too hot or the batter will brown before the onions are cooked. When the onions are ready, drain on towels.

Lay the cooked green beans in a gratin dish; season with salt and pepper. Pour the sauce over the beans and top with the onion rings. Bake in a preheated oven for 20 minutes, until the mixture is well warmed.

RATATOUILLE OF PORK AND VEGETABLES

Ratatouille Charcutière

An excellent dish to accompany roast chicken and noodles. Serve a French cider to drink.

INGREDIENTS	SERVES 6

¼ pound pancetta or lean salt pork, ½-inch lardons
½ cup stock, good homemade (see page 331), or dry white wine
¼ cup green beans, ½-inch julienne
1 cup cooked dry beans
1 cup fresh peas, blanched
½ cup crème fraîche
Chopped parsley, chervil, and tarragon
Salt and freshly ground pepper

METHOD

In a heavy skillet, sauté the pork lardons slowly until they brown lightly and are crisp. Remove and reserve. Drain the fat.

To the pan the bacon was cooked in, add the stock, green beans, cooked dry beans, and peas. Season with salt and simmer covered until the vegetables are tender. Add more liquid as necessary, but the liquid should be entirely evaporated when the vegetables are done. Add the crème fraîche; toss and cook a few minutes longer. Add the pork and sprinkle with the herbs in any combination. Correct the seasoning and serve.

GREEN BEANS IN RED WINE

Haricots Verts Bordelais

This has the makings of a first class dish. Be careful with the sauce: it has eggs, which can overcook and become hard. Serve these beans with veal chops.

INGREDIENTS	SERVES 6

½ cup red wine
3 tablespoons wine vinegar
1 pound green beans, cut in ½-inch lengths
4 tablespoons butter
1 cup muscat grapes (or other variety)
2 egg yolks
⅓ cup heavy cream
Chopped parsley
Salt and freshly ground pepper

METHOD

In a small saucepan, combine the wine and vinegar and bring to a boil. Reduce it over slow heat to ¼ cup and set aside.

Blanch the beans in a large pot of boiling water. When the water returns to a boil, add salt and cook 5 to 8 minutes, or until tender. Drain into a colander and allow to dry.

Melt the butter in a skillet and let it brown lightly. Add the beans and gently roll in the butter. Add the wine/vinegar mixture and season with salt and pepper. Add the grapes and mix well. Remove from heat.

In a small bowl, mix the yolks with the cream; then stir into the skillet with the vegetables and toss to coat everything well. Return to the heat and cook gently until the sauce thickens and the eggs cook. Be careful, as the eggs can hard cook. Serve the beans on a heated platter and sprinkle with chopped parsley.

SWEET AND SOUR GREEN BEANS

Haricots Verts Aigre-Doux

Serve with a roast chicken and steamed and herbed baby potatoes, accompanied by a cool and crisp Pouilly Fumé.

INGREDIENTS	SERVES 6

1 pound string beans
2 bunches scallions
2 medium tomatoes, chopped
⅛ teaspoon cayenne
1 tablespoon Worcestershire sauce
1 tablespoon cider vinegar
1 tablespoon freshly squeezed lemon juice
1 tablespoon peanut oil
1 tablespoon sugar
1 teaspoon Dijon mustard
Salt and freshly ground pepper

METHOD

Clean the green beans, trim the ends, and cut them on a steep diagonal about ⅙-inch wide (French cut). Blanch the beans in boiling salted water until tender, about 3 to 4 minutes. Drain into a colander and reserve.

In a saucepan, simmer the remaining ingredients, except for the mustard, until the water from the tomatoes evaporates, about 10 to 15 minutes. Add the green beans to the sauce along with the mustard and rewarm the vegetable. Serve hot or cold.

Beets

BEETS WITH BECHAMEL

Gratin de Betteraves à la Sauce Béchamel

INGREDIENTS	SERVES 6

2 pounds small beets
1 to 2 tablespoons butter
1 cup béchamel (see page 208)
⅓ cup grated Gruyère cheese
Salt and freshly ground pepper

METHOD

Preheat the oven to 325 degrees.

Cook the whole beets in their skins in the preheated oven or in boiling water until tender. Remove to a cutting board, and when cool enough to handle, peel and cut into a 1-inch dice.

Set the oven to 375 degrees.

In a skillet, warm the beets in butter; season with salt and pepper. Put into an oven-proof gratin dish. Cover them lightly with béchamel and sprinkle with the grated cheese. Bake for 10 to 15 minutes, until they have evenly browned, or place under the broiler for a few minutes.

A SALAD OF BEETS AND CREAM

Betteraves à la Crème

Serve this dish as a first course, followed by a filet of sole with orange butter, and pour an Alsatian Riesling to drink.

Lettuce leaves
2 hard-boiled eggs
3 tablespoons crème fraîche
1 tablespoon Dijon mustard
1 tablespoon lemon juice
1 tablespoon chopped chives or green of scallions
1 tablespoon breadcrumbs
6 medium beets, cooked and cut in slices, small dice, or julienne
2 tablespoons peanut oil
Salt and freshly ground pepper

METHOD

Wash and dry the lettuces and keep ready. Prepare the hard-boiled eggs; when they are cool, chop one of the eggs coarsely. In a bowl, mix the crème fraîche, mustard, lemon juice, chives, breadcrumbs and the chopped egg; season with salt and pepper. Toss in the beets.

Line a salad bowl with the lettuce leaves. Arrange the beets on the bed of lettuce.

Separate the white and yolk of the second egg and chop each separately. Sprinkle the reserved chopped egg white over half of the beets. Sprinkle the chopped yolk over the other half.

Cabbages

RED CABBAGE WITH CHESTNUTS

Chou Rouge Alsacienne

Serve with veal sausage, steamed potatoes, and a cold Alsatian beer.

INGREDIENTS	SERVES 6

8 ounces whole chestnuts, peeled (see page 77)
4 tablespoons butter or goose fat
1 pound red cabbage, shredded
½ pound apples, peeled, cored, and chopped
1 cup red wine
1 teaspoon salt
½ teaspoon pepper
2 to 4 tablespoons butter, optional

METHOD

Remove skins from chestnuts by cooking them in boiling water for 15 to 20 minutes. Peel the skin and cut the nuts into chunks.

Melt 4 tablespoons butter or goose fat in a heavy 4-quart saucepan. Add the cabbage and stir to coat with the fat. Add the apples, chestnuts, wine, and salt. Cover and cook over low heat for about 20 to 25 minutes. Correct seasoning, add more butter if desired, and give a grinding of pepper.

CURRIED CABBAGE

Légumes à la Pondichéry

The inspiration for this *jardinière* of winter vegetables comes from the Indian colony that the French held in the nineteenth century. This dish goes well with a stew of red meat, garnished with rice, and served with a heartier Côtes-du-Rhône from Châteauneuf-du-Pape.

| INGREDIENTS | SERVES 6 |

4 tablespoons butter or peanut oil
3 onions, chopped
3 cloves garlic, minced
2 tablespoons curry powder
1 teaspoon cumin seed, crushed
1 small head of cabbage, finely sliced
½ cup white wine
1 cup chicken stock, good homemade (see page 331)
3 carrots, diced
1 white turnip, diced
1 cup green beans, ½-inch pieces
1 cup cooked dried beans
Juice of 1 lemon
Salt and freshly ground pepper

METHOD

In a heavy skillet, melt the butter. Add the onions and the garlic and sauté until translucent. Add the curry and cumin; cook over a low heat 2 to 3 minutes to activate the curry.

Add the cabbage; cover and continue to cook on a slow flame 10 to 15 minutes. Add the stock and the white wine, bring to a simmer, and cook covered for 15 to 20 minutes. Add the carrots, turnip, green beans, and cooked beans for the last 5 to 10 minutes. Make sure the vegetables are cut so they cook to the perfect crunch when the cabbage is ready. Stir to blend all the ingredients. Check once or twice to make sure the vegetables don't stick to the bottom of the pan. Add the lemon juice; correct the seasonings and serve.

RED CABBAGE AND PEARS

Chou Rouge à la Franc-Comtoise

Red cabbage is good served with a freshwater fish, a salmon or mountain trout with bacon and herbs, accompanied by steamed potatoes and a bottle of mountain wine, a vin de Jura, Chardonnay from Burgundy, a Crépy from the Savoie, a Riesling from the Alsace, or a cider from the pays d'Auge in Normandy.

INGREDIENTS	SERVES 6

1 head red cabbage thinly sliced
½ cup Burgundy
2 tablespoons butter, soft
1 tablespoon peanut oil
2 pears, peeled, cored and sliced
⅛ teaspoon *quatre épices* (see following recipe)
1 onion, thinly sliced
1 tablespoon brown sugar
⅓ cup water
Salt and freshly ground pepper

METHOD

Preheat oven to 250 degrees. Remove the outer leaves of the cabbage if they are flawed. Cut the cabbage in quarters and remove the core. Cut the quarters into fine julienne strips. Put the cabbage in a large bowl with the wine and ½ teaspoon salt; toss and let it rest for an hour.

Rub a large soufflé dish with butter and add the oil. Set in a layer of cabbage, followed by a layer of pear slices; season with a pinch of salt and pepper, *quatre épices*, and a few onion slices. Repeat the layers of cabbage, pears, and seasonings until everything is used up. Sprinkle with the brown sugar and pour over the wine in which the cabbage marinated and the water. Bake in preheated oven for 2 hours, until the cabbage is thoroughly cooked and soft. If it becomes too dry during the cooking, add more liquid.

About Quatre Epices

Quatre épices is a mixture of finely ground spices for which there seems to be no set formula. I often prepare it as follows: 1 tablespoon whole cloves, 2 whole nutmegs, 4 tablespoons ground ginger, and 3 tablespoons ground cinnamon.

Mix everything in the blender to a fine powder. Store in an airtight container.

Sometimes I add dried herbs to the mixture before it is blended, particularly a generous pinch of tarragon and a small pinch of oregano or marjoram.

BRETON RED CABBAGE

Salade de Chou Rouge à la Morbihanaise

The cooked egg sauce called for here is like a *sabayon* and is used to show off the simple cabbage. However, the sauce is made with cider vinegar to satisfy a Breton taste.

INGREDIENTS   SERVES 6

6 slices bacon or pancetta
2 whole eggs
⅓ cup sugar
½ cup water
⅓ cup cider vinegar
1 small red cabbage, shredded
1 bunch scallions, in ⅙-inch slices
2 cups cauliflower flowerets
2 to 4 tablespoons peanut oil
Salt and freshly ground pepper

METHOD

In a skillet, sauté the bacon until crisp; drain off the fat, crumble, and reserve.

Blend the lightly beaten eggs with the sugar, water, and vinegar; cook in the top of a double boiler, whisking until creamy and allow to cool.

Shred the cabbage and combine in a bowl with the scallions and cauliflower. Sprinkle the vegetables with the bacon, add enough oil to coat the vegetables, and season with salt and pepper. Then add the sauce and toss everything well.

CABBAGE FOR PIERROT

Chou Vert Pierrot

Excellent with roast duck or roasted birds accompanied by quartered potatoes sautéed in duck fat. Serve with a white wine with some sweetness—from Loupiac Gaudiet, for example, or from Cérons.

| INGREDIENTS | SERVES 6 |

4 tablespoons butter
1 small green cabbage, thinly sliced
1 onion, sliced
Rind and juice of 1 lemon
1 cup crème fraîche
1 cup Sauternes
⅓ cup Dijon mustard
2 to 3 scallions, finely sliced on the bias
2 tablespoons chopped fresh tarragon
Salt and freshly ground pepper

METHOD

Melt the butter in a large skillet or heavy pot, add the cabbage, onion, and a generous pinch of salt. Sweat the vegetables, cooking covered over low heat until they start to render some water, about 7 to 10 minutes. Add the lemon juice and rind; stir in the crème fraîche, cover, and cook for about 5 minutes. Add the wine and cook until tender, another 10 to 15 minutes. If the cabbage is cooked and too much liquid remains, drain off the liquid and reduce it to sauce consistency. When the liquids have thickened, add the mustard, scallions, and tarragon. Cook for another few minutes; correct the seasonings, give a few grindings of pepper and serve hot.

FROM JOSEPHINE'S NOTES ON CAULIFLOWER

When preparing cauliflower to be eaten raw, use only the flowerets. The rest of the leaves and stalk can be used for soup or as a vegetable. Separate all the flowerets and soak in lemon or vinegar water. This helps keep them white and tender. Before using, drain and dry thoroughly, and sprinkle with coarse sea salt.

In Brittany, the cauliflower is of a very superior quality and the Bretons refer to it as *fleur de Bretagne,* the flower of Brittany. When eaten raw, it is very nourishing and refreshing. It can be eaten by itself or in combination with other ingredients. Cauliflower can be prepared in many ways that are both appealing to the eye and gratifying to the tastebuds.

CAULIFLOWER WITH ANCHOVIES

Chou-Fleur Bayonnaise

Bayonne is in the Basque country. This dish of cauliflower seasoned with anchovy is intended to evoke the tastes of that region. The hams of Bayonne are famous for their taste and are coated bright red with dry peppers. Serve this dish with medallions of pork with sweet peppers, a gratin of potato with Roquefort, and a cold French cider. This little menu has many tastes to evoke a place—Bayonne—that enjoyed a historical relationship with port-to-port sailors from Brittany, which perhaps explains the shared taste for cider in both places.

INGREDIENTS	SERVES 6

1 head cauliflower
6 tablespoons butter
1 teaspoon anchovy paste
1 tablespoon white wine vinegar
½ olive oil
1 clove garlic, minced
2 to 4 tablespoons chopped parsley
2 to 3 anchovies, cut into small pieces
Salt and freshly ground pepper

METHOD

Trim the cauliflower head, cutting the branches into flowerets. Place the trimmed vegetable into a large pot of boiling water. After the water returns to a boil, add a teaspoon of salt and gently boil for 10 to 15 minutes, or until tender. Drain in a colander and sauté until dry in a skillet; keep warm.

In a small saucepan, brown the butter slightly, mix in the anchovy paste. In a small bowl, mix the vinegar, olive oil, garlic, and parsley; add to the butter and pour over the cauliflower, tossing to mix thoroughly. Place a garnish of the pieces of anchovies over the cauliflower and serve.

CAULIFLOWER WITH BEARNAISE SAUCE

Chou-Fleur Clémentine, Sauce Béarnaise

This dish is made with a head of cauliflower cooked whole and presented on a platter. It is carved, sauced, and served like a roast. It is a wonderful event. It makes a fine garnish to any white meat roast. Since the cauliflower has its own sauce, the meat doesn't require another. Pour a first class Burgundy to go with it.

INGREDIENTS   SERVES 6

1 large cauliflower

Blanc
4 tablespoons lemon juice
½ cup flour
8 cups cold water
1 tablespoon marjoram
1 sprig of thyme
1 bay leaf
1 teaspoon salt

4 tablespoons butter
3 hard-boiled eggs, cut in half
4 tablespoons chopped parsley
Salt and freshly ground pepper
Béarnaise Sauce (recipe follows)

METHOD

Remove the core and leaves of the cauliflower and reserve for another use. Break off 6 flowerets from the base of the vegetable to be used whole as a garnish.

Prepare the *blanc*. Add the lemon juice and flour to the cold water in a large pot. Put in the herbs, bay leaf, and salt; bring to a boil. Blanch the whole head in the *blanc* until tender, about 15 to 20 minutes depending on the size of the cauliflower. During the last 5 to 8 minutes, add the flowerets. Remove from the *blanc* with a slotted spoon and allow to drain.

In a skillet, melt the butter and let it brown slightly. Roll the flowerets in the butter, making sure they are well coated.

To assemble and serve, place the cauliflower head in the center of a large serving platter, season with salt and pepper, set the egg halves around the edge, and garnish the outer edges with flowerets. Spoon the sauce over all of the vegetable and sprinkle generously with parsley.

Béarnaise Sauce

3 tablespoons tarragon vinegar
3 tablespoons white wine
1 tablespoon minced shallot
1½ teaspoons dry tarragon
1 teaspoon chopped fresh chervil
2 tablespoons chopped parsley
Pinch of salt
8 to 10 cracked white peppercorns
2 egg yolks
9 tablespoons unsalted butter, melted

Garnish

1 teaspoon dry tarragon
½ teaspoon chopped fresh chervil
Pinch cayenne pepper

In a small saucepan, make an infusion of vinegar, wine, shallot, tarragon, chervil, salt, and pepper. Cook until 2 tablespoons of liquid are left. Strain into a small bowl and cool. Return the infusion to a clean saucepan. Over a low flame whisk in the egg yolks until the mixture thickens. Remove from heat. Drizzle in the butter, whisking thoroughly. Add the garnish of herbs and cayenne.

CAULIFLOWER WITH BUTTERED BREADCRUMBS

Chou-Fleur Polonaise

The crunch of the breadcrumbs contrasted with the soft crispness of the flowerets is a pleasant treat. This dish can be served with a sauté of pork and noodles garnished with tomatoes and herbs. Pour an Alsatian Pinot Blanc.

INGREDIENTS   SERVES 4 TO 6

1 cauliflower
4 tablespoons butter
1 tablespoon breadcrumbs
Salt and freshly ground pepper

METHOD

Cut the cauliflower into flowerets. Put the cut cauliflower into boiling salted water and simmer for 8 to 10 minutes, until tender. Remove to a colander and drain.

Melt the butter and add the breadcrumbs; stir until well coated. Pour over cauliflower, mixing well, correct seasonings, and serve at once.

SOUFFLED CAULIFLOWER

Chou-Fleur Zéphyr

A zephyr is not a typical soufflé, but is instead a light, delicious way to prepare many vegetables. Serve the souffléed Cauliflower as a first course with a garnish of fresh green beans and walnut butter, and a white wine from the Loire, such as a Sancerre.

INGREDIENTS   SERVES 6

Blanc:
4 tablespoons lemon juice
½ cup flour
8 cups cold water
1 tablespoon marjoram
1 sprig thyme
1 bay leaf
1 teaspoon salt

1 large cauliflower
Salt, freshly ground pepper, and nutmeg
6 tablespoons butter
¼ cup cream
3 eggs, separated

Aurore sauce

2 tablespoons butter
2 shallots, finely diced
1 teaspoon flour
2 tomatoes, peeled, seeded, and chopped
1 tablespoon tomato paste
2 teaspoons chopped fresh oregano
¼ cup dry white wine
4 ounces crème fraîche

METHOD

Preheat oven to 375 degrees.

Prepare a 2-quart *blanc*. Add lemon juice and flour to the cold water in a large pot; add the herbs. Bring to a boil; add the cauliflower and salt, and cook 15 minutes, or until very well done. Remove to a colander and drain; mash half the cauliflower thoroughly. Reserve the other half as a garnish.

Put the mashed cauliflower in a dry skillet and heat to dry. Season with salt and pepper and a few gratings of nutmeg. Add 2 to 3 tablespoons of butter broken into pea-size bits and toss well to incorporate the butter. Remove to a 3-quart bowl.

In a small bowl, mix the cream and egg yolks; then add to the mashed cauliflower. Beat the whites stiff in a clean copper bowl with a pinch of salt; fold into the cauliflower mixture. Place the mixture in a buttered soufflé dish or other straight-sided oven-proof dish. Bake in the upper half of a preheated oven for 20 to 25 minutes.

While the cauliflower bakes prepare the Aurore sauce. Heat the butter in a 1-quart saucepan; sauté the shallots and season with a bit of salt. Add the flour, mix well, and cook for 2 to 3 minutes. Add the tomatoes, tomato paste, oregano, and wine, and simmer for 10 minutes. Before serving, stir in the crème fraîche and heat thoroughly.

A few minutes before the zephyr is done baking, set the flowerets in a dry skillet; rewarm and toss with 1 to 2 tablespoons butter, season with salt and pepper, and keep ready. When the zephyr is done, remove from the oven and serve very hot with a garnish of flowerets. Spoon the sauce over individual servings.

CREAM OF CAULIFLOWER AND WATERCRESS SOUP

Crème de Chou-Fleur et Cresson

The origins of this dish are probably the farm. It is the use of chopped watercress that makes me think that. The liaison of the eggs and cream speaks of Paris. The result is an elegant soup, accompanied either by a French cider or by a fine Loire Valley white wine, such as a Savennières.

At the restaurant, Josephine served the soup with a Roquefort butter. The flavors are also found again with Cauliflower Custard with Watercress (see page 297) served on a bed of watercress with crumbled Roquefort and a garnish of tomato.

INGREDIENTS   SERVES 6

1 bunch watercress
1 large cauliflower
4 cups velouté sauce (recipe follows)
4 cups chicken stock, good homemade (see page 331)
½ cup crème fraîche
2 egg yolks
Salt and freshly ground pepper

METHOD

Remove the leaves of the watercress and mince them coarsely; they are a garnish for the soup. Chop the stems; they are blanched with the cauliflower. Prepare the cauliflower. Remove the first few leaves, trim the stems, and cut into pieces; then cut the flowerets. Blanch the vegetable along with the watercress stems in boiling salted water for 10 to 15 minutes, until tender. Drain in a colander and then purée in a food processor.

Make the velouté, add the puréed vegetables and simmer for 15 minutes to allow the flavors to infuse. Thin out the soup if desired with additional stock.

Make a liaison of eggs and crème fraîche, whisking the cream into the yolks to incorporate completely. Ladle two scoops of hot soup into the liaison, to raise the cooking temperature of the eggs, and then add the liaison to the soup. Warm the soup for another 5 minutes, but do not let it boil. Just before serving, correct the seasoning and give several grindings of pepper.

Ladle the soup into bowls and sprinkle each with the minced watercress leaves, and present piping hot as an elegant first course. If you don't serve the soup immediately, do not add the liaison or butter until the soup is reheated and ready to serve.

VELOUTE SAUCE

Sauce Velouté

A velouté sauce is used as a sauce in its own right and is the mother to any number of other sauces made with herbs, cream, cheese, tomatoes, wine, and so on. This sauce can also be the base of a soup. For example, a volume of velouté, mixed with an equal volume of cooked celery root, yields a creamy and delicious celery root soup. At Le Trou restaurant, we finish it with a hazelnut butter. Velouté is a very good recipe to have in your repertoire because it can do so much. See the notes on béchamel (see page 208), because the rules that apply to béchamel also apply to the velouté. It is like a béchamel made with stock instead of milk.

INGREDIENTS

2 leeks, white part only, thinly sliced or 1 onion, cut in small dice
4 tablespoons butter
⅓ cup flour
4 cups chicken stock, good homemade (see page 331)
Bouquet garni: 6 to 8 sprigs of parsley, 1 bay leaf, and 1 sprig of thyme tied in a celery stalk
Salt and freshly ground pepper

METHOD

In a saucepan, sauté the leeks in butter until translucent, but do not brown. Stir in the flour and cook 3 to 4 minutes. Add the warmed stock, stirring well to maintain a smooth liquid, free of lumps. Add the bouquet garni and simmer for 15 to 20 minutes over a slow flame, stirring to prevent the flour from sticking to the bottom of the pan. Strain through a sieve.

Carrots

CARROTS WITH CIDER

Carottes Normandes

The recipe is also excellent if small white onions are substituted for the carrots. They are called Normandy Carrots in French because cider is an ingredient.

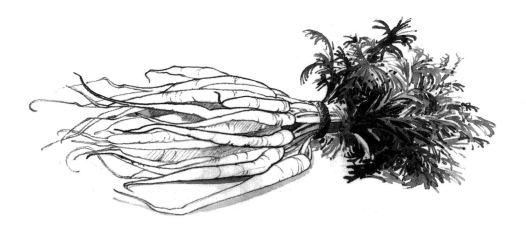

2 pounds thumb-size carrots
4 to 6 tablespoons butter
½ to 1 cup French cider
2 teaspoons sugar
4 tablespoons chopped parsley
Salt and freshly ground pepper

METHOD

Wash, scrape, and trim the carrots. If the carrots are large, quarter and cut into 1½-inch pieces.

In a saucepan, melt the butter and add the carrots, stirring to coat. Add enough French cider to cover two thirds of the carrots; don't hesitate to add more liquid during cooking. Add a light seasoning of salt and the sugar; cover and simmer over low heat for 10 to 15 minutes, or until cooked through. Remove the lid and let the carrots absorb the cider. When the carrots are tender, correct the seasonings, give a grinding of pepper, and sprinkle with parsley. Serve very hot.

GLAZED CURRIED CARROTS

Carottes Glacées à l'Indienne

Serve this dish with any spicy stewed meat or poultry, along with plain rice for sopping up sauces. Pour a red table wine, a Mediterranean wine from Corbières, or the pays d'Oc.

INGREDIENTS   SERVES 6

2 pounds small carrots
4 tablespoons butter
1 teaspoon curry powder
1 teaspoon minced fresh ginger
½ cup sherry
Rind and juice of 1 orange
1 teaspoon freshly squeezed lemon juice
2 tablespoons sugar
¼ cup chopped parsley
Salt and freshly ground pepper

METHOD

Wash and scrape the carrots. Cut in 2-inch lengths, then in quarters lengthwise. Blanch in boiling, salted water until tender, 5 to 8 minutes. Drain them and reserve.

While the carrots are blanching, prepare the glaze in a separate saucepan. Melt 2 tablespoons butter and add the curry and ginger, allowing the flavors to develop over medium slow heat for a minute or two. Add the blanched carrots, sherry, orange rind and juice, lemon juice, sugar, and a pinch of salt. Allow the liquids to reduce slowly until they form a glaze. If there is too much liquid, the sauce can be thickened with 1 teaspoon cornstarch diluted in 1 tablespoon cold water. When the sauce is ready, toss in dots of butter, lots of parsley, and season with pepper.

CARROTS MIXED WITH OTHER VEGETABLES

Carottes en Macédoine

Serve the dish to accompany beef with a ragout of mushrooms and pour a Côtes de Bordeaux to drink.

INGREDIENTS	SERVES 6

¾ pound green beans
1½ bunches carrots
6 to 8 small new potatoes
4 tablespoons butter
⅔ cup sherry
   Walnut-size piece of butter
¼ cup finely chopped fresh chervil
Chopped parsley
Salt and freshly ground pepper

METHOD

Prepare and trim the beans; cut into 1-inch lengths. Wash and scrape the carrots, and cut in 1-inch lengths. Parboil the potatoes in their jackets until barely tender. Peel when sufficiently cooled.

Melt 4 tablespoons butter in a large saucepan; add the carrots and sherry, and salt lightly. Bring to a boil; cover, reduce heat, and simmer 3 to 4 minutes. Add the green beans and potatoes, and continue to cook 4 to 5 minutes more, until tender. Stir in the walnut-size piece of butter before serving. Sprinkle with chervil and parsley.

Celery Root

CELERY ROOT WITH CREAM SAUCE

Céleri-Rave à la Sauce Normande

This celery root can accompany a plain roast beef garnished with sautéed chard or spinach with apple, or a ragout of wild mushrooms. Pour one of your best red wines from Bordeaux, perhaps a Pomerol.

INGREDIENTS	SERVES 6

1½ pounds celery root, preferably small ones
1 to 2 shallots, finely chopped
4 tablespoons butter
2 tablespoons flour
¾ to 1 cup hot milk
⅓ cup chopped chervil and parsley
½ cup heavy cream
Salt, freshly ground pepper, and nutmeg

METHOD

Select small celery roots for this dish. Scrub them well and blanch whole in boiling salted water 15 to 20 minutes, depending on their size. They should be firm to the touch when done. Peel and cut into quarters.

In a 1-quart saucepan, sauté the shallots in 2 tablespoons butter for a few minutes, being careful not to let them brown. Add the flour and cook together for a minute or so, whisking to form a smooth paste. Gradually stir in the hot milk. Season the sauce with salt, pepper, and nutmeg to taste. Leave to thicken over a slow heat for 10 minutes. Stir occasionally to prevent scorching.

After 10 minutes, stir in all but 2 tablespoons of the chopped herbs. Thin with cream to sauce-like consistency, i.e., it coats a spoon.

Melt the remaining butter and sauté the celery root until it starts to brown. Remove to a heated serving platter and top with the sauce. Sprinkle on the remaining chopped herbs.

CELERY ROOT WITH MARROW

Céleri-Rave à la Moelle

Serve this dish with roast beef and wild mushroom sauce, and an elegant red wine from Bordeaux, such as a Saint-Emilion.

INGREDIENTS	SERVES 6

2 bones with marrow
2 medium celery roots or 1 bunch celery
Juice of 1 lemon
1 to 2 tablespoons butter
Mirepoix: 1 carrot and 1 small onion, ¼-inch dice
¼ cup *glace de viande,* veal stock, or meat juices (see page 333)
6 toast rounds: 3- to 4-inch rounds made with toasted French bread
Salt and freshly ground pepper

METHOD

Poach the marrow bones in water 5 to 10 minutes to loosen the marrow. Remove from the pot and push out the marrow and set aside.

Prepare the celery root; peel the skin, cut into ½-inch slices, and then ½-inch squares. Blanch in boiling salted water acidulated with the juice of 1 lemon; cook until tender. Drain and keep ready. If using bunch celery, remove the leaves. Remove the strings by peeling the stalks horizontally. Slice the stalks into ½-inch lengths on the diagonal. Place the celery in cold water, bring to a boil, add a pinch of salt, and blanch for 5 minutes until tender. Remove to a strainer and drain.

Melt 1 or 2 tablespoons of butter in a skillet and sauté the *mirepoix* of onions and carrots for a few minutes. Add the blanched celery root and stir to coat the vegetables. Add 2 tablespoons (or to taste) *glace de viande,* veal stock, or meat juices. Cover and cook slowly about 10 minutes to rewarm the celery and for the flavors to infuse. Season with salt and a generous amount of pepper.

Slice the marrow and place one slice on a toast round. Brown these toasts under the broiler, and season with salt and pepper. Place the celery on a heated platter and surround the vegetable with the marrow toasts.

BRAISED CELERY ROOT WITH MUSHROOMS

Céleri-Rave Braisé aux Champignons

Serve the mushrooms and celery root side-by-side in a serving dish as an accompaniment to roast pork and sautéed potatoes; pour a red Côtes du Rhône. The vegetables are blanched first and then braised. This is a simple dish that yields great flavors.

INGREDIENTS	SERVES 6

1 large celery root or 1 bunch celery
¾ pound mushrooms
2 cloves garlic, finely chopped
½ cup chopped parsley
1 to 2 tablespoons butter
Mirepoix: 1 small carrot and 1 onion, ¼-inch dice
1 to 2 tablespoons peanut oil
¼ cup veal stock or 2 tablespoons *glace de viande* (see page 333)
Salt and freshly ground pepper

METHOD

Preheat oven to 375 degrees.

Prepare the celery root by trimming the outer skin. Cut the vegetable in a large dice, ½-inch square. Blanch in water acidulated with the juice of 1 lemon, until tender. If using celery, remove the tough outer stalks and leaves. Remove the strings by peeling the stalks horizontally. Slice the stalks into ½-inch lengths on the diagonal. Place the celery in cold water, bring to a boil, add a pinch of salt, and blanch for 5 minutes. Remove to a strainer and drain.

In a dry skillet, sauté the mushrooms over high heat, giving them a pinch of salt to help draw moisture. Sauté a minute or two longer before adding some chopped garlic and parsley. Season generously with salt and pepper and toss well; remove from the heat.

Heat 1 to 2 tablespoons butter in a small saucepan and sauté the *mirepoix* for 2 to 3 minutes. Place it in the bottom of a shallow braising dish with a tight-fitting lid. Add the celery, mushrooms, and stock or *glace de viande*; season lightly with salt. Cover the braising pan and bake in a preheated oven for 15 minutes.

Chard

CREAMED SWISS CHARD WITH CHEESE

Bettes au Fromage

Swiss chard and cream is a combination that allows for limitless possibilities; the cream can be augmented with cheese; a Roquefort works well. The cheese could be replaced by walnuts, *quatre épices,* or whole grains of mustard. The vegetable can always accompany a roast duck and sautéed potatoes, and a wine such as a Cahors or Madiran.

INGREDIENTS	SERVES 6

2 bunches Swiss chard
1 to 2 tablespoons butter
1 medium onion
½ cup béchamel (see page 208)
⅓ cup grated cheese
1 egg
⅓ cup cream
Salt, freshly ground pepper, and nutmeg

METHOD

Prepare the chard by removing the center stalks. Reserve for another use. Blanch the greens in boiling salted water until limp. The cooking time depends on the tenderness of the green. If they are young plants, cook only a minute or two; if they are older and more fibrous, they may require more time to blanch. When they are done, remove to a colander and flush them under cold water to stop their cooking. Remove to a cutting board and chop coarsely. In a dry skillet, dry sauté until the leaves render their water; set aside.

In the same skillet, melt 1 to 2 tablespoons butter and sauté the onion for a minute or two. Add the chard, which should be well drained. Stir in the béchamel and cheese; toss well to coat with the sauce. Season with salt, pepper, and nutmeg to taste.

Combine the egg and cream and stir into the chard mixture. Once the egg is added, do not cook. It can be warmed, but if subject to too much heat, the eggs will hard cook. Adjust the seasonings and serve hot.

Note: The recipe calls for both béchamel and an egg and cream liaison. One or the other can be used alone, or both can be replaced by heavy cream reduced until it coats a spoon.

An alternative to cream or béchamel is a flavorful oil, such as extra virgin olive oil, walnut oil, hazelnut oil, or colza oil.

Chestnuts

CHESTNUT OMELETTE

Omelette à la Reine

Ellen Szita, the photographer, took a series of photographs of Josephine making this omelette at the restaurant. The series (and the omelette) is called *Omelette à la Reine.*

Serve this omelette with a green vegetable and a light red wine, such as a Pinot Noir. It is perfect for a vegetarian supper.

INGREDIENTS	YIELD: TWO 3-EGG OMELETTES

Béchamel

4 tablespoons butter
⅓ cup flour
1½ cups heated milk or cream
Salt, freshly ground pepper, and nutmeg

4 to 8 tablespoons butter
¼ pound chestnuts, peeled, cooked, and broken into pieces
   (page 77)
2 tablespoons *glace de viande* or ¼ cup veal stock (page 333)
2 to 4 tablespoons chopped parsley
6 eggs
2 to 3 tablespoons light cream
Salt and freshly ground pepper

METHOD

Prepare the béchamel as described on page 208.

While the béchamel cooks, melt 2 to 3 tablespoons butter in a skillet. Add the cooked chestnuts, broken into coarse pieces; moisten the pan with the *glace de viande* or veal stock. Season with salt and heat until the chestnuts are warmed through. Add some chopped parsley and toss again.

In a 1-quart metal bowl, beat the eggs with a fork to liquify slightly. Add a small amount of cream and season with salt and a generous amount of pepper. Whisk to incorporate the cream. Melt 2 to 4 tablespoons butter in a skillet for each omelette. Cook an omelette, and fill it with the warmed chestnuts before folding. Place the finished omelette on a heated platter.

Thin the béchamel with as much cream or milk as necessary to sauce the omelette. Sprinkle with chopped parsley.

The Story of an Omelette

Everyone must have a technique for preparing an omelette. The eggs are beaten lightly with a fork, seasonings are added, and a few tablespoons of light cream are whisked in until the mixture is liquified; it doesn't take long. The skillet is heated to medium, a bit of butter is tossed in; it foams, and when the foam subsides, it is at heat and ready for the eggs. The eggs are poured in at once and the skillet is left alone for 10 seconds, long enough for a light skin to be formed on the bottom of the omelette. The skillet is then shaken forward and backward on the burner while the egg cooks. It soon starts to form soft curds. You decide how much moisture your omelette will have. When you're ready, you put in a warm filling if you are using one. The skillet is tipped forward and the top of the omelette is coaxed into folding over the bottom. It is carefully slid onto a plate and finally it is enjoyed for being a simple and wonderful phenomenon.

Eggplant

EGGPLANT WITH BREADCRUMBS AND HERBS

Aubergines à la Toulousaine

Serve this eggplant with leg of lamb and a red wine and mushroom sauce. Pour an excellent Saint-Emilion wine.

6 tablespoons butter
1 tablespoon peanut oil
1 large eggplant, peeled and cut into ½-inch slices
¼ cup flour
2 cloves garlic, minced
1 tablespoon chopped parsley
2 tablespoons breadcrumbs
Chopped fresh *fines herbes*: tarragon, chervil, and chives
Salt and freshly ground pepper
Cayenne

METHOD

In a large skillet, heat the butter and oil. Dip the eggplant in the
flour, shake off the excess, and brown the vegetable, turning to each side
every minute or two. Continue to cook thoroughly but it should hold
its shape. Season very lightly with salt each time it is turned and finish
with pepper and cayenne. Place eggplant in a warm shallow serving dish.

In a skillet, melt the 4 tablespoons butter; add the garlic, parsley, breadcrumbs and herbs. Mix well, spread over the eggplant, and serve.

EGGPLANT WITH CREAM

Aubergines à la Crème

Serve with a plain roast of chicken with fresh herbs, and pour a Savennières from the Loire valley.

INGREDIENTS	SERVES 6

2 large eggplants
2 tablespoons butter

Béchamel
2 tablespoons butter
2 tablespoons flour
½ cup warm milk mixed with ½ cup heavy cream and a walnut-size piece of butter
Salt, freshly ground pepper, and nutmeg

(1 cup heavy cream may be substituted for béchamel)
2 tablespoons chopped parsley
Salt and freshly ground pepper

METHOD

Peel the eggplant and cut into 1-inch slices. Sprinkle both sides generously with salt and let stand for 30 minutes. Wash under cold water to completely rid them of salt; dry thoroughly by blotting with a towel.

Melt the butter in heavy skillet. Roll eggplant in butter and let simmer for 10 to 15 minutes so that it cooks completely and retains its shape.

While the eggplant cooks, prepare the béchamel or the cream. To prepare the béchamel, melt 2 tablespoons butter in a 2-quart saucepan. Add 2 tablespoons flour and cook for 3 to 4 minutes. Add the warm milk mixed with the heavy cream and butter; slowly incorporate it into the flour base with a whisk. Season with salt, pepper, and nutmeg; cook over a slow flame until it is the consistency of thick heavy cream.

To prepare the reduced heavy cream, put a cup of heavy cream in a saucepan and cook until it is reduced by half. Flavor with salt, pepper, and nutmeg.

When ready to serve, nap the eggplant with béchamel or reduced cream, and garnish with parsley.

The Use of Béchamel versus the Use of Cream

It seems that the use of a béchamel has all but disappeared from the repertoire of French cooking except in soups or as a soufflé base. I was thrilled that a recipe for béchamel was included in a recent cookbook from a three-star French restaurant.

Béchamel is made from equal amounts of butter and flour cooked together for a few minutes; long enough to cook the flour. Warm milk is slowly whisked in to completely blend in the flour. It is seasoned with salt, freshly ground pepper, and nutmeg, and allowed to simmer on a slow flame for 10 to 15 minutes. It yields a beautiful sauce or a base for soups and soufflés.

The formula for the béchamel is an easy one. You can use 1, 2, or 3 tablespoons flour for each cup of liquid. A béchamel made with 1 tablespoon flour (and of course, 1 tablespoon butter) is suitable for enriching soups. A béchamel made with 2 tablespoons flour is suitable for sauces; and with 3 tablespoons flour, it makes a stout base for a soufflé.

It is possible to have even higher expectations for the simple béchamel. If the butter is flavored with a *mirepoix* (see page 15) of aromatic vegetables, such as onion and carrots, before the flour is added, the flavor will be boosted. If it is then cooked with a bouquet garni (parsley, thyme, and bay leaf inside a branch of celery bound with kitchen string) and then seasoned with salt, pepper, and nutmeg, the result is a first class sauce.

EGGPLANT SOUFFLE

Soufflé d'Aubergines

Serve the dish as a first course with a southern rosé wine, such as a Corbières or Bandol.

INGREDIENTS	SERVES 8

8 Japanese eggplants or 2 medium eggplants
1 cup thick béchamel (see page 208)
1 large onion, chopped
2 to 3 tablespoons olive oil
1 clove garlic, minced
¼ pound prosciutto, ground
1 teaspoon paprika
1 tablespoon tomato paste
2 tablespoons butter
3 egg yolks
2 egg whites
¼ cup freshly grated cheese
Salt and freshly ground pepper

METHOD

Bake the eggplants in a preheated 375-degree oven for 30 minutes, until they collapse. While the eggplants bake, prepare the béchamel in a 1-quart saucepan.

Separate the eggplant flesh from the skins. If you are using Japanese eggplants, make a slit from one end to the other, remove the skin, and reserve. If using large eggplants, cut them lengthwise into quarters and remove the flesh to a bowl. Take the skins and line a shallow oven-proof dish that has been buttered. Set the dish aside.

In a small skillet, sauté the onion in the oil until translucent. Add the garlic and cook for another minute. Add the eggplant flesh and the prosciutto. Season this mixture lightly with salt and pepper to taste; be aware that the ham is salty. Add the paprika, tomato paste, and butter.

Stir in the béchamel. Remove from heat and stir in the egg yolks, one at a time. Beat the egg whites until stiff and fold into the mixture.

Spoon the eggplant mixture into the oven-proof dish, smoothing the mixture evenly. Sprinkle the top generously with the grated cheese and bake it in a preheated oven 15 to 20 minutes. This dish can also be prepared in individual ramekins and baked for a shorter time.

HALVED EGGPLANT WITH TOMATOES AND HERBS

Aubergine à la Nîmoise

Eggplant in the style of Nîmes reveals its Provençal origins, not just by its flavors, but by its simplicity of preparation and presentation. Serve it warm or cold as a first course, or as an accompaniment to a roast chicken with herbs and a rosé from Côtes de Provence.

INGREDIENTS	SERVES 2

1 eggplant, halved
Flour for dusting
   1 to 2 tablespoons olive oil
3 to 4 tomatoes, peeled, seeded, and chopped
1 teaspoon chopped fresh thyme
1 tablespoon chopped parsley
1 clove garlic, minced
¼ cup breadcrumbs
¼ cup grated cheese

METHOD

Preheat oven to 375 degrees. Trim the stem from the eggplant and slice the vegetable in half lengthwise. Dust the surface with flour. In a large skillet, heat 1 to 2 tablespoons of oil and slowly sauté on the cut surface 5 to 10 minutes, until the eggplant collapses.

Carefully scoop out the flesh and mix it with the tomatoes, thyme, parsley, and garlic. Add the breadcrumbs. Fill the eggplant shell with this mixture and sprinkle with grated cheese. Place in a preheated oven until the cheese has browned, about 20 minutes.

Endive

ENDIVE WITH CHEESE SAUCE

Endives Mornay

Serve this gratin of endive with roast pork, cornichons, and herbed steamed potatoes, and, for wine, a good Fleurie from Burgundy.

INGREDIENTS	SERVES 6

12 small endives, whole, or 6 large endives cut in half
3 tablespoons butter plus 2 tablespoons broken into small bits
1 cup béchamel (see page 208)
½ cup heavy cream
¼ pound Gruyère cheese, grated
4 tablespoons breadcrumbs
Salt, freshly ground pepper, and nutmeg

Preheat oven to 375 degrees.

Trim the root of the endives, remove any flawed leaves, and drop the vegetable into a pot of boiling water. Add salt and blanch 5 to 7 minutes, until tender. Remove to a colander and drain.

In a dry skillet, heat the endives to rid them of any excess water; add 2 to 3 tablespoons butter when they are dry, and sauté on medium heat until they start to turn a golden brown. Season with salt, pepper, and nutmeg to taste. Remove to a buttered gratin dish and keep ready.

In a saucepan, warm the béchamel and stir in the cream and half of the grated cheese. Reserve the rest of the cheese for the top. Pour the sauce over the vegetables; sprinkle with the reserved cheese and then the breadcrumbs. Dot with small pieces of butter and bake in a preheated oven for 15 minutes, or until the top is golden brown.

Lettuce

CREAMED LETTUCE

Laitues à la Crème

The dish makes a first class presentation of the lettuce and it is a delicious accompaniment to roasted birds. Serve with a light Beaujolais.

This recipe reflects the kind of economy that doesn't permit waste. You can use any trimmings and greens.

2 heads lettuce or equivalent amount of leftover greens from Boston
  lettuce, escarole, or romaine
4 tablespoons butter
1 rounded tablespoon flour
¼ cup cream

Fresh bread croutons (optional)
Salt, freshly ground pepper, and nutmeg

METHOD

The lettuce greens can be salvaged from leaves that might otherwise be thrown away. Wash, dry, and refrigerate until there are enough to use. Blanch the lettuce as you would spinach; the cooking time depends on the variety. Strain, squeeze dry, and chop. In a skillet, sauté in 3 to 4 tablespoons melted butter. Sprinkle with flour, season with salt, pepper, and nutmeg, and mix everything well. Before serving, stir in the cream. If desired, the croutons can be incorporated into the greens or crumbled and sprinkled on top.

Mushrooms

CHEESE SOUFFLE WITH MUSHROOMS

Soufflé au Fromage et aux Champignons

Serve this as a first course with crêpes and fresh tomatoes, or as the main course for a vegetarian supper, accompanied by Swiss chard. Select a red wine from Chinon.

| INGREDIENTS | SERVES 6 |

Béchamel

4 tablespoons butter
¼ cup flour
1 cup warm milk
Salt, freshly ground pepper, and nutmeg

Butter and freshly grated Parmesan cheese for 6-cup soufflé dish
½ pound mushrooms, sliced or quartered
2 tablespoons butter with 1 tablespoon olive oil
2 to 3 large garlic cloves, minced
2 to 3 tablespoons chopped fresh *fines herbes:* parsley, fennel,
    tarragon, and chives (any combination)
6 egg whites
4 egg yolks
½ cup grated Gruyère cheese
Salt and freshly ground pepper

| METHOD |

Preheat oven to 375 degrees. Prepare the béchamel as described on page 208. While the béchamel simmers, butter the soufflé dish and sprinkle lightly with Parmesan cheese. Set aside.

In a skillet, sauté mushrooms in the butter and oil until they give up their liquid. Add garlic and herbs and season with salt and pepper. Toss everything well and keep ready.

Remove the béchamel from the heat and let cool. Beat the egg whites with a pinch of salt until stiff and keep ready. In a large bowl, mix the yolks into the béchamel one at a time. Stir in the cheese and adjust the seasonings. Add one third of the beaten whites and fold to lighten the mixture. Gently fold in the rest of the whites. Pour half of this mixture into the soufflé dish. Gently spoon a layer of mushrooms over it; any leftover mushrooms can be used to garnish the dish. Add the rest of the soufflé mixture. Place on the middle rack of a preheated oven and bake for 20 to 25 minutes.

Cooking Mushrooms Dry

White button mushrooms often lack flavor, perhaps because of the way they are cultivated. If they are sliced and dry sautéed, however, and allowed to cook in their own juices, they develop a much more flavorful finish.

The technique calls for heating a skillet on a high flame until it is very hot. Toss the sliced mushrooms in the skillet with a bit of salt, which helps draw out moisture. After a minute or two the mushrooms give up all their water. If you sauté them until the water evaporates, they brown nicely in their own juices and concentrate their flavors. When the water completely evaporates, remove from the heat, season with salt and pepper; add garlic and parsley, and, if desired, some butter. Toss everything together. The mushrooms are ready, exploding with aroma.

Another way to flavor these mushrooms is to infuse them with the water used to revive dry mushrooms. Put dried mushrooms, either a single variety or a blend, in a bowl and pour boiling water over them. Let sit to revive and soften. Once revived, pour off the water through a coffee filter and save. Flush the revived mushrooms with water to rid them of sand.

Prepare the white mushrooms as described above and toss in a dry skillet with a pinch of salt. At the first sign that they are sweating little beads of water, pour the filtered mushroom water over them. Then add the revived mushrooms and cook everything over high heat until the water evaporates. In this way, the ordinary white mushrooms take on the flavor of *cèpes*, *porcini*, or other varieties of dry mushrooms. Finish with an addition of garlic and parsley.

Notes on Making Soufflés

Mathematics for Preparing a Soufflé: There are formulas for making soufflés that take the mystery out of making them. A soufflé dish has a calculable volume, i.e., it is a 1-, 2-, or 4-cup soufflé dish, and so on. If you don't know how big your soufflé dish is, pour water into it by the measuring cupful to determine its volume.

A soufflé is made up of two parts; the base, which is inactive and where the flavor is found; and the whites, which are the active element of the dish. Moreover, a soufflé is made from ingredients whose volumes can be measured. The volume of a beaten egg yolk yields about ⅛ cup; a beaten egg white measures about ⅔ to 1 cup. If the white is beaten to its maximum volume, and if it is handled properly in the folding, it loses about ⅓ of its volume. This loss of volume can be corrected by adding extra whites.

We have, for example, a 6-cup soufflé dish. It needs a certain amount of base, béchamel or roux, and flavoring, such as cheese, herbs, and seasoning. There is a saying that soufflés like to be a little drunk, and if you give them a bit of sherry they will always rise. (I subscribe to the notion.) We need ¾ cup of base (béchamel) and ¾ cup of flavoring (yolks plus cheese) for the 6-cup soufflé dish. There are 4½ cups left. The 6 egg yolks use approximately ¾ to 1 cup of volume. So now there are 3½ cups remaining for the egg whites. At ⅔ cup per white, we need exactly 7 whites. We add an additional egg white to account for the loss in volume in handling, folding, and pouring of the soufflé. Our recipe for a 6-cup soufflé dish must read:

⅔ cup béchamel
½ to ¾ cup grated Gruyère cheese
2 to 4 tablespoons chopped *fines herbes*: chives, scallions, parsley, chervil, and tarragon
4 tablespoons dry sherry
6 egg yolks
8 egg whites
Salt and freshly ground pepper

Always butter the soufflé dish and coat with breadcrumbs or grated Parmesan cheese so the eggs can cling to the side of the dish as they climb. Put the base, béchamel, into a large bowl. Add the egg yolks, one at a time. Add the cheese, herbs, seasonings, and sherry; then everything is nicely folded.

Beating Egg Whites: Beat the egg whites stiff with a pinch of salt in a copper bowl. If you don't have a copper bowl, use any glass or metal bowl, but not plastic. Scour the inside of the bowl with ¼ cup salt and ½ cup vinegar to degrease; rinse the bowl thoroughly in hot water and wipe dry.

Next add the egg whites, along with a pinch of salt, and whip the whites with a whisk until they are stiff, i.e., when you lift the whisk from the beaten whites, a peak forms on the blades. If the peak holds its shape when moved from the 6 o'clock position to the 12 o'clock position, the whites are stiff. If they are not, continue to whip until they are at least stiff enough to hold the peak. Technically, they should be beaten until they hold an egg without letting it sink; try it and you will quickly learn to judge for yourself.

Folding Techniques for Soufflés: Folding is an important technique to understand. It makes the base lighter by getting it to accept the air bubbles that are in the beaten egg white. It is the egg whites that cause the soufflé to rise when subject to the heat of the oven. Put the soufflé base in a bowl that is large enough to handle the volume of the base and the whites. Add ⅓ of the whites and fold in with a spatula.

Before there were spatulas, people used their hands to do this sort of work. With your fingers extended flat like a spatula and vertical to the dish, cut through the center of the base and whites, reach to the bottom, and lift the base, scooping it gently. Lift and turn the wrist so that the base falls in a fold over the top of the whites. Imagine the same action when working with a spatula. With the spatula firmly held in your hand, cut through to the center of the mixture, to the bottom and scoop some of the base, and as you lift away from the center, turn your wrist so that there is actually a fold when the base is set on top of the whites. Give the bowl a quarter turn each time this action is performed. Don't twirl the spatula like a baton; it's a wasted action. Don't swirl the mixture with the spatula, it is self-defeating. The idea is to lighten the base with the whites; the weight of one material folded on top of the other is all that is required to mix these different densities. First add only ⅓ of the whites to lighten the base; mix in by folding and turning, then add the remaining ⅔ of the whites in the same way.

This technique lightens the base without sacrificing all of the egg whites. Even if properly handled, ⅓ of the volume of the whites is lost.

Carefully ladle the soufflé mixture into the prepared soufflé dish. The volume should fill the dish to within an inch of the top. There are tricks for giving its final crown different shapes. You can prepare a collar to prevent the soufflé from climbing out of the dish and spilling over the sides. If a soufflé dish of the proper size is used and if it is filled within an inch of the top, it won't spill over. Put the soufflé on the middle shelf of a preheated oven and bake.

Baking Techniques: There are two methods of baking soufflés. They can bake at a high temperature, 375 degrees, for a short time, 25 to 30 minutes for a 6-cup soufflé. Or, they can bake at a lower temperature, 325 degrees, for a longer time, 45 to 50 minutes for a 6-cup soufflé. The longer baking time cooks the soufflé all the way through; and the shorter time leaves the soufflés creamy in the center. Since the soufflés are not usually served with a sauce, leave them creamy in the center and the creaminess functions as a sauce.

Make a thousand soufflés to discover all their quirks. Do it with my encouragement and don't be afraid; whether or not you have the perfect soufflé, you will at least wind up with a wonderful omelette. You will love them all.

MUSHROOMS WITH CREAM

Champignons à la Crème

This recipe lends itself to a number of subtle variations. One version calls for reducing the cream. Another version has mushrooms sautéed dry, with just a little salt to draw their juices. In yet another version, the *persillade* is sautéed crisp, or tossed in, uncooked, at the last moment to give the fresh taste of the herb and garlic. Try all versions.

INGREDIENTS	SERVES 6 TO 8

1½ pounds small mushrooms
1 tablespoon olive oil
4 tablespoons butter
2 large cloves garlic, minced
2 to 4 tablespoons finely chopped parsley

1 tablespoon flour
¼ cup heavy cream
Salt and freshly ground pepper

METHOD

Prepare and clean the mushrooms. Remove the stems and finely chop, reserving the caps. Coat the bottom of a skillet with the oil and add half the butter. When the butter is hot and the foam starts to subside, add the chopped mushroom stems, season lightly with salt, and sauté quickly until they give up their liquid. Remove to a bowl. Add the remaining butter to the skillet; when it is hot, add the mushroom caps, garlic, and 1 tablespoon parsley. Sauté quickly on high heat until tender. Add the cooked stems.

Add a light dusting of flour, and then the cream. Continue to heat 3 to 4 minutes, stirring until the liquid starts to bind and the flour has a chance to cook. Correct the seasoning and give a few grindings of pepper. Place on a heated platter and sprinkle with the remaining chopped parsley.

MARINATED MUSHROOMS

Champignons Marinés

These make a wonderful first course by themselves; they can also be the garnish for a composed salad served with toast. They make the best picnic food.

INGREDIENTS	SERVES 6

1 tablespoon cider vinegar
3 tablespoons peanut oil
1 shallot, minced
1 teaspoon Dijon mustard
Few drops Worcestershire sauce
1 clove garlic, minced
¼ cup chopped parsley
1 pound mushrooms, sliced if large, left whole if small
Salt and freshly ground pepper

METHOD

In a bowl, combine all the ingredients except the mushrooms. Mix well, then add the mushrooms. Cover and let marinate at least overnight.

If this salad is to be served within 24 hours don't cook the mushrooms; if it is kept longer than a day, blanch the mushrooms for 5 minutes in acidulated water and drain well before adding to the marinade.

Onions

BRAISED ONIONS

Oignons Braisés

This is a delicious dish with Provençal flavors. It is satisfying and simple. Serve with a red wine from Corbières.

INGREDIENTS	SERVES 6

4 large onions, whole
4 tablespoons olive oil
2 tablespoons butter

1 eggplant, ½-inch dice
1 green pepper, ¼-inch julienne and peeled
1 zucchini, halved lengthwise and cut in half moons
2 to 3 small tomatoes, peeled, seeded, and chopped
1 large clove garlic, crushed
1 pinch cinnamon
1 tablespoon fresh basil, shredded, or mixed *herbes de provence*
1 teaspoon dry marjoram
A few green olives
Salt and freshly ground pepper

METHOD

Preheat oven to 325 degrees. Peel the onions and brown whole in 1 tablespoon oil and the butter until golden brown. Remove from the pan and reserve. Dice the eggplant; slice the green pepper and remove the skins. Cut the zucchini into ½-inch half moons. Sauté eggplant separately in the remaining oil and remove to a shallow baking dish. Then sauté the pepper and zucchini in the same skillet. Stir in the rest of the ingredients along with the eggplant. Arrange everything in the oven-proof dish. Place the whole onions on top. Cover and bake for 1½ hours, until the onions are completely cooked. Add more fresh herbs if desired and serve.

CREAMED ONIONS AND PEAS

Oignons et Pois, Sauce Piquante

The combination of these tastes is classic in French cooking. It makes a delicious and satisfying dish. Serve with salmon and a Pinot Noir from the Alsace for good company.

INGREDIENTS	SERVES 6

Béchamel
   4 tablespoons butter
   ⅓ cup flour
   1½ cups light cream
   ½ teaspoon fresh dill, finely chopped
   ½ teaspoon fennel seeds, finely chopped
   ½ teaspoon Dijon mustard
   ½ cup Sauternes
   Salt and freshly ground pepper

   1 pound small white onions
   1 pound fresh peas, shelled
   3 tablespoons butter

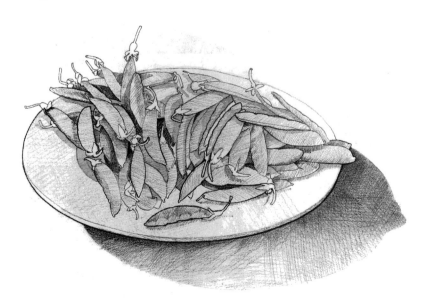

1 cup breadcrumbs
½ teaspoon rosemary
Salt and freshly ground pepper

METHOD

Make the béchamel. Add the dill, fennel, mustard, and the Sauternes, mixing well. Keep ready. Peel and cook the onions in boiling salted water until tender, so that when a cake tester is inserted it gets only the slightest resistance; then drain.

In a bowl, pour boiling water over the peas and let stand for 5 minutes. Drain well and then add to the sauce. Heat the butter in a skillet, add the breadcrumbs and toast until brown; sprinkle with rosemary. Put the onions in a serving dish. Pour the sauce over the onions and serve topped with the flavored breadcrumbs.

ONION RAGOUT

Ragoût d'Oignons

Serve hot with roast lamb and noodles with a mustard cream. Pour a Côtes-du-Rhône.

INGREDIENTS   SERVES 6

2 pounds small white onions
4 tablespoons butter
2 tablespoons flour
1 cup chicken stock, good homemade (see page 331)
1 pound tomatoes, peeled, seeded, and quartered
¼ teaspoon ground cloves
¼ teaspoon cinnamon
1 bay leaf
Salt and freshly ground pepper

Peel the onions; score an "X" in the root end. In a deep skillet, slowly sauté the onions in the butter until they are a deep golden brown. Stir in the flour, whisking well. Add the stock to the onions, and then the tomatoes and the remainder of the ingredients. Cover the pan and simmer for about an hour, until the onions are soft and cooked through but still whole. If necessary, add a little water or stock to the onions during the cooking.

ALSATIAN ONION TART

Tarte à l'Oignon Alsacienne

This tart would love an Alsatian wine, a Riesling or Pinot Blanc. It can be an appetizer, or served with a salad or kohlrabi flavored with lemon and dill for a light supper.

INGREDIENTS   SERVES 6

Pastry Crust
   1½ cups flour
   Pinch of *quatre épices* (see page 184)
   Pinch of salt
   8 tablespoons butter, in walnut-size pieces
     1 whole egg

   6 leeks or 6 white onions, thinly sliced
   4 tablespoons butter
   3 eggs
   1 cup cream
   ½ teaspoon nutmeg
   2 to 3 slices bacon, browned and cut into small pieces
   1 cup grated Gruyère cheese
   Salt and freshly ground pepper.

Prepare the pastry crust by mixing the flour, *quatre épices,* and salt. Work the butter into the flour until it is completely mixed and grainy in texture. Mix the egg into the dough. When it is homogeneous, let it rest for 30 minutes in the refrigerator before rolling it out.

Preheat oven to 400 degrees. Line a pie pan with the dough. Prepare the leeks. Trim to remove the root and cut the tops where the dark green begins. Save the tops for flavoring stocks or soups. Cut the leeks in half lengthwise and wash by flushing thoroughly under cold running water. Cut the leeks in ⅙-inch slices, cut on the diagonal. If using white onions, cut them in half, peel away the papery outer layers, and slice in ⅙-inch slices. Sauté the leeks in butter until soft. In a bowl, beat the eggs with the cream, adding salt, pepper, and nutmeg.

Add sautéed leeks to the egg mixture. Sprinkle the bottom of the pastry crust with small pieces of bacon. Pour the leeks and egg mixture into the shell. Sprinkle with grated cheese. Bake in a preheated oven for 15 minutes, then turn the oven to 325 degrees and cook 15 more minutes, until it is set.

Parsnips

Most of the parsnips the French eat are cooked in a *pot-au-feu,* but they go very well with all types of stews and grilled red meats. Use them as you use salsify (oyster plant)—fried or creamed. Parsnips can be cooked in boiling water or braised in butter. They are also used to make parsnip pancakes.

PARSNIPS WITH MEAT GLAZE

Panais au Jus

INGREDIENTS	SERVES 6

1 pound parsnips, peeled and sliced
1 quart water acidulated with 1 tablespoon vinegar
4 tablespoons butter
1 small onion, finely chopped
½ cup beef or veal stock (see page 331) or 2 tablespoons *glace de viande* or meat juices (see page 333)
2 teaspoons torn fresh basil
Salt, freshly ground pepper, and nutmeg

METHOD

Parboil the parsnips in the acidulated water for 5 minutes. Melt the butter and add the onion and sauté for a minute. Drain the parsnips and add them to the pan. Season to taste with salt, pepper, and nutmeg. Stir in the beef stock and/or *glace de viande.* Cover and cook 10 to 15 minutes, or until desired doneness. Add the basil just before serving.

Peppers

GREEN PEPPERS WITH EGGS

Terrine de Poivrons Verts aux Oeufs

To taste peppers without their skins is to experience their luxury. You can peel them or roast them black over a flame and put them inside a paper bag to sweat the skin off (see below).

Bake the custard slowly and you will achieve a very unctuous texture. I would search for a Cantal cheese for this recipe; lacking that use cheddar

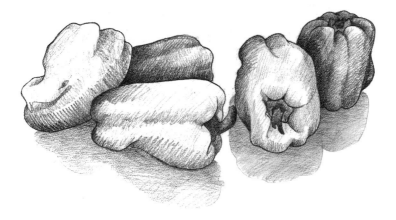

mixed with an equal amount of Roquefort. These are cheese tastes that particularly like peppers. Drink something red from the southwest, a Côtes de Bordeaux, or enjoy a French cider.

INGREDIENTS   SERVES 6 TO 8

1 to 2 tablespoons butter
6 sweet bell peppers, red or green, or mild green chilies, cut in strips, seeded, and peeled
1½ cups melting cheese, grated (see above)
6 eggs
2 cups milk
Salt and freshly ground pepper

METHOD

Preheat oven to 300 degrees. Generously butter a casserole. Put a layer of peppers on the bottom; then add a layer of cheese. Repeat this layering until all the ingredients are used.

Beat the eggs in a bowl with a fork. Add the milk, salt, and pepper; pour the mixture over the peppers and cheese. Bake in a slow oven for 1 hour, or until the eggs are set. Test by placing a skewer into the center of the dish, it should come out warm to the touch and show no trace of uncooked egg.

Peeling Skins from Peppers: Place the peppers in a hot oven, turning on all sides until the skin begins to blister. The peppers can also be skewered with a fork inserted into the stem end and placed directly over the burner flame or coil. Turn constantly so that the heat is even and makes the skin blacken and blister over the entire surface of the pepper. Place the pepper in a paper bag, close the top, and let stand for 15 minutes. Peel off the skin, remove the seeds, and cut the vegetable into strips.

PEPPERS WITH MIXED VEGETABLES

Ratatouille Provençale

This dish is typical of the Mediterranean provinces or departments, and has the advantage of being delicious served hot, or cold as an hors d'oeuvre. It rewarms nicely.

At the restaurant I prepare the vegetables separately, and then arrange them in a visually pleasing way. A layer of eggplants set straight across the gratin dish alternates with a layer of zucchini, then a layer of tomato slices; repeat the pattern until all the vegetables are used up. Just before serving, season with a few grinds of pepper and drizzle a little extra virgin olive oil for flavoring.

INGREDIENTS	SERVES 6 TO 8

1 large eggplant
1 large onion
4 tomatoes
3 medium zucchini
3 sweet peppers, sliced and peeled
Persillade: 2 cloves garlic, minced, and 2 to 4 tablespoons chopped
   parsley
¼ cup olive oil
Salt and freshly ground pepper

METHOD

Prepare all the vegetables. Slice the eggplant into 1-inch slices; cover with salt to draw out the juices; wash completely in cold water; wipe dry and cut into 1-inch cubes. Cut the onion in half lengthwise; then cut into thin slices. Remove the stem end of the tomatoes and chop coarsely. Cut the zucchini in half lengthwise, then cut into 1-inch half moons. Remove the stem of the sweet pepper; cut into quarters and remove seeds and cottony ribs. Cut into ½-inch strips; lift the skin off with a paring knife. Mince the cloves of garlic and add to finely chopped parsley.

Preheat oven to 300 degrees. In a large skillet, pour in enough olive oil to just cover the bottom. Be sure the oil is hot before adding the vegetables. Apart from the tomatoes, which should be added to the casserole uncooked, mix all the vegetables together and sauté in batches. Season each batch lightly with salt. Lightly brown the vegetables and transfer to an oven-proof casserole; add the tomatoes. Top the dish with the *persillade*. Bake in a preheated oven for at least 1 hour.

Potatoes

ALSATIAN POTATO FLUFFS

Floutes Alsaciens

INGREDIENTS   SERVES 6

2 pounds potatoes
3 tablespoons butter
¼ cup crème fraîche
1 whole egg
2 tablespoons finely chopped parsley
1 to 2 tablespoons melted butter
Salt, freshly ground pepper, and nutmeg

Preheat oven to 350 degrees. Boil the potatoes whole until done, peel, and mash with butter and mix in a little cream. Add the egg, parsley, and spices. If the potatoes appear dry, they may take more crème fraîche a little at a time; the mixture should have body and not be runny. Make sure everything is mixed well.

Butter a large cookie sheet. Using a tablespoon, drop the potato mixture by spoonfuls onto the baking sheet. Bake in a preheated oven for about 12 minutes. Brown under the broiler if necessary. Pour the melted butter over them and serve piping hot.

POTATO CASSEROLE WITH ANCHOVIES

Purée Parmentier

The lattice design for this potato dish makes a pleasing presentation. Serve these potatoes with roast leg of lamb and drink a Bandol *rouge* from the *domaine* at Pibarnon in Provence.

INGREDIENTS   SERVES 6

2 pounds potatoes
4 to 5 tablespoons butter
1 egg, slightly beaten
Leaves from several sprigs of fresh oregano
10 to 12 anchovy fillets
2 to 3 cherry tomatoes, thinly sliced
2 to 3 pitted olives, sliced
Freshly grated Parmesan cheese
Salt, freshly ground pepper, and nutmeg

METHOD

Boil or steam the potatoes whole in their jackets. Peel them, and while the potatoes are still warm, mash with 3 tablespoons butter. Stir in the egg and half the oregano. Season with the salt and pepper to taste and a few gratings of nutmeg.

Preheat oven to 350 degrees. Butter a 10-inch, shallow baking dish and spread the potato mixture evenly. Lay the anchovies across the top in a lattice-like design. Inside the spaces left by the anchovies, alternately place a slice of tomato or olive. Dot the tomatoes with the remaining butter. Sprinkle the remaining oregano and the Parmesan cheese over the top. Bake 15 to 20 minutes.

CATALAN STUFFED POTATOES

Pommes de Terre Catalane

Serve the baked potatoes with a loin of veal and orange sauce, and pour a southern red wine, such as a Corbières.

INGREDIENTS   SERVES 4

2 potatoes
1 shallot, finely chopped
1 pimento, peeled and finely chopped
2 tablespoons butter
4 to 6 anchovies, finely chopped
2 hard-boiled eggs finely chopped
1 tablespoon chopped chives
4 tablespoons béchamel (see page 208) or 4 tablespoons reduced
   heavy cream
Salt, freshly ground pepper, and nutmeg

Preheat oven to 375 degrees. Bake the potatoes until a skewer can pierce them with no resistance. While the potatoes are baking, sauté the shallot and pimento in a little butter until limp. Keep ready.

After the potatoes have baked, remove from the oven and turn the heat to 350 degrees. When the potatoes are cool enough to handle, halve and scoop out the potato shell. First combine the potato with all of the ingredients except the béchamel and butter. Then add enough béchamel to bind. Place the potato mixture back into shells and dot with the butter. Place in the oven until heated through and slightly browned on top.

POTATOES WITH CREAM

Pommes de Terre à la Crème

Serve with a plain roasted chicken garnished with wild mushrooms and a Chardonnay from Mâcon.

5 to 6 medium-size russet potatoes
4 tablespoons butter
⅓ cup flour
1½ cups warm milk
⅓ cup white wine or sherry
1 tablespoon chopped parsley
1 tablespoon chopped tarragon
½ cup of crème fraîche, mascarpone, or clotted cream
Salt and freshly ground pepper

Preheat oven to 350 degrees. While the potatoes boil, prepare the sauce. Melt the butter in a saucepan, blend in the flour, whisking until smooth, and season with a bit of salt. Cook over slow heat 3 to 4 minutes but don't let it brown or discolor. Add the warm milk, a small amount at a time, until a creamy consistency is obtained. Add the wine and cook 10 to 15 minutes on a slow flame, stirring occasionally so that the sauce doesn't scorch or stick to the bottom of the pan. The final sauce shouldn't be too thick so don't hesitate to add more milk during the cooking. Correct the seasoning; add the pepper and herbs.

When the potatoes are cooked, peel and slice them in ¼-inch slices; put in a gratin dish, cover with the sauce, and dot with the crème fraîche. Bake in a preheated oven until the top is brown, about 15 minutes.

GRATIN DAUPHINOIS

Gratin Dauphinois

Slice the potatoes thin enough so that when you hold a slice horizontally, the tip of it droops slightly. It is hard to imagine naming this dish in English anything but *Gratin Dauphinois*. It is such a satisfying dish—potatoes, cheese, and milk, all baked together. It can also be done with cream, which makes something wonderful that you might not want to eat as often, but makes you dream of the dish between times.

INGREDIENTS   SERVES 6

1 clove garlic, slightly crushed
8 potatoes, peeled and thinly sliced
6 to 8 tablespoons butter
1½ cups boiled milk or cream
1 egg, beaten
½ cup grated Gruyère cheese
Salt, freshly ground pepper, and nutmeg

METHOD

Preheat oven to 350 degrees. Butter a two-quart round casserole and rub with the garlic. Lay a double layer of potatoes on the bottom of the casserole and dot with small pieces of butter. Continue layering until three-quarters full. Mix the hot milk with the egg, and season to taste with salt, pepper, and nutmeg. Add the cheese and pour over the potatoes. Cover and cook in a preheated oven for 45 minutes to 1 hour. Uncover and brown lightly under the broiler.

POTATOES WITH ENGLISH SAUCE

Pommes de Terre à la Sauce Anglaise

Serve the dish with roast beef and a friendly Burgundian wine, such as Saint Joseph. This dish makes great sense when organizing a menu because it can be held in the oven, freeing you to assemble the remainder of the meal.

INGREDIENTS	SERVES 6

4 medium new red potatoes
1 medium onion, finely chopped
4 tablespoons butter
1 tablespoon oil
2 eggs, lightly beaten
3 tablespoons Lea and Perrins sauce
Juice of 1 lemon
Mixed *fines herbes*: tarragon, chervil, and parsley
Salt and freshly ground pepper

METHOD

Preheat oven to 350 degrees. Boil the potatoes in their jackets, starting them off in cold water. While the potatoes cook, sauté the onion until limp in 1 tablespoon butter mixed with 1 tablespoon oil. When the potatoes are done, remove them from their jackets and make a purée mixing in 2 tablespoons butter. Then mix in the eggs and the remaining ingredients, folding everything well.

Butter a baking dish and spread the potatoes in an even layer. Dot the top with the last of the butter broken in tiny pieces. Bake in a preheated oven until the top browns nicely. Cut into squares and serve piping hot.

POTATO GNOCCHI

Gnocchi de Pommes de Terre

These gnocchi make a great dish because they lend themselves to so many variations. Spinach can be added to the dough instead of cheese, bacon, or raisins. They can be served with or without a sauce; by themselves or as the garnish to a main course. This is a very versatile dish to have in your repertoire. The only trick in cooking gnocchi is to keep the water at a simmer so they poach and are not boiled.

INGREDIENTS   SERVES 6 TO 8

1 pound potatoes
3 egg yolks
½ teaspoon salt
1 cup sifted all-purpose flour
4 tablespoons butter, melted
1½ cups grated cheese: Gruyère, cheddar, or Parmesan

METHOD

Boil potatoes in their jackets until tender. Peel and mash. Beat in the egg yolks and salt; stir in the flour, butter, and ½ cup cheese. Shape the potato mixture into small balls the size of walnuts and place on a floured board.

Preheat oven to 375 degrees.

Bring a 6- to 8-quart pot of water to a boil; salt it lightly and turn down the flame until the water simmers. Drop the dumplings into the water and poach in the simmering water for 5 minutes. The gnocchi should feel firm to the touch when done. If the water boils, it could make the dumplings crumble. Drain the dumplings when they are cooked, and arrange in a buttered casserole. Sprinkle cheese between the layers and bake in a preheated oven 10 to 15 minutes, or until brown.

POTATOES WITH TWO HEADS OF GARLIC

Purée de Pommes de Terre à l'Ail

Cooking the minced garlic in cream allows the garlic to sweeten by the time it is added to the potatoes. Serve with a roasted leg of lamb and a sunny southern red wine, such as one from Tricastin.

INGREDIENTS   SERVES 6

¾ cup cream
2 heads garlic, peeled and finely chopped
3 pounds potatoes, boiled and peeled
6 tablespoons butter
Salt and freshly ground pepper

METHOD

In a small saucepan, combine the cream and minced garlic, and cook over low heat until mixture bubbles. Simmer 3 to 4 minutes longer. Meanwhile, sieve or mash the potatoes, adding butter, salt, and pepper to taste. Mix the cream and garlic, half at a time, into the potatoes to make a smooth purée. Check the seasonings and add more cream or milk if necessary to produce the desired consistency.

GARLIC POTATOES, MARSEILLE STYLE

Pommes de Terre Marseillaise

Potatoes cooked in stock have a singular richness. Serve these with a breast of duck, roasted on the bone, and a ragout of sweet peppers. Accompany the meal with a Châteauneuf-du-Pape.

INGREDIENTS	SERVES 6

2 pounds small potatoes
2 tablespoons olive oil mixed with 2 tablespoons butter
1 cup veal stock (see page 331)
5 to 6 cloves garlic, minced
2 to 3 tablespoons chopped parsley
Salt and freshly ground pepper

METHOD

Peel the potatoes and sauté them brown in the olive oil and butter. They require only partial cooking at this point, and need only to be browned. If you are using large potatoes, cut into small ovals. When they are browned, remove from the skillet to a 4-quart saucepan. Add the stock, garlic, and salt; bring to a boil, cover, and simmer 15 to 20 minutes, or until they are done but hold shape. Garnish with parsley, give a grinding of pepper, and serve.

POTATOES WITH MEAT JUICES

Pommes de Terre Parisienne

A volume of good veal or beef stock can be reduced to a point where it is flavorful and like a jelly. These potatoes are coated in that jelly and then used to garnish the platter of a roast.

INGREDIENTS	SERVES 6 TO 8

2 pounds small potatoes, or scoop hazelnut-size rounds from large
   potatoes
4 to 6 tablespoons butter
¼ cup concentrated meat juices or ½ cup veal or beef stock reduced
   by half (see page 331)
2 tablespoons chopped parsley
Salt and freshly ground pepper

METHOD

Sauté the whole potatoes in butter and brown them evenly. As soon
as they are cooked through, add the reduced meat juices, sprinkle with
parsley, season with salt and pepper, and serve.

PUFFED POTATOES

Pommes de Terre Dauphine

These are a good accompaniment to a plain steak with a béarnaise
sauce (see page 190), accompanied by a Pinot Noir from the Alsace.

INGREDIENTS	SERVES 6 TO 8

4 medium potatoes, cooked whole
1 egg
4 tablespoons butter
Salt, freshly ground pepper, and nutmeg

Pâté à Chou

1 cup water
4 tablespoons cold butter, cut in walnut-size pieces
1 cup flour
4 whole eggs

1 to 2 tablespoons finely chopped *fines herbes* (optional)
Oil for deep frying

METHOD

Peel the cooked potato, and mash or sieve into a bowl. Mix in the egg and butter. Season with salt, pepper, and nutmeg.

To prepare the *pâté à choux,* put 1 cup of cold water in a 2-quart saucepan along with the butter and bring to a boil. Remove from the heat, add the flour all at once, and work with a wooden spoon until it is homogeneous. Set the pan back on the heat and cook this paste for 4 to 5 minutes, stirring continuously until it develops a shiny surface. Season the paste with salt and pepper. Remove from heat. Add the eggs one at a time; as each egg is added, stir with a wooden spoon to incorporate it into the paste.

After all the eggs have been added, fold in the potato mixture. Add the herbs if desired. Form this potato paste into walnut-size pieces, about a tablespoon in measure.

Heat the oil for deep frying in a skillet deep enough to hold approximately 2 inches of oil. Bring the oil to about 350 degrees. Push the potato puffs off the spoon into the hot oil with another spoon. Do not crowd the pan. Cook until browned evenly on all sides. As soon as they are cooked, remove to a cookie sheet lined with paper towels, and keep them hot in a warm oven. Just before serving, sprinkle lightly with salt; they should be light and crisp.

POTATO PUFFS WITH ALMONDS

Zéphyr de Pommes de Terre aux Amandes

Josephine says that in Italy they serve a similar potato dish with a well-seasoned tomato sauce. Serve these potatoes with a plain roasted chicken and drink a light Chianti.

INGREDIENTS   SERVES 6 TO 8

5 to 6 potatoes, boiled and peeled
4 tablespoons butter
½ cup light cream
1 egg, beaten
½ cup almonds, walnuts, or other nuts, finely chopped
Salt, freshly ground pepper, and nutmeg

METHOD

Preheat oven to 350 degrees. Make a mashed potato mixture with the butter and cream; season with salt, pepper, and nutmeg. Mix well to make the potatoes fluffy. Beat the egg with a fork until foamy and fold into the potatoes; then fold in the nuts. (To make the potatoes even lighter, add an extra egg white beaten stiff.) Drop the mixture by spoonfuls onto a well-buttered baking sheet. Bake in a preheated oven 15 to 20 minutes, until golden brown. Serve very hot.

RATATOUILLE OF VEGETABLES IN SEASON

Ratatouille de Saison

This ratatouille follows Josephine's counsel that a cook must pay attention to technique and texture. Here the technique calls for sautéing followed by slow cooking until the vegetables have the desired texture or doneness. With that understanding, the cook is free to create any vegetable combination that makes sense to the palate.

INGREDIENTS	SERVES 6

2 to 3 medium new red potatoes
2 to 3 ripe tomatoes
½ pound green beans
1 cup shelled peas
2 to 3 medium zucchini
2 tablespoons butter
2 tablespoons vegetable oil
2 to 3 slices bacon or pancetta
1 bunch scallions, chopped
2 large cloves garlic, minced
Fines herbes: parsley, chervil, tarragon, or chives
Salt and freshly ground pepper

METHOD

The quantities of vegetables can vary depending on availability and freshness. Potatoes and tomatoes are cut into ¾-inch cubes. The remainder of the vegetables are cut into bite-size pieces so they finish cooking at about the same time, accounting for their varying densities.

Melt the butter and oil in a skillet; then pour half into a small bowl and keep it in reserve. Add the bacon to the butter in the skillet and cook slowly until it renders its fat and has browned to desired doneness. Remove the bacon from the skillet and crumble; reserve as a garnish.

Add the scallions to the fat in the pan and sauté 1 minute; then add the minced garlic and continue to cook another minute. Add the potatoes and season with a small amount of salt. Cook at a simmer, turning them often, until the potatoes are almost done. Add the remaining vegetables and continue to simmer until all the vegetables are tender. Sprinkle with *fines herbes* and serve.

POTATO SALAD

Salade de Pommes de Terre

Potato salad should always be made while the potatoes are still warm as they absorb the dressing more easily. The sauce does not penetrate when the potatoes are cold so it wouldn't be as savory. Serve this dish with a cold roast chicken and a tender green salad accompanied by a fresh goat cheese; drink a cold French cider or a Sauvignon Blanc from the Haut-Poitou.

INGREDIENTS	SERVES 6

6 medium potatoes
5 hard-boiled eggs
1 bunch scallions, chopped
2 tablespoons chopped parsley, tarragon, and chervil
1 pound green beans, blanched

Dressing
3 tablespoons vegetable oil
1 tablespoon wine vinegar
1 tablespoon Dijon mustard
2 tablespoons homemade mayonnaise (see page 94)
½ cup light cream
Salt and freshly ground pepper

METHOD

Steam or boil the potatoes whole, peel their skins, and cut into a large dice. While the potatoes cook, hard boil the eggs. In a bowl, mix the potatoes, scallions, and some coarsely chopped parsley and herbs; season with salt and pepper and toss everything lightly.

Shell 2 of the hard-boiled eggs and pass through a strainer; reserve as a garnish.

To make the dressing, combine oil, vinegar, mustard, and mayonnaise in a 1-quart bowl, and whisk with a fork; slowly add the cream while whisking; blend well. Pour most of the dressing onto the warm potatoes and toss to coat everything well. Reserve a small amount of dressing for the green beans.

Arrange the potato salad on a large platter; surround with sliced eggs, alternating with small bunches of blanched green beans. Sprinkle the entire dish with the strained eggs and herbs.

POTATO SOUFFLE

Soufflé aux Pommes de Terre

While the soufflé bakes, sauté a salmon fillet. Time the cooking so they are ready at the same time. Serve the salmon with a parsley sauce and drink an Alsatian Riesling.

INGREDIENTS	SERVES 6

5 medium potatoes, cooked whole
4 tablespoons butter
⅛ teaspoon nutmeg
¼ teaspoon salt
Generous grinding of pepper
¼ cup cream
3 egg yolks
4 egg whites

METHOD

See page 215 for more information on preparing soufflés. Preheat oven to 375 degrees. Sieve or mash the potatoes and add butter, nutmeg, salt, and pepper to taste. Add the cream and mix thoroughly; then add the yolks and mix again. Beat the egg whites with a little salt until dry but not stiff. Fold into the potatoes. Butter an oven-proof serving dish and fill with the mixture. Bake 25 minutes in a preheated oven.

POTATO SPIRALS

Spirales de Pommes de Terre

Serve this recipe with creamed vegetables as a garnish for a plain roast beef. They make a pretty presentation on the plate.

INGREDIENTS	SERVES 6

Recipe for a pastry crust (see Alsatian Onion Tart page 224)
½ cup grated Gruyère cheese
2 cups mashed potatoes
Salt and freshly ground pepper

METHOD

Preheat oven to 450 degrees. Make the pastry dough, adding the cheese to the flour. Allow the dough to rest for 1 hour. Roll out to a 9-inch square and spread with the mashed potatoes. Sprinkle lightly with additional grated cheese. Roll as you would roll a jelly roll. Cut into 2-inch slices. Place each roll, cut side up, on a buttered, heavy baking pan.

Bake at 450 degrees for 10 to 15 minutes. Reduce the heat to 375 degrees and cook an additional 10 minutes.

POTATOES COOKED WITH TOMATOES

Pommes de Terre aux Tomates

The trick to the success of this recipe is to get the potatoes to absorb the liquid the tomatoes give up. The end result, the combined flavor of new potatoes and tomatoes with a bit of basil, is very satisfying. Serve with a confit of duck and drink a vin de Cahors.

INGREDIENTS   SERVES 6 TO 8

3 pounds small new potatoes
4 tablespoons butter
1½ pounds tomatoes, peeled, seeded, and chopped
1 tablespoon fresh basil, torn
Salt and freshly ground pepper

METHOD

Parboil the potatoes for a few minutes to loosen their skins; drain
and peel. Melt the butter in a skillet and sauté the potatoes until they
start to brown lightly. Add the tomatoes; season with salt and pepper to
taste. Cover and cook until the potatoes are just tender. Add the basil,
correct the seasonings, and serve.

Pumpkin

PUMPKIN SOUFFLE

Soufflé aux Potiron

Serve this dessert with a late harvest Alsatian or Californian wine.

INGREDIENTS   SERVES 6 TO 8

Butter and sugar for soufflé dish
2 tablespoons flour

½ cup sugar
1 cup cold milk or cream
1 cup pumpkin purée
4 egg yolks
2 to 4 ounces kirsch
Several gratings of nutmeg
6 egg whites
Pinch of salt
4 to 6 ounces heavy cream whipped with 1 tablespoon sugar and
  1 teaspoon vanilla

METHOD

Preheat oven to 375 degrees. Butter a 4-cup soufflé dish; then dust the inside with sugar. Set the bowl aside and keep ready.

In a saucepan, mix the flour and sugar; add the cold milk or cream, whisking to make a smooth paste. Bring to a boil and slowly cook on a heat diffuser about 10 minutes, so that it thickens and has the same texture as the pumpkin purée.

Remove the pan from the heat and stir in the pumpkin purée; taste for sweetness, adding more sugar if necessary. Put the pumpkin in a bowl and add the egg yolks one at a time. Stir in the kirsch, adding enough so that you can taste it; give a few gratings of nutmeg.

Beat the egg whites with salt to stiff peaks. Fold one third of the whites into the pumpkin mixture. Then gently fold in the rest of the whites. Place in a preheated oven 20 to 25 minutes. Serve immediately with the whipped cream for a garnish.

Spinach

SPINACH CRÊPES

Crêpes Florentine

Drink with these a cold Brittany cider or a dry white Loire Valley wine, a Savennières or Sancerre.

INGREDIENTS	SERVES 6

Mornay sauce
- 1½ cups hot milk
- 4 tablespoons butter
- ⅓ cup flour
- Cayenne
- Nutmeg
- 1 cup grated Gruyère cheese plus 2 to 3 tablespoons for garnish
- Salt and freshly ground pepper

Crêpe batter
- 4 tablespoons butter
- ¾ cup flour
- Pinch of salt
- 3 whole eggs
- 1 cup cold milk

Filling
- 1½ pounds spinach
- 2 tablespoons butter
- 2 tablespoons chopped scallions
- 1 teaspoon anchovy paste
- 2 tablespoons finely ground almonds

METHOD

Make the Mornay sauce first. Warm the milk; set aside and keep ready. In a saucepan, melt the butter; slowly work in the flour and mix well. Cook, stirring over slow heat, 4 to 5 minutes. Add the warm milk, slowly stirring so the sauce is creamy and smooth. Add a little salt, a pinch of cayenne, black pepper, and nutmeg. Add 1 cup cheese and stir until the sauce is smooth and creamy again. Add more warm milk if the sauce gets thicker than heavy cream.

To make the crêpe batter, melt the butter in a small saucepan; remove from the heat and keep ready. In a bowl, mix the flour and salt; beat in the eggs with a fork. When they are well incorporated with no lumps, mix in the cold milk, a little at a time, so the mixture is smooth. Mix in the melted butter. Allow the batter to rest 20 to 30 minutes before making the crêpes. Make the spinach filling while the batter rests.

To make the filling, wash the spinach thoroughly and remove the stems. Blanch 3 to 4 minutes in boiling salted water. Drain, flush in cold water to stop cooking, squeeze dry, and chop coarsely.

Melt the butter and add the scallions, sauté 1 minute. Add the chopped spinach, anchovy paste, and almonds. Add a little Mornay sauce to the spinach to make a creamy but not loose composition. Keep ready.

To cook the crêpes, place a small skillet (about 6-inches across) on a medium to medium-low flame and let it get hot. The idea is to have a steady heat, so let it build up. Whisk the batter with a a fork, put 2 to 3 tablespoons of batter into a measuring cup, and keep it ready. Lightly butter the crêpe skillet when it is hot. After making the first crêpe, you shouldn't need more butter because there is butter in the batter. Take the measuring cup, and, lifting the skillet off the flame, pour the batter into the pan; roll the pan in a circular motion to make the batter fill the bottom. Set the skillet back on the flame and allow the crêpe to cook until the outer edges start to brown. Turn the crêpe over and cook on the other side for about a minute. Remove to a plate. Stack the crêpes with sheets of waxed paper to separate them.

Repeat the process of premeasuring the batter needed to fill the skillet. It makes the crêpes as thin as possible and of uniform size. Stack them on a plate. This batter should make 12 crêpes in a small skillet.

To assemble the dish, fill the crêpes with some of the spinach mixture and roll them closed. Set them seam side down, side by side in a buttered baking dish. Pour the Mornay sauce over the crêpes; sprinkle with additional cheese. Bake in a 350 degree preheated oven for 15 minutes, until the cheese is lightly browned.

SPINACH GRATIN

Epinards au Gratin

In this recipe the spinach is cooked in a ring mold. Fill the center of the finished dish with creamed or buttered carrots, or creamed or honey-glazed onions. Sprinkle with chopped fresh parsley. It makes a beautiful presentation.

INGREDIENTS

1½ cups béchamel (see page 208)
2 pounds spinach
1 cup grated Gruyère cheese
4 eggs, lightly beaten
1 teaspoon Dijon mustard
¼ cup chopped parsley
Salt and freshly ground pepper

METHOD

Preheat oven to 300 degrees. Prepare the béchamel. While it simmers, blanch the spinach, cool under cold water, squeeze dry, and chop.

In a bowl, add the cheese and the beaten eggs to the béchamel. Mix in the remaining ingredients, reserving enough chopped parsley for a final garnish. Pour the spinach mixture into a well-buttered ring mold. Set the mold in a water bath and bake in a preheated oven 45 minutes, until the mixture has set. Allow to cool for 10 minutes in the water bath.

Carefully remove the gratin from the mold by inverting it onto a platter; garnish with the remaining parsley.

A SWEET SPINACH TART

Tarte aux Epinards

There are several instances of a sweet tart based on a vegetable; they are intended as desserts and this one would go well with an orange muscat wine. It is also another instance of a definitely regional pairing of fruit and vegetables.

INGREDIENTS	SERVES 8

1 partially baked pastry crust (see Alsation Onion Tart page 224)
1 cup French pastry cream (see below)
½ cup spinach, blanched, chopped, and dried
1 tablespoon grated lemon or orange rind
½ teaspoon vanilla or rum to taste
  Dash of salt
2 eggs, slightly beaten
⅓ cup heavy cream
Orange or tangerine slices for decoration

French Pastry Cream
  ⅓ cup sugar
  4 teaspoons of cornstarch
  Generous pinch of salt
  3 egg yolks, lightly beaten with a fork
  ¼ cup cold milk
  ¾ cup light cream
  2 teaspoons vanilla

METHOD

Preheat oven to 375 degrees. Blind bake a 9-inch tart shell.

To make the pastry cream, combine the sugar, cornstarch, and salt in a bowl. Add the egg yolks, whisking smooth. Gradually blend in the cold milk, mixing it so that it is free of lumps. Scald the light cream in a heavy saucepan, remove it from the heat, and let it cool a minute. Slowly whisk the scalded liquid into the eggs; then reverse, putting the egg mixture into the pan with the cream. Return to a medium flame and bring just to the boiling point, stirring constantly so that it does not stick to the bottom of the pan or scorch. Remove from the heat, add the vanilla, and continue to whisk for a full minute to cool it down; set aside.

To assemble the tart, combine the pastry cream, spinach, grated rind, vanilla, salt, 2 eggs, and the heavy cream. Pour the filling into the partially baked shell.

Bake the tart 12 to 15 minutes on the top shelf of a preheated oven. Remove, and set the fruit slices around the top. Then bake on the bottom shelf for another 10 to 15 minutes, or until set. Serve warm or at room temperature.

Tomatoes

TOMATO PRESERVE

Conserves de Tomates au Sucre

These tomatoes make a delicious cool dessert by themselves, with any cream, or as a preserve.

INGREDIENTS	SERVES 6 TO 8

2½ pounds cherry tomatoes
4 cups sugar
1½ cups water
1 lemon, cut in slices

METHOD

Pour boiling water over tomatoes and skin them. In a saucepan, melt the sugar in the water, add the lemon slices, and cook at a slow boil 10 to 15 minutes, until it forms a heavy syrup (about 245 degrees on a candy thermometer). Remove the lemon slices.

Add the tomatoes to the sugar syrup and gently simmer, until the tomatoes are just cooked. It should take about 20 minutes; the tomatoes should stay whole. Skim off any scum during this cooking. Ladle the cooked tomatoes very carefully into a bowl to cool. Cover and chill.

SAUCE OF FRESH TOMATOES

Coulis de Tomates

This sauce is best prepared with fresh tomatoes, but it can be made with canned ones. The use of brown stock makes a delicious and unctuous tomato sauce. Use only the best homemade stock for the sauce (see page 331).

INGREDIENTS	YIELDS 3 CUPS

3 tablespoons butter
3 tablespoons olive oil
1 large onion, chopped
2 cloves garlic, minced
2 tablespoons flour
1½ cups beef or veal stock or *glace de viande* (see page 331)
1 pound fresh tomatoes, chopped
Bouquet garni: thyme and bay leaf tied in 2 celery stalks
1 teaspoon oregano
1 teaspoon fennel seed
1 teaspoon sugar
¼ pound mushrooms
1 tablespoon fresh basil, shredded
Salt and freshly ground pepper

METHOD

Melt 2 tablespoons butter with 2 tablespoons oil and sauté the onion. Add 1 clove garlic and the flour. Stir and add the stock, tomatoes, bouquet garni, and herbs. Season with the sugar, and salt and pepper to taste. Simmer for 2 hours, replacing any liquid if it becomes too dry.

Sauté the mushrooms in the remaining butter and oil. Add the second clove of garlic and sauté briefly. Just before serving, stir the mushrooms and garlic into the tomato mixture along with the basil.

COOKED TOMATO SAUCE

Fondue de Tomates

This sauce makes a more concentrated flavoring than the fresh tomato sauce (see previous recipe) and can be added to other sauces to give them flavoring. It can also be reconstituted by adding stock to thin it to the desired consistency for a tomato sauce, soup, and so on.

INGREDIENTS	YIELDS 1½ CUPS

2 tablespoons butter or vegetable oil
2 pounds ripe tomatoes, peeled and coarsely chopped
1 sprig oregano leaves, chopped
1 sprig thyme leaves, chopped
¼ teaspoon salt
Freshly ground pepper

METHOD

Melt butter in a heavy-bottomed saucepan and add rest of the ingredients. Cook slowly over low flame, stirring occasionally, until the liquid evaporates and the mixture thickens. It keeps one week in the refrigerator; it can also be frozen.

BASQUE TOMATO AND PEPPER SAUCE

Pipérade

This recipe makes a good all-purpose sauce to use on meat, on fowl, or as the sauce for an omelette. After a long cooking, everything reduces to a purée. At Le Trou restaurant, this sauce is served with rabbit and a gratin of potatoes (see Potato Cake page 110) made with a layer of Roquefort cheese in the middle. Pour a French cider as a Basque might do with a similar menu.

INGREDIENTS	SERVES 6

1 tablespoon fat (butter, goose fat, chicken fat, or bacon rendering)
4 small onions, chopped
2 cloves garlic, minced
2 large green peppers, peeled, seeded and cubed
2 pounds tomatoes, peeled, seeded, and chopped
1 bay leaf
1 sprig thyme
2 to 4 tablespoons chervil or parsley
Stock, if necessary
Salt and freshly ground pepper

METHOD

Melt the fat in a large heavy pan. Add the onions and garlic and sauté for a few minutes. Add the peppers; sauté until the onions and peppers are soft. Add the tomatoes, bay leaf, thyme, and herbs; season with salt and pepper to taste. Simmer until it tastes good, about 1 hour. Taste again and correct seasonings if needed. If the sauce becomes too dry, moisten with stock.

STUFFED TOMATOES

Tomates Farcies Gabrielle

These tomatoes make an excellent cold first course when tomatoes are at the height of their season. Serve with a crusty dark bread and a rosé wine from Anjou.

INGREDIENTS   SERVES 6

6 medium tomatoes
½ cup homemade mayonnaise, well seasoned with Dijon mustard (see
    page 94)
1 very ripe avocado
Juice of ½ lemon
6 ounces cooked fish, flaked: tuna, salmon, sole, etc.
2 tablespoons chopped parsley
Lettuce or watercress leaves
Salt, freshly ground pepper, and paprika

METHOD

Wash and dry the tomatoes. Cut off the tops and carefully remove
the pulp to hollow out the tomatoes; turn them upside down on a plate
to drain and dry.

Meanwhile, prepare the mayonnaise; season with mustard to taste,
salt, pepper, and paprika. Peel and cut the avocado in small cubes, put
in a bowl, and sprinkle with lemon juice. Add some mayonnaise to the
avocado, the flaked fish, and finally mix in 1 tablespoon of chopped
parsley, tossing everything well to coat with mayonnaise. Lightly season
the inside of the tomatoes with salt and pepper and fill with the mixture.
Serve very cold on a bed of lettuce or watercress leaves. Sprinkle with
the remaining chopped parsley.

TERRINE OF GREEN TOMATOES

Terrine aux Tomates Vertes

This dish could be a main dish for a vegetarian supper, accompanied
by buttered noodles. It could also be serve with roast chicken, Potato
Cake, and a *vin de table* from the Côtes de Bordeaux.

INGREDIENTS	SERVES 6

6 tablespoons butter
½ teaspoon curry powder
Pinch of red pepper (cayenne is best)
2 tablespoons chopped fresh tarragon
1 teaspoon fennel seeds
1 pound yellow onions, peeled and sliced
1 cup chicken stock, good homemade (see page 331)
½ teaspoon paprika
  1 cup cream or crème frâiche
2 to 3 pounds medium-size green tomatoes
1 cup breadcrumbs
½ cup grated Gruyère cheese
1 teaspoon each chopped fresh herbs: oregano, tarragon, chervil, and chives (any combination)

METHOD

In a large pot, melt 2 to 3 tablespoons of butter, add curry, cayenne pepper, tarragon, and fennel seeds; simmer for 1 or 2 minutes on medium heat. Add the onions, give a generous pinch of salt, and pour in the stock; stir and cook until onions are limp. Mix in the paprika and the cream, turn the heat off, and keep ready.

Core the tomatoes, cut in ½-inch thick slices, and keep ready. Mix the breadcrumbs and grated cheese in a small bowl. Chop the fresh herbs, set in a small bowl, and keep ready.

Preheat oven to 350 degrees. Butter an oven-proof dish. Set half of the onions on the bottom; sprinkle with one third of the breadcrumbs and cheese. Layer half of the tomatoes; sprinkle with some of the chopped herbs. Top with another third of the breadcrumbs; lay in the remaining tomatoes and top with the remaining onions and breadcrumbs. Dot the top with pea-size pieces of butter and scatter the remaining herbs. Bake covered for 30 minutes; then uncover and cook another 10 minutes.

Watercress

FROM JOSEPHINE'S NOTES

Under the name of cress there are many species. The watercress and garden cress are used in cooking, as herbs and as salad greens. Both watercress and garden cress are eaten raw, used for garnish, or mixed with other greens. They can also be cooked like spinach or sorrel and added to purées, soufflés, and soups.

WATERCRESS SOUP

Potage de Cresson

This soup is excellent served hot or cold. Finish with a garnish of mustard-flavored crème fraîche, as we do at Le Trou, and drink a mountain wine from the Savoie, such as Apremont.

INGREDIENTS   SERVES 8

4 tablespoons butter
1 small onion, chopped
Green of 1 bunch of scallions or whites of 2 leeks, chopped
2 tablespoons flour
2 medium potatoes, peeled and sliced
2 quarts chicken or veal stock
1 bunch watercress, leaves and stems, coarsely chopped
1 to 2 egg yolks
1 cup heavy cream
Salt, freshly ground pepper, and nutmeg

METHOD

Melt the butter in a heavy saucepan; add the onion and scallions and sauté for a few minutes. Stir in the flour and add the potatoes. Stir in the stock, a little at a time, and bring to a boil. Season with salt, pepper, and nutmeg to taste. Reduce the heat and simmer for 15 to 20 minutes. Add watercress, saving a few leaves for garnish. Simmer 20 minutes or more. Remove from the heat and strain through a fine sieve, or purée in a blender. Correct seasonings if necessary. Up to this point the soup may be made in advance if desired. When ready to serve, reheat the soup. Combine the eggs and cream. Remove the soup from the heat and stir in the egg/cream mixture. Mince the reserved watercress leaves and add to the soup before serving.

WATERCRESS SOUFFLE

Soufflé au Cresson

Savory soufflés can be baked so that they are a little runny, creamy, or soft at the center, which can serve as a sauce (see page 215).

INGREDIENTS   SERVES 4 TO 6

4 tablespoons butter
⅓ cup flour
1 cup hot milk
4 to 6 ounces watercress (approximately 1½ bunches)
   Milk for blending the watercress
Butter and freshly grated Parmesan cheese for soufflé dish
4 egg yolks
6 egg whites
Salt, freshly ground pepper, and nutmeg

Melt the butter in top of a double boiler over medium heat. Stir in the flour and cook for a minute or so. Slowly add the hot milk, stirring constantly. When the mixture is smooth, lower the heat, cover, and cook for 20 to 25 minutes. Meanwhile, cut off the coarser parts of the watercress stems and discard. Blanch the watercress in boiling salted water (to enhance the flavor). Put leaves into a blender container. Add a little cream or milk and blend into a smooth mixture. Season with salt, pepper, and nutmeg to taste. Put in a large bowl and set aside.

Preheat oven to 375 degrees.

Generously butter a 6-cup soufflé dish and sprinkle with Parmesan cheese. When you are ready to assemble the soufflé for baking, stir the egg yolks into the base one at a time. Stir in the watercress purée and correct seasonings. Beat the egg whites with a pinch of salt until stiff; add one third to the watercress mixture. Gently fold in the rest of the whites and pour into the prepared dish. Bake in the upper half of a preheated oven for 20 to 25 minutes. Serve at once.

Zucchini

ZUCCHINI GRATIN

Gratin de Courgettes

This gratin can be presented at the table with roast lamb, accompanied by roasted herbed potatoes, and a friendly Burgundy, Morgon or Fleurie.

1½ pounds zucchini
4 tablespoons butter

1 small onion, small dice
1 cup béchamel (see page 208)
⅓ cup grated Gruyère cheese
1 tablespoon breadcrumbs
Salt and freshly ground pepper

METHOD

Preheat oven to 325 degrees.

Grate the zucchini on the large holes of a grater. Heat 2 tablespoons butter in a large skillet; add the zucchini seasoned with a little salt and cook covered until the vegetable gives up its water. Remove the lid, raise the heat to high, and evaporate the liquid. Remove the zucchini to a bowl, season with salt and pepper, and keep ready.

In the same skillet, heat 1 tablespoon butter; add the onion seasoned with a little salt. Sauté for a few minutes until tender but do not let brown. Add the béchamel to the onion and mix well; keep the sauce warm.

Butter a small oven-proof dish and add the zucchini mixture so it is at least 1-inch deep. Pour a thin layer of béchamel on top of the zucchini and sprinkle the surface with the cheese and breadcrumbs. Dot with the remaining butter broken into pea-size pieces. Set on the middle rack of a preheated oven for 20 to 25 minutes, or until golden brown on top.

ZUCCHINI WITH TOMATOES AND ONIONS

Courgettes à la Provençale

This recipe uses olive oil as a flavoring just before serving. Use it as you might use butter, just drizzle a bit on and allow the fresh taste of the oil to perfume the dish. Use extra virgin olive oil. Serve the zucchini with veal roast and garlic sauce, accompanied by a red wine from Provence, such as a Bandol.

INGREDIENTS	SERVES 6

¼ cup olive oil
1 large onion, coarsely chopped
4 cloves garlic, minced
2 pounds zucchini, sliced into 2-inch pieces
1½ pounds tomatoes, peeled, seeded, and chopped
2 tablespoons fresh herbs: chopped parsley, tarragon, or thyme (in any combination)
Salt and freshly ground pepper

METHOD

Heat 1 to 2 tablespoons olive oil in a skillet and sauté the onion until golden. Add the minced garlic and cook another minute, stirring. Add the zucchini and a little salt; add the tomatoes and toss gently. Flavor with some of the herbs, reserving some. Cover and cook over low heat 5 minutes, until the vegetables give up their water. Remove the lid, raise the heat, and without overcooking, evaporate the liquid. Correct the seasonings and add the remaining herbs and a grinding of pepper; toss with a light drizzling of olive oil and serve at once.

PART III

San Francisco

Josephine and Robert
at Le Trou

Josephine had a special public voice that she reserved for important moments; it was a voice that carried. In the basement of the Liberty House department store during a cooking demonstration, she launched me into my restaurant, Le Trou, with the following introduction to the group amassed before her. "This is *Robeirt*, and he is a great chef, and he is going to open a restaurant." She sat down and signaled me with her finger to bring my face closer to her own. In a smaller voice she said, "Now, *Robeirt,* when will you open that restaurant?"

Mrs. Mortimer Fleischhacker of the San Francisco banking family went to Paris in 1924 looking for a cook. Her quest took her to the Cordon Bleu cooking school. There they recommended she consider Josephine Enizan, who was in the employ of a wealthy family in Paris. Josephine was interviewed and given the position in San Francisco. Moving to the United States represented such a big event for Josephine that Mrs. Fleischhacker allowed her to bring her cousin. The two young women crossed the ocean by ship and the continent by train to get to San Francisco. Josephine was in her early twenties and so was the century.

When Josephine arrived in San Francisco, she had no real competition, although she liked to compete. It was part of her French character. There was no one on the horizon who had experience like hers. She became a star and she stepped into the role without difficulty. She never questioned her position; she had been a star at the Cordon Bleu. The freedom from having to compete allowed her to impart the true spirit of cooking, something simple and pure. She often told stories about being asked to prepare a specialty when she was in San Francisco restaurants in those early days. She would get up from her table and go into the kitchen where she would prepare *crêpes Suzettes* or some other crowd pleaser. Then after the performance she would return to her own party.

In San Francisco Josephine met Charles Araldo and immediately proposed marriage to him. Theirs was a love story for all time. In her inimitable way, she always called him her *gigolo*. Charles once told me that it was a privilege to take care of Josephine, and that they would play at their roles with great humor. Charles drove Josephine everywhere in a green Plymouth. He would get out and open the back door, where Josephine would be sitting as if driven by a chauffeur. She would exit the car, enter the party on her own, and he would go park the car.

A few minutes later Charles would appear with his accordion. While Josephine socialized, Charles would sit in a small chair in an inconspicuous spot and play his music. It was pure sweetness. Over the years Charles seemed to grow smaller and his accordion bigger. One day he arrived with a small cassette player. It weighed a fraction of the accordion and he could plug it in anywhere. With a "Look, Ma, no hands" shrug, he would exude self-satisfaction. He thought it was the greatest thing ever. Charles' death in 1983 was a great loss to Josephine and to all who knew him.

Josephine spent her professional life in San Francisco working for a succession of wealthy families. After the second World War she retired and began teaching. She continued to cook for private families, but gave more and more time to students, thousands of whom passed through her kitchen on McAllister Street. For the next thirty years her name was synonymous with French food in the San Francisco Bay Area. It has been said that the heart of the modern American food world is in California, and that San Francisco and the Bay Area are the movement's lifeblood. And it can also be said that many of the Bay Area's most important cooks, restaurateurs, and food writers of the last thirty years passed through Josephine's kitchen: Marion Cunningham, who revised the *Fannie Farmer Cookbook*; Alice Waters, whose Chez Panisse restaurant set the tone for much that has happened here; Paula Hamilton of the *Oakland Tribune*; Patricia Unterman, the restaurateur and restaurant critic for the San Francisco *Chronicle*, who finished her column for years with the footnote that she had studied with Josephine Araldo. These are a few of the best known of Josephine's students. It was a source of great pleasure for

Josephine to be remembered by her students through the years, and she took great pride in their success.

"Le Trou." I will never hear these words pronounced with such affection by anyone else. "There are lots of these in France, little *trous*. *Trous* for gastronomes." Josephine talked as if this restaurant were her own work of love—and that's not far from the truth. I've always expressed her position at the restaurant by saying, "She is in charge of prayers. She's got God's ear."

She walked into my little restaurant one day in 1984 for classes, peeled off her hat and coat, donned her apron and toque, and without looking over her shoulder issued commands.

"Give me a knife."

"I have to cut something."

"I need a pan."

"Give me a wooden spoon."

"Light this flame."

She was rolling. Suddenly she stopped and gave out a hearty laugh. "Will you listen to me, I haven't been here five minutes and I'm full of orders. And," she said, turning toward me with a theatrical bow and that familiar sparkle in her eyes, "you're the boss!" Then she went back to her preparations. She worked at a furious pace. We had difficulty keeping up with her. She just didn't give out; often she would comment on her energy as she went along. "You know, *Robeirt,* I have been on my feet for a long time and I'm not tired." She had been getting around with a cane, performing shaky turns, wobbling from one spot to the next. At one point she took the cane in her hand and raised it over her head and threw it across the room muttering, "I don't need this damn thing!" Then she looked up at me and said, "Watch me." She balled up her fists, set her jaw and, fiercely determined, walked toward me across the room. Then she went back to work without another word. This was Josephine at eighty-eight, showing the spirit she had all her life.

Sometimes we would come in the day before a class and prep the food. On these days, we would work quietly in the kitchen for a couple of hours, cutting vegetables or preparing bases for sauces. I would stand on one side of the cutting board and slice, julienne, or cut at my pace.

Josephine would stand on the other side, and I could feel her competitive nature. She would begin slowly to get a rhythm going and gradually build up speed. We had a silent contest, a race to get through cutting all the apples. By the time the last were done, she was cutting as fast as I was. Nothing was ever said.

In conversations with her, she kept going back again and again to the images of her grandmother's garden in Brittany, as if she hungered for the memories. She would tell me about other things that grew there, or about eating things from the garden where she played as a child. The more Josephine thought about that garden by the river Scorff, the more she remembered.

Once, on a visit to her apartment at her daughter Jacqueline's house, I found her knee-deep in her papers and books. She took great comfort in her books and notes, those maps of her profession that were as much the tools of her trade as knives and whisks. Though increasingly frail, she often checked the dexterity of her hands by touching each finger to her thumb as if she were a dancer from Thailand or Burma. There was something elegant and exotic about this ritual. She observed that they were not as good as they used to be and followed with a laugh, "Oh what the hell." Then she was off in pursuit of another subject.

Leafing through her books I found a French edition of Prosper Montagné's *Larousse Gastronomique,* a 1907 edition of a Cordon Bleu cookbook, a book by Escoffier, and one by her teacher, Pellaprat. There were books in her library from generations of great chefs including works by Fernand Point and his disciples, Bocuse, Troisgros, and then their disciples. While leafing through a cookbook by Bocuse, the famous contemporary French chef, I noticed a recipe for *Poularde en demi-deuil*— chickens from Bresse so larded with truffles under the skin that they appear to be in "half mourning." It was a dish perfected by a woman chef named La Mère Brazier. In Lyons, the gastronomic capital of France, there were a number of women like her—La Mère Denis and La Mère Fillioux—women chefs who captured the attention of the world, so that other chefs, such as Bocuse, would recreate their recipes.

The first time I went to Madeleine Kamman's restaurant outside Boston. I saw a framed menu hanging upside down. On closer examination, I saw it bore Bocuse's signature. I asked what it was about and was told that Madeleine Kamman turned it upside down as a response to Bocuse's remark that there were no great women chefs. I asked Josephine why she thought Bocuse made the remark. She came back with something about women not lifting huge stock pots. As I tried to imagine her at eighty-five, lifting a 40-gallon pot full of cooked bones, Josephine was off in another direction. "You know, Escoffier had been given the Legion of Honor for his work in his day. Bocuse was given it also, by Giscard d'Estaing. But it doesn't mean the same thing." Josephine had once been in a room with Escoffier in Paris, although she had never met him. We went back to our conversation about puréed peas and lemon-flavored cabbage, and other parts of an Easter menu we were dreaming up.

"You know, *Robeirt,* I'm not going to be around much longer. I'm getting to be pretty old," Josephine would say, pointing heavenward. Whenever she said that, and she would say it fairly frequently, it made me very reflective. The idea that she would no longer be around saddened me. One day, however, I guess I had heard it too many times, or there was a lilting tone in her voice, or I was reminded of the boy who cried wolf, so I just blurted out, "Josephine, I simply don't believe you." She burst out laughing and confessed, "I've been saying that since I was eighteen years old. I think it brings me good luck." When she said it, I looked closely at her and for the first time wondered whether she might not be telling the truth. I asked her what I should do with the new bicycle that I had ordered for her. She replied that I should trade it in for a Cadillac.

When Josephine was no longer able to live alone, she closed up the house on McAllister Street and moved to her daughter's apartment. After several months had gone by I suggested that she come back to the restaurant and teach. She agreed. On the day of her first class, I went to pick her up. We decided to pass by her old house to get some herbs from the garden. Josephine was ahead of me as we entered the alley under the house. The alley sloped forward and at the same time listed to the side. She was walking with a cane, determined and teetering. It made me very nervous—the darkness, the shadowy light, her determined and unsteady step. So I moved along beside her and slipped my hand under her elbow. Without saying anything or slowing down a bit, she jerked her elbow out of my hand and kept going. I could have burst out laughing.

Once we got into the clearing of the back yard, she went into high gear.

"The chervil is under the bush in the shade."

"There is parsley by the fence. Pull it out by the roots and plant it in your own garden."

"There is thyme just beside the flowers."

She was spitting out commands like a machine gun, four at a time and following them with, "What's taking you so long?" When I had my arms full, she thought we should go. She did a quick inventory and realized she was missing tarragon. "Where is it?" she asked as she scanned the little garden she knew like the back of her hand. I was standing at her side and she indicated a spot just in front of me. I bent over to pick. I couldn't have taken five seconds. As I came back up, I realized she wasn't in my peripheral vision. As I turned toward where she had been, I could see her falling over backwards.

Fortunately she had her fall broken by a bush. Instantly the lady upstairs was at her side; the neighbor next door literally came out of her window and was there too. We got her up and brushed her off. I could see that she was having trouble breathing. The fall had winded her. She sidled over to me and whispered, "Get me the hell out of here would you."

We drove along to the restaurant in silence, something I seldom experienced with Josephine. I wondered whether I could even hear her breathing. She was just slumped in the seat looking steadily ahead with all the concentration of her iron will. Finally I took her hand and asked if she was alright. "Why?" she responded sharply. "Because I'm scared," I answered. She turned to me and looked me in the eye, *"Robeirt,* don't let anything dampen your spirits."

We pulled up in front of the restaurant and she announced, "Let's go, we have a show to put on." She taught the class that day, exhausting twelve students in the process with her excitement and attention. At the end, I took her home. When I called her the next day, she was in the hospital; her fall had fractured a disk in her back.

"I want to teach classes again. I should have a chair to sit in between where students work and where they cook." Josephine articulated exactly what she wanted with the beautiful hands that have given shape to her dishes for over seventy years. Her expressions fall on my ears; I respond to them like music. She talked as the afternoon sun poured into her small apartment under her daughter's house, warming her back. She talked about the families she worked for when she came from Paris in the early 1920s and of the women who had a love for the finely prepared foods that Josephine elegantly presented "like a horse on parade."

"My Josephine," they would say with an emphasis on the "my" as a measure of the pride they took in Josephine's work. To which Josephine would reply, with the ironic tone of one who is not totally amused, "But Madame, do you think you own Josephine body and soul?" Mrs. Oppen once observed Josephine preparing a lunch. When Josephine finished, she commented, "Josephine you certainly have your hands in my food an awful lot." Josephine always prayed that her inspiration would never fail her in such moments, and she replied without hesitation, "I'm so sorry, Madame, but they didn't teach me to prepare food with my feet."

Josephine told me that there were 194 vegetable recipes in her manuscript. I told her I thought there were perhaps 200, because I was sure there were some we had left out. "Perhaps," she said, "I can't remember all of them."

"Beets and Currants is not in the book. Nor is . . ." We started going back and forth as if in a tennis match warm-up. Sometimes she could remember easily; at other times she just couldn't bring back the word she was looking for. I'd ask her what it was in French; she would slip into that language to recall what she wanted to remember. She told me about a garlic tart that way. It could be served as an entrée and "also used like a dessert, but dessert is not the word. What's the other word?" We puzzled for a moment, wondering what another word for dessert was and finally I asked in French, "another word for *des sert?*" "Yes," she said, "*entre mets.* The garlic tart can be served like an *entremets.*"

The garlic tart is done by blind baking a pastry shell. It is made with two cups of baked garlic, four eggs, and two cups of cream seasoned with a little salt, some sugar, and a jigger of cognac. It is baked at 325 degrees for 35 to 40 minutes until it is set.

She remembered Salsify and Plums was done by blanching the salsify, then seasoning with salt and pepper, and tossing with chopped plums. Finally they are given some herbs. "Which ones?" I asked. "Oh, tarragon and chervil," she replied.

The mention of radishes brought her attention up. She remembered that they were served with small apples whose name she couldn't recall. I asked her if there was a way to cook the radishes so that they would retain their color. "No," she said. "When you cook them with their skins the color gets pale and thin. So I peel them and cook them white. The apples should be cooked with their skins on."

"How do you make sauerkraut, Josephine?"

"I made it for you before; haven't you made it?"

"Yes. I remember how wonderful it was, but it has been a long time since I made it."

"You put some salt in a crock, then a layer of cabbage, then salt, cabbage, and salt. You make a brine with water, like I showed you, and then pour it over the cabbage. Then you put a weight on top and let it set."

"And herbs?"

"Oh yes. Thyme, bay leaf, and juniper. My grandmother made a sauerkraut of turnips in the same way that was delicious. I remember the chard, but I don't remember what goes with it. I remember that spinach was served with green plums."

The door was always unlocked at Josephine's house on McAllister Street; I simply walked in. The voice from the kitchen sang: "Who is that?" Since I was often the only man for classes, I would sing as I closed the door, "C'est moi." As I turned to cross the entry hall I would hear Josephine continue, "Ah Albert, *comment allez-vous?* How are you?" It felt like a European house; you could sense that it had a center. I entered the dining room and turned left to pass into the kitchen where she was already working. I would continue the ritual responding like a music student practicing finger exercises. "Josephine, there is only one man here and his name is not Albert." Her eyes were lit with a sparkle; I was with my mentor and our day had begun.

In more recent years, we laughed about that Albert phase. I became *Robeirt* when I told Josephine that I was going to France for professional study. Josephine underwent a kind of metamorphosis in those moments while we talked about my plans. There were physical changes that accompanied her new attitude; we were both very aware of it. Life was never the same for us. Things never reverted, they only evolved. In the quiet of her kitchen she concluded the conversation saying, "Because you are going to be with the best, I will treat you differently."

Josephine's responses were sometimes deliberate and careful. I remember once facing a disappointment and talking with her about it. She remained silent for a moment; the only time that I remember her at even a temporary loss for words. She looked ahead out of the car window for a minute before she said to me, "It's okay, you have me."

I called Josephine on the telephone. "I want you to give me my toque, please. I didn't get one when I was in France."

"Alright, my dear, when would you like to do it?"

"Today is my birthday," I said. "I would like to see you."

"I have to be somewhere," Josephine answered, "but you could come before I go."

I sat in her living room. The house was very still. She went to the back of the house and returned with a collection of toques. Josephine sat beside me on the couch and handed me the chef's hats one by one to try on.

"This one is too big," I said.

"Too small."

She offered another: "This one you can adjust."

"This one Pellaprat gave me," she continued.

"This one's just right."

"Thank you, Josephine, for doing this."

"You're welcome, *Robeirt*. I must go now, my dear." She was tired and resigned, and I knew it had to do with her husband's illness. She got up. There was strength in her posture; she personified faith.

"*Je vous embrasse*, Josephine. I hug you, Josephine." I said this as a way of saying both I love you and goodbye.

Contemporary Recipes

The recipes in the San Francisco section reflect my work with Josephine over the years at Le Trou Restaurant Français. These recipes tell a story of the combinations of taste designed by minds who knew well how to satisfy palates. The instincts and intelligence that give them form are mostly lost to us, but the ideas have withstood the test of time, and finally these ideas gave rise to food that continues to be immensely satisfying. We no longer have La Mère Jacquette, but we do have her ideas, as carried to us by Josephine. The culinary voice of Josephine, simple and straightforward, had the capacity to be more modern, more sensible, more simple than any other I have known. "Don't tell me about nouvelle cuisine," she would say. "Isn't that what my grandmother did with her carrots and persimmons?"

Artichokes

ARTICHOKE AND AVOCADO SALAD WITH GRAPEFRUIT

Salade Algérienne

Depending on its ingredients, each salad needs its own balance of acidity in the dressing. Neither acid nor oil should dominate, but instead they should achieve a pleasing balance with the addition of salt, mustard, herbs, and the like. The vinaigrette in this recipe is deliberately more acidic.

INGREDIENTS   SERVES 6

1 to 2 whole ripe grapefruit
1 to 2 ripe avocados, quartered
2 heads limestone lettuce
4 cooked artichoke bottoms, sliced (see Marinated Artichoke Bottoms page 160)

Vinaigrette
1 tablespoon cider vinegar
3 tablespoons freshly squeezed grapefruit juice
1 teaspoon mustard
Persillade: 2 tablespoons chopped parsley and 1 clove garlic, minced
2 tablespoons chopped chives
½ cup peanut oil
Salt and freshly ground pepper

METHOD

Peel and section the grapefruit over a bowl to save the juices. Slice the avocado lengthwise and coat with juices of the grapefruit to keep it from discoloring. Make a bed of lettuce on a serving platter; decorate with alternating slices of grapefruit and avocado. Place the artichokes in the center. Make the vinaigrette in a bowl by mixing the vinegar, juice, mustard, herbs, salt, and pepper with a fork. Slowly whisk in the oil. When you are ready to serve, garnish the salad with vinaigrette.

ARTICHOKE HEARTS WITH DUCK CUSTARD

Foie de Canard Pompadour

This dish of duck custards garnished with artichokes and Gruyère cheese drew its inspiration from Josephine's Artichoke Hearts with Foie Gras (see page 152). This combination is often served at Le Trou with a sweet wine from the southwest of France, a Loupiac Gaudiet or Cérons.

INGREDIENTS	SERVES 6

2 ounces duck livers
¾ cup light cream
2 egg yolks
1 tablespoon of butter
½ cup artichoke flesh (see Artichoke and Broccoli Fritters page 16)
1 teaspoon each juniper berries, coriander, and sage, ground fine in a mortar
3 to 4 tablespoons grated Gruyère cheese
Salt and freshly ground pepper

METHOD

Preheat oven to 275 degrees. Butter six 2-ounce timbale molds; set them in a water bath lined with 2 to 3 layers of paper towels to protect the bottoms of the custards from the oven heat; keep them ready.

Clean and trim the livers. Place them in a blender along with the cream, salt, and pepper; liquify for a full minute. When the mixture is completely blended, add the egg yolks and pulse the machine only long enough to liquify the yolks, 10 or 15 seconds.

Pour the mixture into the buttered molds and bake in a preheated oven until set, 30 to 45 minutes. A knife inserted into the center will come out clean when they are done. Remove from the oven and keep ready.

Melt the butter in a skillet and rewarm the cooked artichoke flesh. Season it with a generous pinch of the ground juniper mixture, salt, and pepper.

Unmold the liver custards on individual plates and garnish with the artichoke. Sprinkle a generous grating of Gruyère cheese over the vegetable and serve the custards hot as a first course.

About Timbales, Custards, and Savory Flans

One time when I visited Josephine, she was very impatient for me to try something she had prepared. "It's in the refrigerator," she said with all the excitement of a child, "and I want you to tell me what it's made from." I found the custard she had made and sat down to taste it. She was squirming with delight. It was creamy, sweet, and delicious; I scanned my palate to determine the flavors. "Well," I finally said, "I can tell you what it isn't made from." "What do you think," she asked. "It's not made with garlic," I answered. She was delighted. "You're wrong. That's exactly what it is made from."

Josephine liked those molded dishes, and at Le Trou I have used them in every possible way—as courses by themselves, as appetizers, as the main part of a vegetarian dinner, in salads, and as desserts. I make them using meats, seafood, vegetables, cheeses, or fruits. They are very versatile and lend themselves to endless flavors, particularly those unusual combinations that I learned from Josephine. Sometimes we call them pillows on the menus at the restaurant, because they seem to be as light as air, and because when you eat them they seem to make you dream.

Molded custards are basically made in small oven-proof containers; Pyrex custard cups will work if that's what you have. I call for the use of molds in different sizes, but I have made them in everything, including demitasse cups and butter cups, when metal or glass molds weren't available. The basic formula I use is that 3 eggs will bind a cup of cream.

Heavy or light cream can be used, depending on the main flavoring ingredient. Custards should be set to bake in a water bath, otherwise known as a bain marie. Line the bottom of a water bath with paper towels to protect the bottom of the custard, which will take the most direct heat. The technique of slow baking results in a dish that is creamy and shimmeringly soft. The custards can certainly be cooked faster for a different texture. Set the filled custard cups in the pan for the water bath on top of 2 or 3 layers of paper towel, and add hot water to a depth of about 1 inch. The custards bake at 275 to 300 degrees until they are set and a knife inserted into the center comes out clean.

NOODLES WITH SAUSAGE, ARTICHOKES, AND HERBS

Les Pâtés aux Artichauts Lyonnaise

This dish draws its ideas from Josephine's Artichokes Stuffed with Onions and Meat (see page 159); it uses all the same elements and flavorings. Serve the noodles and drink a white Côtes-du-Rhône.

INGREDIENTS   SERVES 6

2 to 3 medium artichokes, blanched (see Boiled Artichokes page 11)
4 to 6 tablespoons butter
Grated rind of 1 lemon
3 medium white onions, thinly sliced
½ cup veal stock, good homemade (see page 331)
2 tablespoons chopped fresh tarragon
2 tablespoons chopped parsley
1 clove garlic, minced
½ pound sausage of choice
1 pound noodles, fresh or dried
Salt and freshly ground pepper

METHOD

Cook the artichokes in boiling salted water until tender. Drain under cold water; remove the leaves and scrape the edible tips and reserve. Remove the choke and discard it. Quarter the bottoms and add to the trimmings. Grate the rind of a lemon and toss with the artichoke trimmings; season with salt and pepper, and keep warm.

Prepare the onions by trimming the stem end. Cut in half from root to stem; lay flat and remove the tougher, papery exterior. Cut in thin slices. Select a skillet with a tight-fitting lid; over a medium-low flame, melt 2 tablespoons butter. Add the onions and sauté with a pinch of salt for a few minutes, until they start to turn golden. Add the stock and simmer covered until tender. The stock should mostly evaporate. Correct the salt if necessary and give a few grindings of pepper. Keep the onions warm.

While the onions cook, prepare the fresh herbs, chopping them coarsely. Mince the garlic and mix with the herbs; reserve for the noodles.

Cook the sausage in a skillet until it browns lightly, and when it is done, cut it into ½-inch pieces. Cook the noodles in boiling salted water until done. Drain and remove to a bowl. Add the remaining butter and herbs and toss to coat. Put the noodles on a platter and set the artichokes in the center. Garnish this bed of artichokes with the sausage and glazed onions. Give a final grinding of pepper and serve.

CREAM OF ARTICHOKE SOUP WITH MUSHROOMS AND HAM

Crème d'Artichauts aux Champignons

The flavors for this soup are drawn from Josephine's recipe for Artichokes with Stuffing (see page 145). Here the elements are rearranged to prepare an elegant soup for the first course of a special event. The fullness of the soup's flavor depends on the slow browning of the artichoke meat.

6 medium artichokes, blanched tender (see Boiled Artichokes
   page 11)
2 ounces pancetta, thinly sliced
4 tablespoons butter
½ pound mushrooms, sliced
2 medium tomatoes, peeled, seeded, and chopped
¾ cup dry white wine
2 to 4 shallots, small dice
Rind of lemon, 1-inch wide and 2-inches long
1 tablespoon chopped fresh tarragon
6 cups veal stock
¼ cup crème fraîche
2 tablespoons chopped chervil or parsley
Salt and freshly ground pepper

METHOD

Prepare all the vegetables and keep them ready on a tray. Blanch the
6 artichokes in acidulated water until they can be pierced by a cake tester
at the stem end. Remove to a colander and run under cold water. Remove
all the leaves and scrape the flesh from each leaf with a spoon, discarding
the leaves as they are cleaned. Put the scrapings into a bowl. Scrape and
discard the choke and cut the hearts into 4 or 5 slices.

While the artichokes are cooking, prepare the garnish. Sauté the
pancetta in 2 tablespoons of the butter and chop it finely. Sauté the
mushrooms in a hot skillet, salting lightly. Cook the mushrooms until
they give up their water and it has evaporated. Season with freshly ground
pepper. Coarsely chop the mushrooms in a food processor; mix with
pancetta. Mix the tomatoes with the mushrooms and set aside.

In a soup pot, sauté the artichoke hearts and scrapings in 2 tablespoons
butter. Pour the white wine into the pan with the artichokes and deglaze,
using a wooden spoon to scrape all the caramelized particles. Add the
shallots, the lemon rind, and the tarragon. Season lightly with salt, pour

in the veal stock, and bring the liquid to a boil; turn it to a simmer and cook slowly for 15 minutes.

After the flavors have infused, purée the soup in a blender until it is absolutely smooth and creamy. Correct the seasonings. Ladle the soup into bowls; garnish the soup with a dollop of crème fraîche and the sautéed mushroom and tomato mixture. Give a sprinkling of chopped chervil or parsley, then a grinding of pepper, and serve hot.

ARTICHOKE TIMBALE WITH SPINACH AND HAZELNUTS

Timbale d'Artichauts avec des Epinards

At Le Trou I have reinterpreted the ideas in Josephine's recipe for Puréed Artichokes (see page 164). I love the trio of artichoke, tarragon, and hazelnuts. In this recipe, I use the artichokes to make a custard flavored with tarragon, and set it on a bed of spinach with a hazelnut butter. It can be served as an entrée accompanied by a crisp white wine from the Savoie, such as an Apremont.

INGREDIENTS	SERVES 10

3 to 4 artichokes, cooked flesh only
2 cups light cream
5 eggs
2 tablespoons chopped fresh tarragon
10 hazelnuts, toasted
3 tablespoons butter
2 tablespoons chopped fresh chervil or parsley
2 shallots, fine dice
1 bunch spinach, washed and stemmed
Salt and freshly ground pepper

METHOD

Preheat oven to 300 degrees. Butter ten 2-ounce timbale molds and set aside.

Place the cooked artichoke flesh (see page 16) in a blender with the cream. Season with salt and pepper, and purée completely. Add the eggs and turn the machine on only long enough to liquify the ingredients, 10 to 15 seconds. Add the tarragon and give it one final pulsing. Taste for the seasoning and correct if necessary.

Pour the artichoke mixture into the buttered molds and set in a water bath lined with 2 to 3 layers of paper towels. Pour in hot water so that it half fills the pan. Bake the custards in a slow oven until they are set, 20 to 30 minutes. The custards are done when a cake tester inserted into the middle comes out clean. Remove from the oven and let them sit in the water.

Prepare the garnish while the custards bake. Toss the hazelnuts in a dry skillet, and brown on medium heat; peel the skins off while hot; allow to cool and grind fine. Make a compound butter by mixing the nuts with 2 tablespoons butter and keep ready. Coarsely chop the chervil or parsley and keep ready.

Melt 1 tablespoon butter in a skillet and sauté the chopped shallots for about a minute. Add the spinach; season lightly with salt. Put a lid on the pan and cook 1 to 2 minutes, until the spinach collapses. Once the spinach has collapsed, add the hazelnut butter broken into small pieces and toss everything until the vegetable is well coated. Correct the seasonings and give the spinach a generous grinding of pepper.

Unmold the custards onto individual plates and garnish each portion with the spinach. Serve hot as an hors d'oevre or as an accompaniment to a main course.

Beans ═══════════════════

LENTILS WITH SWEET COD

Cabillaud aux Lentilles

It is difficult to think about Brittany without some reference to the sea and the products that derive from it. I made this dish for Josephine because it has simple elements that she liked. She had never eaten the combination before but when she was finished, she offered, "It was unsurpassed." I offered her a French beer to drink with it. "Very good, my dear," was her final comment as she returned the plate, which had been mopped with the bread.

INGREDIENTS	SERVES 6

1 pound small French lentils
1 onion, small dice
½ carrot, small dice
¼ celery root, small dice
2 cloves garlic, chopped
Bouquet garni: thyme, bay leaf, and rosemary tied in two celery stalks
2 to 4 tablespoons chopped parsley
1 to 2 tablespoons chopped fresh tarragon
2 shallots, finely minced
½ cup crème fraîche
6 portions sweet whitefish, such as cod
Salt and freshly ground pepper

METHOD

Add the lentils to a pot with the onion, carrot, celery root, garlic, and the bouquet garni. Pour in cold water to cover the vegetables by about 2 inches and bring to a boil. Simmer the lentils, without adding any salt, for about 20 minutes. Drain in a colander; set lentils and veg-etables in a bowl; discard the bouquet garni.

Season the lentils with salt and pepper. Add a generous amount of parsley, tarragon, and minced shallots, and the crème fraîche.

When the lentils are ready, poach or sauté the fish until it is cooked, but moist. Place a bed of lentils on a plate and set the cooked fish on top, so it is surrounded by the lentils. Season the fish, if desired, and give a grinding of pepper. Serve hot.

Beets

BEET CUSTARDS WITH BLACK CURRANTS

Timbales de Betteraves aux Cassis

At Le Trou I serve this dish with lamb, veal, or chicken. The idea for this recipe came from Josephine's repertoire of foraged dishes from her grandmother. You can also use berries that are like currants—dark, round sweet berries. Sometimes I find a variety of local berries, blue-berries or loganberries, in season in California. I have also found currants in jars from Poland, Hungary, and the Soviet Union. If you have access to good local berries, I recommend your trying them with this dish.

INGREDIENTS	SERVES 8

2 or 3 medium beets
1½ cups light cream
3 whole eggs
2 to 3 tablespoons butter
1 clove garlic, minced
2 shallots, chopped
1 tablespoon good quality vinegar
1 cup greens, beets, chard, or spinach, coarsely chopped
½ cup black currants
2 tablespoons chopped fresh tarragon

2 tablespoons chopped parsley
Salt and freshly ground pepper

METHOD

Preheat oven to 275 degrees. Butter eight 2-ounce timbale molds and set them into the pan used for a water bath lined with 2 to 3 layers of paper towels (see page 280). Keep ready.

Bake the beets for 40 minutes, until tender enough to be pierced with a knife. Smaller beets can be wrapped in foil and baked until tender. The beets can also be blanched whole in boiling salted water until tender. After they are cooked, peel and chop into coarse dice. Put in a blender with the light cream and purée well. Add the eggs, season with salt, and give a generous grinding of pepper. Purée again for about 10 seconds, until the eggs are blended.

Fill the individual molds with the mixture, pour 1 inch of water in the water bath, and bake in a slow oven until they are set, about 30 to 45 minutes.

In a large skillet heat the butter. Add the garlic and shallots and sauté in the butter for 1 to 2 minutes. Add the vinegar and mix well. Put the chopped greens in the skillet, toss to coat them with butter, and sauté gently until they collapse. Then add the currants. Season the dish with salt and pepper; add the tarragon and parsley, and give everything a final toss to mix the flavors.

Unmold the custards onto individual plates. Garnish each custard with the greens and serve at once.

BEET CUSTARDS

Timbales de Betteraves à la Crème

Beets and cream make one of those heavenly marriages that survive in a number of ways and with great style into modern cooking. The beets in this recipe can be served with sautéed greens, as the vegetable accompaniment to a main course roast breast of duck. They provide an element on the plate that is visually stunning as well as stunning to the palate.

INGREDIENTS   SERVES 6

5 ounces of beets, peeled and cut in ½-inch dice
¾ cup heavy cream
2 eggs
2 tablespoons butter
1 bunch of greens, chard or spinach
Pinch of *quatre épices* (see page 184)
¼ cup grated Gruyère cheese
Salt and freshly ground pepper

METHOD

Preheat oven to 275 degrees. Butter six 2-ounce timbale molds. Line a water-bath pan with two or three layers of paper towels, and set aside, (see page 280).

Put the diced beets into a saucepan with the heavy cream and simmer covered until the beets are cooked, about 15 to 20 minutes. They are tender when they can be pierced with a cake tester with no resistance.

Pour the beets and cream into a blender and purée completely. Add the eggs, salt and pepper, and 1 tablespoon butter; purée again for 10 seconds or so, just long enough to incorporate the eggs.

Fill each mold with the cream mixture and set it into the water bath. Pour in ½ inch of boiling water. Bake the custards on the middle rack of a preheated oven, until they set, 30 to 45 minutes. Remove from the oven and let them rest in the pan.

Coarsely chop the greens. Melt 1 tablespoon butter in a skillet and when it is warm, add the greens, lightly season with salt, and sauté until they collapse. The cooking time depends on the tenderness and type of green. When they are done, give a pinch of *quatre épices,* correct the seasonings, and finish with a grinding of pepper.

Unmold the custards onto individual plates and garnish them with the sautéed greens. Sprinkle the greens with a small amount of grated Gruyère cheese and serve hot.

Cabbages

BRUSSELS SPROUTS WITH WATER CHESTNUTS AND GINGER

Choux de Bruxelles à l'Orientale

This strikes me as a recipe that Josephine developed in San Francisco because of the use of the water chestnuts. Serve with roast chicken, a gratin of potato, and drink a rosé from Provence.

INGREDIENTS	SERVES 6

1 large onion, thinly sliced
4 tablespoons butter

1 tablespoon peanut oil
½ pound fresh water chestnuts, sliced
1 cup chicken stock, good homemade (see page 331)
1 tablespoon fresh ginger, finely minced
1½ pounds brussels sprouts, blanched (see Brussels Sprouts in Cream
    page 43)
½ pound mushrooms, sliced
¼ cup chopped watercress
Salt and freshly ground pepper

METHOD

In a skillet, sauté the onion in 1 tablespoon butter and the oil until translucent; add the water chestnuts, stock, and ginger. Season lightly with salt and continue cooking until the chestnuts are tender but retain a crispness.

While the chestnuts cook, blanch the brussels sprouts in boiling salted water until tender, 10 to 15 minutes. Drain when done; add the sprouts to the water chestnuts.

In another skillet, melt 1 to 2 tablespoons butter and sauté the mushrooms with a pinch of salt until they start to give up their water. Remove them to the pan with the water chestnuts and brussels sprouts. Mix everything together and let simmer, covered, for a few minutes. Just prior to serving, add the watercress; give everything a generous grinding of pepper and serve at once.

BRUSSELS SPROUTS AND CUCUMBERS WITH LIME

Choux de Bruxelles et Concombres au Citron Vert

This dish lends extraordinary life to vegetables that are often the staples in winter climates. It allows us to taste something unexpected and shows Josephine's imagination. Serve it with game, white meats, or salmon. I would select an Alsatian Riesling to drink.

INGREDIENTS   SERVES 6

1 pound brussels sprouts, blanched (see Brussels Sprouts in Cream
   page 43)
4 tablespoons butter
1 medium onion, thinly sliced
2 cucumbers, peeled and coarsely chopped
1 tablespoon chopped fresh fennel or dill weed
1 tablespoon juniper berries, crushed, or 2 to 3 tablespoons gin
Juice of 1 lime
1 tablespoon chopped fresh tarragon
2 tablespoons chopped parsley
Salt and freshly ground pepper

METHOD

Trim the stem end of the brussels sprouts of any dried flesh. Score
the stem with an "X" ⅙-inch deep with a small knife. Remove any brown
or flawed leaves. Drop the brussels sprouts in boiling salted water, turning
the heat to a simmer after the water returns to a boil. Cook until tender,
about 10 to 15 minutes. Drain and refresh under cold water.

Melt 2 tablespoons butter in a large skillet, add the onion, and sauté
until golden. Add the cucumber, brussels sprouts, fennel, juniper berries,
and lime juice. Season lightly with salt. Cover and simmer the vegetables
until they are tender and to taste, about 5 to 7 minutes. Correct the
seasoning and give a grinding of pepper. Toss in 1 to 2 tablespoons butter
broken into pea-size pieces, along with the tarragon and parsley. Toss
everything to coat and serve at once.

CABBAGE WITH APPLES AND GOOSEBERRIES

Chou aux Pommes et aux Groseilles

This dish originated in the kitchen of La Mère Jacquette. I have found fresh gooseberries in California to use in it; I have also found jars of gooseberries packed in a light syrup that come from Poland and Hungary that are not overly sweet. Serve with poached salmon and a purée of potatoes, and pour an Alsatian Pinot Blanc.

INGREDIENTS	SERVES 6

1 head green cabbage
1 cup French cider or white wine
2 to 3 green apples
6 tablespoons butter
1 cup gooseberries, ripe and sweet
2 to 4 tablespoons chopped *fines herbes:* parsley, chervil, and chives (any combination)
1 teaspoon each juniper and coriander seeds and dried sage, finely ground
Salt and freshly ground pepper

METHOD

Prepare the cabbage, peeling away any flawed outer leaves. Cut in half, then in quarters; remove the core. Shred the cabbage fine and put it in a heavy-bottomed pot with a tight-fitting lid. Add the French cider and a pinch of salt, and cook slowly until it is tender, about 30 to 45 minutes.

Peel and core the apples and cut into quarters. Melt 2 tablespoons butter in a skillet and add the apples and sauté slowly until they are tender but still firm. Add them to the cooked cabbage, along with the gooseberries, herbs, and spices. Add 2 to 4 tablespoons butter, broken into pea-size pieces, according to your taste. Correct the seasoning and give a generous grinding of pepper. Toss everything well and serve hot.

RED CABBAGE AND BLACK CURRANTS

Chou Rouge Saint-Nazaire

One day Bart Evans, a friend from Vermont, and I visited Josephine. During our conversation Josephine told him that there were no currants to be had in this country. He told her he had a bush of them growing at his home in Vermont. She expressed surprise and asked for cuttings. A few weeks later I received a package with cuttings carefully wrapped. I brought them to Josephine and she was delighted. She put them in water and kept them alive; months later she was still coaxing them along. Finally, they were moved to her property in Santa Cruz; she always kept track of them.

It was an ongoing story for years. When the first crops of Bart's berries came in, Josephine advised him how to make a currant liqueur. A few months later we received a bottle of his liqueur in an old Nehi soda bottle. I brought it to Josephine and we sipped it with great delight. It made her cheeks pink and her laughter merry.

You can never go wrong serving cabbage and roast pork. Accompany them with noodles flavored with cream, mustard, and herbs, and drink an excellent Alsatian Pinot Noir. The original idea for the dish has its roots in the regional cooking of Josephine's grandmother, La Mère Jacquette.

INGREDIENTS   SERVES 6

---

1 head red cabbage
1 medium onion, thinly sliced
2 to 4 tablespoons butter
1 cup French cider or red wine
1 cup black currants
2 to 4 tablespoons chopped parsley
Salt and freshly ground pepper

METHOD

Slice the cabbage to a fine shred. Cut the onion in half lengthwise, peel, and slice thin across the grain.

Heat 2 tablespoons butter in a skillet, add the onion, season lightly with salt, and sauté until translucent. Add the cabbage and French cider or wine, and a pinch of salt; cover and cook slowly until the cabbage is completely tender, about 30 to 45 minutes. By the time the cabbage is cooked, most of the wine will have evaporated. If the liquid completely evaporates, don't hesitate to add more.

When the cabbage is tender, add 2 to 4 more tablespoons butter broken into pea-size pieces. Cabbage likes to be fattened, so flavor to taste. Add the currants and parsley; toss everything to melt the butter and coat the vegetables. Correct the seasonings and finish with a grinding of pepper.

CABBAGE SOUP WITH SAUTERNES FOR PIERROT

Crème au Chou pour Pierrot

Josephine's Cabbage for Pierrot (see page 185) makes use of the humble cabbage at one end of the scale and the elegant Sauternes at the other; this embrace of extremes has always attracted me. I love the dish as she prepared it. At Le Trou, I have served the same combination of ingredients as a soup, mixing the flavorings of mustard, scallions, and tarragon into the cream as a garnish for the puréed cabbage soup.

INGREDIENTS   SERVES 6

4 tablespoons butter
1 medium head green cabbage, thinly sliced
2 onions, thinly sliced
Rind and juice of 1 lemon
1 cup Sauternes
6 cups veal stock, good homemade
⅓ cup Dijon mustard
2 to 3 scallions, finely sliced on the bias
2 tablespoons chopped fresh tarragon
1 cup crème fraîche
Salt and freshly ground pepper

METHOD

Melt the butter in a large skillet or a heavy pot, add the cabbage, onions, and salt. Cook the vegetables slowly over low heat, covered, until they render some water, about 7 to 10 minutes.

Add the lemon juice and rind; then add the wine and stock. Season lightly with salt, cover and simmer about 25 minutes. When the cabbage is well cooked, remove to a blender and purée smooth; return to the heat to keep warm. In a bowl, mix the mustard to taste, scallion, and tarragon into the cream. To serve, fill the soup bowls and garnish with a dollop of the flavored cream, give a few grindings of pepper and serve hot.

CAULIFLOWER SOUP WITH APPLES AND CURRY

Crème au Chou-Fleur et au Cari

Josephine prepared cauliflower with curry, so I thought these ingredients would make a light perfumed soup. Serve with a plate of buckwheat crêpes and a chilled French cider.

INGREDIENTS	SERVES 6

3 tablespoons butter
1 tablespoon fine curry powder
1 medium onion, small dice
2 apples, grated
1 head cauliflower, in flowerets
Bouquet garni: parsley, thyme, and bay tied in two celery stalks
Freshly grated nutmeg
6 cups chicken stock, good homemade (see page 331)
⅓ cup crème fraîche
2 to 4 tablespoons chopped parsley or chervil
Salt and freshly ground pepper

METHOD

Heat the butter in a large pot until it starts to brown. Add the curry and onion with a sprinkling of salt, and cook for a minute. Add the grated apples and the cauliflower. Add the bouquet garni, nutmeg, and a light seasoning of salt; simmer 10 to 15 minutes. Pour the stock into the pot. Allow the soup to simmer 15 minutes, and then discard the bouquet garni and purée the soup in a blender. Return the soup to the pot; heat and keep warm. If the soup is too thick, add more stock. Ladle the soup into bowls and serve with a dollop of crème fraîche and chopped chervil.

CAULIFLOWER CUSTARD WITH WATERCRESS

Flan au Chou-Fleur et au Cresson

Josephine prepared cauliflower and flavored it with Roquefort. At Le Trou I use those flavors for a custard. I use watercress as a garnish in the same way that chopped parsley is used.

INGREDIENTS	SERVES 6

1 cup cauliflower, cut in flowerets and blanched tender
1 cup light cream
2 tablespoons butter mixed with 2 tablespoons Roquefort
2 egg yolks
1 egg
4 tablespoons chopped watercress leaves for garnish
2 very ripe tomatoes, peeled, seeded, and diced
Salt and freshly ground pepper

Preheat oven to 300 degrees. Butter six 2-ounce timbale molds and prepare a water bath, lined with 2 to 3 layers of paper towels (see page 280).

Blanch the cauliflower flowerets in boiling salted water 5 to 7 minutes, until tender. Drain in a colander and purée in a blender; add the cream, processing until smooth. Season with salt and pepper. Add the butter and Roquefort, and purée again until smooth. Add the egg yolks and whole egg, and purée only long enough to incorporate the eggs, about 5 seconds.

Fill the molds and set into a water bath and pour in 1 inch of boiling water. Bake in a preheated oven until the custards have set. Unmold the custards onto individual plates. Toss the tomatoes with the chopped watercress. Season with salt and a grinding of pepper; present each custard with a tablespoon of the tomatoes.

A GARDEN OF VEGETABLES

Ratatouille de Légumes aux Fines Herbes

Serve with roasted chicken or other fowl with herbs, and pour a fresh white Burgundy, a Mâcon-Viré.

INGREDIENTS   SERVES 6

2 cups chicken or veal stock (see page 331)
1 head cauliflower, in flowerets
½ cup green beans, cut into 1-inch pieces
2 onions, halved and thinly sliced
Juice of 1 lemon
1 cup cooked dry beans
1 cup shelled green peas
2 tablespoons butter
2 tablespoons fresh dill or fennel

2 tablespoons chopped parsley

2 tablespoons tarragon

1¼ cups crème fraîche (or 1 cup sour cream mixed with ¼ cup sweet
  cream)

Salt and freshly ground pepper

METHOD

Preheat oven to 300 degrees. In a large pan, heat the stock. Add the cauliflower, green beans, and onions. Sprinkle with lemon juice and simmer for about 10 minutes, until the vegetables are tender but still retain crispness. Add the cooked dry beans and peas, stirring to blend all the vegetables. Simmer until the peas are cooked. Drain the vegetables.

Set the vegetables, flavored with a little butter, into an oven-proof casserole. Add the herbs and crème fraîche. Correct the seasoning and keep gently warm in a preheated oven until ready to serve.

Cardoons

FROM JOSEPHINE'S NOTES

Cardoons come from the stalk of the thistle. They look like celery but have a flavor that is related to artichokes. Like celery, they also have a fibrous outer layer that needs to be removed to make them more digestible. They discolor quickly when they are exposed to the air, so they need to be kept in acidulated water while being prepared, and they should be cooked in a *blanc* (see page 189). There are a number of ways to prepare cardoons, including with cream and lemon, with a white sauce, or with marrow.

RAW CARDOON, PIEDMONT STYLE

Cardons Crus à la Piémontaise

Charles, Josephine's husband, was born in the Piedmont region of Italy; hence Josephine's interest. His own specialty was a minestrone soup, which he prepared every week and invited anyone to share with him at the drop of a hat. Josephine always said Italian food was the best. When people wondered how a French chef of her merit could make such a remark, she would get that twinkle in her eyes and reply: "I didn't say they were the best cooks."

INGREDIENTS	SERVES 6

1 bunch cardoons
Juice of 1 lemon
1 recipe Piedmontese Warm Sauce (see below)
1 slice bread for each serving

METHOD

Clean and peel the cardoons. Cut the stems into 2-inch lengths. Plunge immediately into water mixed with the lemon juice. When ready to serve, drain and place on a dish. Eat them dipped into Piedmontese Warm Sauce. Each guest takes a piece of vegetable with a fork and dips it into the sauce. Place the vegetable on a piece of bread and bring it to the plate, each time without spilling any of the sauce. Josephine said this is a very Piedmontese way of eating raw vegetables, such as cardoons, sweet peppers, celery, carrots, and tomatoes, at the table.

Piedmontese Warm Sauce

12 tablespoons butter
⅔ cup olive oil
4 cloves garlic, finely chopped
4 anchovy filets (more if desired), chopped
2 to 4 tablespoons chopped parsley
Salt and freshly ground pepper
Chafing dish or other warm serving dish

Warm the butter and olive oil in a saucepan and add garlic, anchovy, parsley, salt, and pepper. Put it in the chafing dish and keep it warm.

Carrots

CARROT SOUP WITH CIDER

Crème aux Carottes Normandes

Many times I have seen Josephine use French cider as a cooking medium when any liquid was called for. It makes sense that a marriage of cider and carrots would be pleasing in a soup, and Josephine agreed when she tasted it.

INGREDIENTS   SERVES 6

2 pounds small carrots
4 to 6 tablespoons butter
2 medium onions, sliced
½ cup celery root, diced
1 cup French cider
2 teaspoons sugar
6 cups chicken stock, good homemade (see page 331)
2 to 4 tablespoons chopped parsley
Crème fraîche for garnish
Salt and freshly ground pepper

METHOD

Wash, scrape, and trim the carrots, and then cut into 1½-inch pieces.
In a large pot, melt the butter and add the carrots, onions, and celery root, stirring to coat with butter. Add French cider to the vegetables; don't hesitate to add more liquid if necessary. Add the sugar and a light seasoning of salt to taste. Cover and simmer over low heat 10 to 15 minutes, or until they are cooked through. Add the stock and allow the

soup to steep for another 10 minutes; then purée in a blender and return to the heat. Correct the seasonings, give a grinding of pepper, and sprinkle with chopped parsley. Garnish with a tablespoon of crème fraîche and serve very hot.

CURRIED CARROT SOUP

Crème aux Carottes a l'Indienne

The idea for this soup came directly from a dish of Josephine's that no doubt had its origins in the Indian colonies of France (see Glazed Curried Carrots page 197). At Le Trou restaurant, we use the curried carrots as a base for a delicious soup that can be served hot or cold.

INGREDIENTS	SERVES 6

4 tablespoons butter
1 teaspoon minced fresh ginger
1 teaspoon curry powder
2 pounds of carrots, washed, scraped, and cut in ½-inch pieces
½ cup sherry
1 teaspoon freshly squeezed lemon juice

Rind and juice of 1 orange
2 tablespoons sugar
6 cups chicken stock, good homemade (see page 331)
2 to 4 tablespoons chopped parsley
Salt and freshly ground pepper

METHOD

Melt 2 tablespoons butter in a large pot; add the ginger and curry and cook over medium-low heat for a minute or two, allowing the flavor of the curry to develop. Add the carrots and a pinch of salt; let the carrots sweat 4 to 5 minutes on very low heat. Add the sherry, lemon juice, orange rind and juice, sugar, stock and salt, and cook another 10 to 15 minutes.

When the carrots are tender, purée in the blender, correct their seasoning, and return to the heat. When the dish is finished, toss in dots of butter, lots of parsley, season with a grinding of black pepper, and serve.

CARROT SOUP WITH PLUMS

Crème aux Carottes du Verger

Josephine made her grandmother's dish of carrots and plums (see Carrots with Fruits page 67). At Le Trou I work with those tastes to make a puréed soup of carrots and turnips, flavored with orange. The remaining flavors, honey, mustard, and herbs, flavor a butter that garnishes the soup along with the plums. I pour a pink Sancerre from the Loire, or just as easily a French cider.

| INGREDIENTS | SERVES 6 |

Rind and juice of 2 oranges
1 pound small carrots
1 to 2 small turnips
6 cups chicken stock, good homemade (see page 331)
1 tablespoon honey
2 tablespoons Dijon mustard
2 to 4 tablespoons chopped parsley
1 to 2 tablespoons chopped fresh tarragon
2 to 3 tablespoons butter
6 to 8 pitted plums
Salt and freshly ground pepper

METHOD

Grate the rind from the oranges. Squeeze ¼ cup fresh orange juice. Clean the carrots and trim the stems. If the carrots are small, cook whole; if they are larger, cut into any shape so they will cook in about 10 minutes. Peel the turnips and cut into ½-inch dice. In a saucepan, cook the vegetables in the orange juice on slow heat until tender. Add the chicken stock and let the vegetables steep on a slow flame another 10 to 15 minutes. Remove to a blender and purée until smooth; correct the seasonings.

Make a compound butter by combining the orange rind, honey, mustard, and herbs with softened butter. Halve the plums and then slice each half into thin slices that can be fanned out. Ladle the soup into bowls; garnish with a piece of the compound butter and the plums.

CARROTS AND MIXED VEGETABLES

Carottes Panachées

A dish named for having panache deserves a modern presentation with panache. This dish would be a good accompaniment to a roast beef; pour a southern Rhône wine, such as Châteauneuf-du-Pape.

INGREDIENTS	SERVES 8

½ cup green beans, cut in ½-inch pieces
½ cup carrots, cut in ½-inch dice
6 to 8 small new potatoes
2 to 3 tablespoons butter for the potato
½ cup warm light cream for the potato
1 cup cold light cream
4 tablespoons butter
4 eggs
2 tablespoons sherry
¼ cup finely chopped fresh chervil and parsley
Salt and freshly ground pepper

METHOD

Preheat oven to 300 degrees. Butter sixteen 1-ounce timbale molds. Prepare a water bath large enough to hold the molds and line the bottom with two or three layers of paper towels (see page 280).

Blanch the green beans and carrots separately in boiling salted water until tender, 5 to 8 minutes. Drain, refresh under cold water, and reserve. Parboil the potatoes in their jackets until tender. Peel them and mash in a bowl along with the butter, and add enough light cream to get a smooth purée; season with salt and pepper, and keep ready.

Put ½ cup of the cold cream and the green beans into a blender; purée until smooth. Toss in 1 tablespoon butter and season with salt and pepper; add 2 eggs and purée again for 5 to 10 seconds. Pour into eight of the buttered molds and set into the water bath.

Put the remaining ½ cup of cold cream, the cooked carrots, and sherry in the blender and purée until smooth. Toss in 1 tablespoon butter and season with salt and pepper; add 2 eggs and purée again for 5 to 10 seconds. Pour into the remaining buttered molds and set into the water bath.

Place the water bath in a preheated oven, pour in 1 inch of hot water, and bake until set, 15 to 20 minutes.

When ready to serve, put the hot purée of potatoes into a pastry bag. Unmold one carrot and one green bean timbale on each plate and garnish with the potato purée piped decoratively from the pastry bag. Garnish with the chopped herbs.

Celery Root

CELERY ROOT SOUFFLE

Soufflé au Céleri-Rave Normande

This recipe translates the ideas of Josephine's dish for Celery Root with Cream Sauce (see page 199) into a soufflé. A soup can also be made from these ingredients (see Celery Root Soup with Chervil Butter page 308).

INGREDIENTS	SERVES 6

Butter and 2 to 3 tablespoons breadcrumbs for the soufflé dish
1 medium celery root, blanched

Stiff béchamel

1½ tablespoons butter
1½ tablespoons flour
½ cup warm cream
Salt, freshly ground pepper, and nutmeg

2 tablespoons butter
3 shallots, small dice
4 tablespoons chopped chervil or parsley
6 eggs, separated
2 to 3 tablespoons Madeira
2 additional egg whites

METHOD

Preheat oven to 325 degrees. Prepare an 8-cup soufflé dish by buttering the bottom and the sides and dusting with breadcrumbs. Set aside and keep ready.

Blanch the peeled celery root whole in boiling salted water; chop coarsely and purée in a food processor. Remove to a bowl.

Prepare the béchamel, following the description on page 208.

In a small skillet, melt 1 tablespoon butter and sauté the shallots. Add to ½ cup puréed celery root and season generously with salt, pepper, and the herbs. Mix in ½ cup béchamel; then add the egg yolks one at a time, blending everything well. Add the Madeira.

In a copper bowl beat the egg whites with a pinch of salt until they hold stiff peaks. Fold in one third of the whites to the base; once the base accepts the whites, add the remaining two thirds, folding carefully.

Pour the mixture into the prepared soufflé dish and bake in a preheated oven about 45 minutes, until it has set. Remove from the oven and serve at once.

CELERY ROOT SOUP WITH CHERVIL BUTTER

Crème au Céleri-Rave Normande

If the celery roots are large, peel them raw, cut them into small cubes, and keep them in acidulated water so they don't discolor before cooking. This ensures a soup that has a beautiful white creaminess. The celery root can also be cooked in a *blanc* or milk; you can use the milk to thin the soup.

INGREDIENTS	SERVES 6

1 large celery root, peeled and diced
Blanc (see page 189)

Béchamel
    6 tablespoons butter
    6 tablespoons flour
    3 cups light cream or milk
    Bouquet garni: parsley stems, thyme, and bay leaf tied in 2 celery
      stalks

2 cups warm chicken or veal stock
¼ cup coarsely chopped fresh chervil
4 tablespoons butter
Salt, freshly ground pepper, and nutmeg

METHOD

Peel and dice the celery root; cook in a *blanc* until tender; drain and purée in a blender.

In a 2-quart saucepan, prepare the béchamel with a bouquet garni as described on page 332. Remove the bouquet garni and mix in puréed celery root. Thin out the soup to the consistency desired with hot chicken stock (or additional light cream).

Mash the chervil and butter into a paste with the flat edge of a knife to make a compound butter.

Bring the soup to serving temperature on a low flame. Correct the seasonings and give a grinding of pepper. Ladle the soup into individual bowls; top each one with a pat of chervil butter and finish with a dusting of finely chopped chervil or parsley. Serve hot.

Chard

SWISS CHARD WITH MUSTARD

Bettes Epicées

Swiss chard is an interesting vegetable that lends itself to a great variety of flavors. This dish could accompany a roast duck with sautéed potatoes and a wine from duck country, such as a Cahors or Madiran.

INGREDIENTS	SERVES 6

2 bunches Swiss chard
1 to 2 tablespoons whole grain mustard
Persillade: 1 clove garlic, minced, and 4 tablespoons chopped parsley
Pinch of *quatre épices* (see page 184)
2 to 4 tablespoons flavorful oil: colza, walnut, olive, or peanut
Salt and freshly ground pepper

METHOD

Wash the Swiss chard, trim the stems, and set aside. If the greens are young and tender, they are best left wet from the washing and sautéed in a dry skillet until they wilt. Cover the pan and cook for a few minutes; remove the lid and allow the moisture to escape.

If the greens are large and more fibrous, blanch in boiling salted water until limp, and then run under cold water to stop the cooking. Rewarm in a dry skillet to rid them of any excess water.

Add the mustard and *persillade*; correct the seasoning, give a few grindings of pepper, and add the *quatre épices*. Toss in enough oil to coat the greens and serve at once.

Eggplant

FLAMBEED EGGPLANT WITH PLUMS

Aubergines Agenoises

The first time Josephine mentioned a dish of eggplant and plums, I was intrigued. I didn't ask her what the recipe was or how to do it; I wanted to go off and discover it for myself. This recipe is a result of that discovery. I use eau de vie made by Saint George Spirits in California for flambéing the eggplant. Flambéing eggplant in brandy is an old country technique from France. It was done often with *marc,* a brandy made from the crushed wine grapes.

INGREDIENTS	SERVES 6

2 medium eggplants
2 to 4 tablespoons extra virgin olive oil
¼ cup eau de vie or *marc*

Persillade: 2 to 4 tablespoons finely chopped parsley, and 2 cloves garlic, minced
6 to 8 fresh plums, pitted and quartered
Salt and freshly ground pepper

METHOD

Peel the skin from the eggplant and slice into 1-inch slices. Salt them on each side and let sit for about 30 minutes to draw their water. Then rinse well under cold water and dry.

Cut the eggplant slices into a large dice, about 1-inch square. Pour the olive oil into a skillet over a medium flame. When the oil is hot, add enough eggplant to cover the bottom of the pan. Toss well with wooden spoons so the eggplant is coated with oil. Sauté, shaking the pan to prevent the vegetable from sticking to the bottom. Cook until the eggplant starts to brown.

Once it has browned, carefully flambé the vegetable with half the eau de vie. When the flame goes out, cover the pan, turn the heat to low and continue cooking until the eggplant collapses. Don't cook it so long that it turns to mush; it should hold its shape. When cooked, set the vegetable aside. Repeat the procedure for the second and subsequent batches until all the eggplant is cooked.

Put all the eggplant back into the skillet and rewarm. Toss in the *persillade*; when completely warm, toss in the quartered plums and serve at once.

EGGPLANT WITH TOMATO AND CREAM SAUCE

Aubergines à la Fontainebleau

This is a version of Josephine's recipe Eggplant with Cream (see page 207) with a modern leanness. These *faux* fries are deliciously highbrow; serve them with ground lamb patties garnished with a *persillade* and chard flavored with blanched slivers of lemon rind. All of which go very well with a red wine from Corbières.

INGREDIENTS   SERVES 6

1 cup heavy cream
2 pounds ripe tomatoes
4 tablespoons butter
1 large onion, finely chopped
3 small eggplants
Flour for dredging eggplant
2 tablespoons olive oil
½ cup grated Gruyère cheese
4 tablespoons chopped parsley
Salt and freshly ground pepper

METHOD

Pour the heavy cream into a small saucepan and reduce it slowly by half over a low flame; keep warm on reserve.

Peel, seed, and coarsely chop the tomatoes. In a saucepan, heat 2 tablespoons butter, add the onion, and sauté until translucent. Add the tomatoes, season with salt, and cook until the tomato liquid evaporates, about 10 minutes. Season with pepper and keep ready. Mix half the reduced cream into the tomatoes; reserve the remaining cream.

Peel the eggplant; cut in half lengthwise, then cut each half into quarters, and cut each quarter into thirds. Dredge in flour; season with salt and set on a cake rack.

In a skillet, sauté the eggplant slices in the remaining butter mixed with the olive oil on medium heat until they are browned; lower the heat and continue to cook until tender. Season lightly with salt and pepper.

Add the grated cheese to the hot reserved cream and mix until it melts. If it is too thick, thin with a bit more cream. Pour a layer of the tomato/cream mixture into a baking dish. Arrange the cooked eggplant slices neatly in a line. Cover half the surface of the eggplant with the tomato mixture and then cover half of that surface with the cream/cheese sauce. Brown the dish under the broiler 2 to 3 minutes; sprinkle with parsley and serve piping hot.

EGGPLANT PUREE

Purée d'Aubergines

Serve the purée warm or cold with toasted bread. It can be an appetizer or an accompaniment to roast lamb and saffron-flavored zucchini with raisins. Pour a Bandol rosé.

INGREDIENTS	SERVES 6

2 large eggplants
8 tablespoons butter
1 to 2 cloves garlic, minced
Juice and rind of 1 lemon
2 to 4 tablespoons *fines herbes*: chopped parsley, tarragon, and/or chervil
Salt and freshly ground pepper

METHOD

Preheat oven to 400 degrees. Prick the eggplant all over with a fork. Set on a baking sheet and bake in a hot oven until they collapse, about 30 to 40 minutes. Remove from the oven and scrape the flesh from the skin.

Put the eggplant in a large bowl, add the butter broken into pieces along with the remaining ingredients. Make a purée by whisking until everything is well blended. It can also be puréed in a blender or food processor, but the coarser texture of the hand mixing makes a more agreeable purée.

Endive

BRAISED ENDIVE WITH CARROTS

Endives Braisées Crécy

This dish makes a great one-dish supper, as Josephine suggested. As a variation, Josephine would make a delicious luncheon dish by placing chopped leftover meat between the vegetable layers and serving it with a tossed green salad and a crisp white wine, perhaps a Riesling from Alsace.

INGREDIENTS   SERVES 6

2 quarts boiling water
2 tablespoons white vinegar or juice of 2 lemons
6 endives
4 tablespoons butter
2 shallots or equivalent whites of scallions, chopped fine
2 cups finely diced carrots
1 cup sherry, Madeira, or orange juice
1 cup stock
¼ cup grated Swiss cheese
½ cup breadcrumbs
½ cup grated almonds
1 tablespoon chopped *fines herbes*: chervil, tarragon, and parsley (any combination)
Salt and freshly ground pepper

METHOD

Preheat oven to 350 degrees. Bring two quarts of water to a rolling boil; add the vinegar, endives, and a teaspoon of salt. Blanch for about

5 minutes to eliminate the bitterness of the endives. Drain and allow to dry.

Heat 2 tablespoons butter in a skillet and sauté the shallots for 1 to 2 minutes, until they soften. Add the carrots and another tablespoon butter, if desired, and cook on a medium-low flame until lightly browned. Add ½ cup sherry and simmer for 3 to 5 minutes. Remove the carrots and shallots with a slotted spoon, and arrange them in the bottom of an oven-proof braising pan that has a tight fitting lid.

In the skillet, add the stock and remaining sherry to the cooking liquid and reduce by half.

Arrange the endives on top of the bed of carrots and pour over the reduced stock/sherry mixture. Cover the braising pan with a tight-fitting lid and braise the endive in a preheated oven for 45 minutes.

To serve the dish, combine the cheese, breadcrumbs, and almonds. Spread this mixture on top of the vegetable and dot with butter. Place under the broiler for 2 to 3 minutes, until brown. Sprinkle the surface with the fresh herbs and present it piping hot at the table.

Jerusalem Artichokes

JERUSALEM ARTICHOKES WITH BANANAS

Topinambours aux Bananes

Josephine talked about her grandmother's kitchen and the fact that it had a *cheminée* so large that all sorts of meats, sausages, and bacon could be hung there to smoke. When it was winter, the table was moved close to it and people sat along benches to receive its warmth, and her grandmother would regale them with stories. This recipe is from one of those stories.

Serve this dish with fillet of sole in a chervil sauce.

INGREDIENTS	SERVES 6

1½ pounds whole Jerusalem artichokes
2 small ripe bananas
4 tablespoons Chablis
Nutmeg
Salt and freshly ground pepper

METHOD

Blanch the Jerusalem artichokes until tender, and then peel and cut into a dice and reserve in a saucepan, keeping warm. Cut the bananas into quarters lengthwise; then cut each quarter in half. From the halves cut *batons,* or sticks, about the size of your little finger. With one or two of these *batons* make a sauce by mashing the banana with the Chablis, working it so that it is creamy, not thick and pasty or thin and runny. Flavor with nutmeg. Season the artichokes with salt and a few grindings of pepper. Add the banana sauce and *batons* to the artichokes. Toss to coat with the banana mixture.

JERUSALEM ARTICHOKES WITH GUAVAS

One day I found guavas at the market. I phoned Josephine and when she answered, I immediately asked, "If you had guavas today, what would you like to eat them with?" "Jerusalem artichokes" was the ready reply. I am always astonished by the combinations of tastes that she would recall. The earthiness of the Jerusalem artichoke is complemented perfectly by the bright, floral taste of the fruit. Serve with roast pork and pour a Pinot Noir to drink.

INGREDIENTS	SERVES 6

1 pound Jerusalem artichokes, whole
3 to 4 fresh ripe guavas
2 to 3 tablespoons butter
2 to 4 tablespoons *fines herbes:* parsley, chervil, tarragon, and chives (any combination)
Salt and freshly ground pepper

METHOD

Blanch the artichokes whole in boiling salted water until they are tender and can be pierced by a cake tester. While they blanch, peel the guavas and cut the flesh into a small dice; then chop the herbs. When the artichokes are tender, drain and peel them. Cut into slices or dice. Toss in a dry skillet over slow heat to rid them of any excess moisture. Toss in the butter broken into pieces, adding enough to coat the vegetable. Then add the guavas and herbs; finally, season with salt and pepper.

Mushrooms

MUSHROOMS IN CREAM

Champignons à la Bordelaise

I remember eating with a friend in a small neighborhood restaurant in Paris. It was family-operated, and the mother ran the dining room. We ordered mushrooms. The mother came out of the kitchen at a brisk clip carrying our order. The steam wafted off the plates as she passed each table, and all heads turned. She delivered two plates of small *champignons de Paris* that had been sautéed and perfumed with sweet garlic. On her way back to the kitchen, each diner asked her what she had served us as if the aromas were a mystery. "Just calm yourselves," she finally said to the whole dining room. "It is only the aroma of garlic that has you excited." This dish of Josephine's carries that same magic.

INGREDIENTS	SERVES 6 TO 8

¾ cup heavy cream
1½ pounds small mushrooms

Persillade: 2 large cloves garlic, minced, and 2 to 4 tablespoons of parsley, finely chopped
Salt and freshly ground pepper

METHOD

Put the heavy cream in a small saucepan and reduce by half over a low flame, until it has the consistency of a sauce; keep ready.

While the cream reduces, clean the mushrooms. Remove the stems and finely chop them. Reserve the caps. Add the chopped mushroom stems to a dry skillet, season lightly with salt, and sauté quickly on medium-high heat until they give up their liquid. Remove to a bowl. Add the mushroom caps to the same skillet, salt lightly, and sauté quickly on medium-high heat until they give up their liquid; cook until tender. Add the stems and rewarm.

Remove from heat; give a generous grinding of pepper and a generous amount of *persillade;* toss everything well. Add the reduced cream to coat the mushrooms and serve hot.

MUSHROOM SOUP WITH OYSTERS

Soupe aux Champignons et aux Huîtres

Josephine's recipes often tell a story about flavors. For example, this recipe tells us that oysters can be served with mushrooms, bacon, cream, lemon, and herbs; a cook can apply these flavor combinations to many dishes, such as a soup, soufflé, or tart.

Serve this soup with a spicy Gewürztraminer from the Alsace.

INGREDIENTS   SERVES 6

1 pound mushrooms, trimmed and sliced
3 or 4 shallots, minced
½ teaspoon cumin seed, crushed
6 cups warm chicken stock, good homemade (see page 331)
4 thin slices pancetta
1 tablespoon butter
6 to 8 fresh shrimp, shelled and deveined
4 to 6 fresh oysters
2 egg yolks
¾ cup heavy cream
4 tablespoons chopped parsley
6 slices rye bread, lightly toasted
Salt, freshly ground pepper, and cayenne

METHOD

Dry sauté the mushrooms in a heavy-bottomed pot on medium-high heat. After a few minutes they will give up their liquid; continue to cook, stirring, until they start to brown in their juices. When the juices evaporate, turn down the heat and toss in shallots and cumin seeds. Season lightly with salt, pepper, and a pinch of cayenne. Slowly add the heated chicken stock and allow the soup to simmer 10 minutes so the flavors infuse the broth.

Prepare the garnishes. Brown the bacon in a skillet and remove to a plate lined with paper towels; crumble it and keep ready. Discard the fat from the skillet, but don't wipe the pan clean. Add a tablespoon of butter to pick up the bacon flavor. Sauté the shrimp in butter until they have just cooked; remove and keep ready. Remove the oysters from their shells and set in the same batter used for the shrimp; heat them on a low flame until they turn opaque but barely cook; reserve.

In a separate bowl, mix the egg yolks into the cream with a whisk. Bring the mushroom soup to a boil, take off the heat and slowly whisk in the cream and egg mixture. Put the soup back on low heat and let it steep for 2 to 3 minutes, being careful not to boil or the egg will curdle.

Correct the seasonings and ladle the soup into individual bowls. Garnish each bowl with an oyster, some shrimp, crumbled bacon, and parsley. Serve it hot with rye toast.

MUSHROOM AND OYSTER TARTS

Tartes aux Champignons et aux Huîtres

INGREDIENTS   SERVES 6

6 individual tart shells, prebaked
½ pound mushrooms, thinly sliced
Persillade: 1 small clove garlic, minced, and 2 tablespoons chopped parsley
½ cup heavy cream
1 teaspoon grated lemon rind
2 to 3 tablespoons finely grated Gruyère cheese
6 fresh oysters
2 to 3 slices bacon, cooked crisp
1 tablespoon butter
1 to 2 tablespoons cognac
Salt, freshly ground pepper, and cayenne

METHOD

Prebake the individual tart shells made from the pastry crust of your choice; keep them warm and ready. Dry sauté the mushrooms in a skillet, adding only a pinch of salt, and cook on high heat, tossing until they give up their water. Continue cooking on high heat until they start to brown and the water evaporates. Remove from heat, season lightly with salt, a fresh grinding of pepper, a pinch of cayenne, and the *persillade*; toss everything well.

In a saucepan, reduce the heavy cream over a low heat to ¼ cup. Add a teaspoon of grated lemon rind and the finely grated Gruyère cheese and blend completely. Keep this mixture warm and ready.

Remove the oysters from their shells over a sieve set in a bowl to catch their liquor. Strain the liquor to remove any coarse material. Sauté the bacon in a skillet until it browns; remove to paper towels and crumble it. Discard the bacon fat from the skillet; add the butter, and then add the oysters when the butter is hot. Turn the heat to medium low and gently cook until the oysters turn opaque and the edges shrink, 1 to 2 minutes. Remove the oysters from the pan. With the heat on high, add the oyster liquor along with the cognac to deglaze the pan, whisking and scraping to collect all the particles on the bottom.

Assemble the tarts by spooning some of the mushroom mixture and then some of the cream onto each tart shell. Set an oyster on top of the bed of mushrooms, pour over a little of the deglazing juices, and sprinkle with crumbled bacon. Serve warm.

Onions

ONION AND RASPBERRY TARTS WITH BACON

Tarte aux Oignons et aux Lardons

I use a California eau de vie made by Saint George Spirits to flavor this onion tart. It could be served alone as an appetizer, or with a salad for a light supper. It would love an Alsatian wine, a Riesling, or Pinot Blanc.

INGREDIENTS   SERVES 6 TO 8

¼ pound pancetta in one piece
2 to 4 tablespoons butter
2 to 3 medium white onions
¼ cup raspberry eau de vie
3 eggs
1 cup heavy cream
6 individual tart shells, prebaked
Salt and freshly ground pepper

METHOD

Preheat oven to 275 degrees. Butter six 2-ounce timbale molds. Set them in a water bath, lined with 2 or 3 layers of paper towels (see page 280) and keep ready.

Cut the pancetta into ½-inch pieces to yield lardons. Blanch the lardons in boiling water 10 to 15 minutes. Then sauté slowly in 1 to 2 tablespoons butter so they turn golden outside and remain creamy inside. Remove with a slotted spoon to paper towels to drain.

Pour off all but 1 to 2 tablespoons bacon fat, add another 1 to 2 tablespoons butter, and set aside.

Cut the onions in half and slice them in ⅙-inch slices. Sauté in the skillet with the reserved bacon fat and butter until they start to go limp. Turn the heat to high, add the eau de vie, and ignite with a match until all the alcohol burns entirely. Continue to cook to evaporate any liquid. Remove to a plate and divide into two batches, one for the custards and one for the garnish.

In a bowl, mix the eggs with 1 cup heavy cream and season lightly with salt and pepper. Mix in half the onions; then spoon into the buttered timbale molds. Set to bake in a water bath with 1 inch of water, in a preheated oven, until they are set, 20 to 30 minutes.

Set the prebaked tart shells on individual plates and unmold an onion custard on top of each one. Mix the remaining onions with the sautéed pancetta and season with salt and pepper. Garnish each tart with onions and serve warm.

Salsify

SALSIFY WITH PLUMS

Salsifis aux Prunes

Josephine's memory for this dish, the combination of salsify and plums, came out of a conversation we had in French. Salsify is a root vegetable shaped like a young carrot; its flesh is white, and it has a delicate flavor. It is also called oyster plant in English.

This combination of plums and salsify is perfect with roast chicken and a white Loire wine, such as a Savennières.

INGREDIENTS	SERVES 6

1½ pounds salsify
Juice and rind of 1 lemon
2 tablespoons cider vinegar
2 tablespoons butter
2 to 3 tablespoons *fines herbes*: chervil, tarragon, chives, and parsley (any combination)
8 plums, stoned and quartered

METHOD

Trim and peel the salsify. Put into a bowl with fresh water and lemon juice to keep from discoloring. Cut into 1-inch lengths, putting the cut vegetables back in the acidulated water. Blanch the prepared vegetable in boiling salted water to which the cider vinegar has been added. Blanch until tender and drain.

Put the salsify in a dry skillet and heat on a medium flame until any excess water evaporates. Add the butter and toss until well coated. Season with salt and pepper; mix in the herbs and the plums. Toss everything again, remove to a bowl, and serve at once.

Spinach

SPINACH WITH HAZELNUTS

Epinards Noisettes

This dish is served at Le Trou with handmade noodles for a vegetarian supper, or as an accompaniment to roast veal. For a wine, select a Beaujolais.

INGREDIENTS	SERVES 6

1 pound fresh spinach, washed, and stems removed
3 eggs
1 cup light cream
2 tablespoons butter
8 toasted hazelnuts, finely minced
Salt, freshly ground pepper, and nutmeg

METHOD

Preheat oven to 300 degrees. Wash and trim the spinach; sweat it in a dry skillet with some salt until it is limp, 1 to 2 minutes. Strain off the liquid and cook until the moisture evaporates. Put the spinach on a cutting board and chop coarsely. Season with salt, pepper, and nutmeg.

In a small bowl, whisk the eggs and cream until well mixed; add half the spinach to the mixture. Fill the timbale molds and set in a water bath to bake in a preheated oven until set, 30 to 45 minutes.

Toss the remaining spinach with the butter broken into pieces and the hazelnuts. Unmold the timbales on individual plates and garnish with the spinach.

Zucchini

ZUCCHINI CASSEROLE

Terrine de Courgettes

This makes a wonderful hot or cold presentation. Made to accompany a rabbit braised in cider and garnished with little dumplings, it could be served with a wine from Chinon.

INGREDIENTS	SERVES 6

- 4 tablespoons butter
- 3 medium red onions
- 2 pounds zucchini
- 1 pound tomatoes
- 2 tablespoons oregano or marjoram

2 tablespoons chopped parsley
1 clove garlic, minced
½ cup Gruyère cheese, grated
Salt and freshly ground pepper

METHOD

Preheat oven to 375 degrees.

Melt the butter in a skillet and sauté the onions until limp. Season with salt and pepper and reserve.

Cut the zucchini into ¼-inch slices. If the vegetable is particularly large, slice in half lengthwise, then slice in ¼-inch half moons. Slice the tomatoes to the same thickness as the zucchini. Butter the bottom of an oven-proof gratin dish. Using half the onions, make a layer in the bottom of the gratin dish. Set alternating rows of zucchini and tomatoes, repeating the pattern until the baking dish is entirely filled. Make a second layer if necessary. Season the surface of the vegetables with salt and pepper; sprinkle with the herbs, garlic, and grated cheese; cover with a layer of sautéed onions. Bake in a preheated oven for 20 to 30 minutes, until the vegetables have cooked and the cheese has melted.

ZUCCHINI SOUP WITH TOMATOES

Soupe aux Courgettes et aux Tomates

The combination of zucchini and tomatoes makes a good basis for a number of dishes. Josephine's recipe for Zucchini with Tomatoes and Onions (see page 261) is made into a soup at Le Trou. Serve with a rosé from Corbières.

INGREDIENTS   SERVES 6

2 medium onions, thinly sliced
3 cloves garlic, minced
¼ cup extra virgin olive oil
1 pound zucchini, finely grated
1 tablespoon chopped fresh marjoram or oregano
¼ cup chopped fresh parsley
6 cups chicken or veal stock, good homemade (see page 331)
4 medium tomatoes
Salt and freshly ground pepper

METHOD

In a 4-quart soup pot, sauté the onions and 2 cloves garlic in 3 tablespoons olive oil, until soft. Add the finely shredded zucchini, marjoram, and half the parsley; cook on medium heat until the vegetables gives up water, 3 to 5 minutes. Pour in the warm stock and simmer 5 to 10 minutes.

While the soup simmers, plunge the tomatoes in boiling water for 10 seconds, remove and run under cold water to stop any cooking. Peel, seed, and dice the tomatoes. In a bowl, toss the tomatoes with an additional clove of garlic mixed with the remaining parsley.

Purée the soup in a blender; correct the seasoning and give it a grinding of pepper. Ladle the soup into individual bowls. Garnish each bowl with a generous portion of tomatoes, seasoned at the last minute with salt and pepper. Just before serving, very lightly drizzle the surface of the soup with olive oil and serve. This is a wonderful summer soup that can also be served cold.

ZUCCHINI PILLOWS WITH FRESH TOMATOES

Timbales de Courgettes aux Tomates

Again working with the flavors of Josephine's Zucchini with Tomatoes and Onions (see page 261), I shred the zucchini and cook them dry, with or without tomatoes. The resulting "hash" is mixed into a base for an egg custard baked in individual timbale molds. Serve hot or cold with a salad of mesclum and a chilled rosé from Provence.

INGREDIENTS   SERVES 6

2 tablespoons extra virgin olive oil
1 medium onion, finely sliced
2 cloves garlic, crushed
6 tablespoons chopped parsley
2 tablespoons chopped fresh marjoram
3 medium zucchini, finely shredded
3 eggs
1¼ cups heavy cream
3 medium tomatoes
1 clove garlic, minced
2 tablespoons finely chopped tarragon
2 tablespoons raisins
1 tablespoon cognac
Salt and freshly ground pepper

METHOD

Preheat oven to 275 degrees. Butter six 2-ounce timbale molds and set them in a water bath, lined with 2 or 3 layers of paper towels (see page 280). Keep a kettle of boiling water ready to fill the water bath before it is put in the oven.

To a skillet on medium heat, add 2 tablespoons olive oil and the onion and crushed garlic; cook for a minute until the onions start to go limp. Add 4 tablespoons chopped parsley, the marjoram, and the shredded zucchini. Season lightly with salt and allow to cook covered 2 to 3 minutes, until the vegetable gives up its water. Remove the lid and evaporate the water completely. Remove the zucchini to a bowl.

Mix the eggs, one at a time, into the zucchini mixture; add the cream and mix everything well. Taste for salt and give a generous grinding of pepper.

Spoon the zucchini mixture into the molds and bake in the water bath in a preheated oven until barely set, 20 to 30 minutes. Remove from the oven and allow to rest in the water bath if serving warm.

While the timbales bake, drop the tomatoes in a pot of boiling water for 10 seconds; remove and flush them under cold water to stop the cooking. Peel, seed, and dice the tomatoes. Mince one clove of garlic and mix it with the remaining parsley and the chopped taragon. Add raisins and cognac.

Unmold the timbales onto individual serving dishes and garnish with the tomatoes, seasoned at the last minute with salt and freshly ground pepper. Serve hot or cold.

GOAT CHEESE WITH SAFFRON, ZUCCHINI, AND TOMATOES WITH BASIL

Zucchini with Tomatoes and Onions (see page 261) is the foundation for this dish with the aromas of Provence. At Le Trou, we serve this dish with an interesting bread, a fougasse, or a walnut bread, and offer a wine from the vineyards at Pibarnon in Bandol to accompany the plate.

INGREDIENTS   SERVES 6

2 ounces goat cheese, a Crottin, soft and fresh if possible; or a sheep's milk cheese, a Banon
1 medium onion, sliced
Pinch of finest quality saffron threads
2 tablespoons extra virgin olive oil
3 zucchini, finely shredded
4 tablespoons chopped parsley
4 tablespoons torn basil leaves

3 medium tomatoes
Salt and freshly ground pepper

METHOD

Use Crottin for the goat cheese; it is a soft cheese. A sheep's milk cheese, such as a Banon, can also be used. It should be a soft and creamy cheese. Keep ready.

In a skillet, sauté the onion and saffron in the olive oil until transparent. In a large bowl, salt the shredded zucchini heavily and set aside for 30 minutes. The zucchini will give up their water and get limp as though cooked. Flush in several changes of cold water until they no longer taste salty; leave to drain completely. Return them to the bowl and add the onion and half the chopped parsley. Correct the seasoning and give a grinding of pepper. Drizzle lightly with olive oil.

Peel, seed, and dice the tomatoes. Put them in a bowl and add the remaining parsley along with the basil. Season with salt only when the dish is assembled.

Garnish individual plates with the saffron zucchini on one side and the herbed tomatoes on the other. Put a portion of the goat cheese onto each plate and season lightly with freshly ground pepper.

Notes on Stock

There are many uses for good homemade stock. At its simplest level it is mother's chicken soup—no more, no less. She put a chicken in a pot with water to cover; then added onions, carrots, celery, parsley, salt, and pepper, brought it to a boil, and cooked the bird at a simmer until it was tender. The cooking yielded a great stock. When it is chilled, it leaves fat on top that can be used for cooking. When I prepare duck broth this way, I save that fat and use it for sautéing potatoes; it can also be used in a duck confit.

Veal, beef, or some other meat stock is prepared in the same manner, i.e., with onions, carrots, celery, salt, and pepper. Cook veal stock for a longer time than one made from chicken, because the ingredients are denser and require more time to release the richness of their proteins.

Stocks are more elaborate in a French context: they involve a bouquet garni, a *mirepoix* of vegetables, and wine—all things that lend flavor. Also, the French roast the meats and bones sometimes, because the stock ends up golden brown and more flavorful. Whether or not you roast the bones, the rewards are more than commensurate with the effort; particularly if like me, you feel that a well-prepared and flavorful stock provides one of life's great and simple pleasures.

Bouquet Garni in Stock: A bouquet garni is a flavoring device. Cut a clean stalk of celery in half and lay the two pieces side by side. Place a half dozen or so sprigs of parsley in the piece of celery with the bigger groove. Lay a few sprigs of thyme on top of the parsley. Then add a bay leaf. Place the narrower branch of celery on top.

Cut a piece of kitchen string about 24 inches long. Grab the celery securely with one hand, dead center so that it extends from both sides of your hand, and wrap the string three or four times around one end, leaving a 6- to 8-inch lead. Turn your hand, exposing the other end of the celery branch, and wrap the string around it three or four times. It should leave a 6- to 8-inch trailer of string.

Set the bouquet down on the counter and tie the lead and trailer strings in the middle, making two knots to secure it. Tie a slip knot to join the two strings.

Now you can pick up the bouquet by the string and drop it into a pot of boiling liquid, and conversely, you can slip a fork's tines into a boiling pot and catch the string to remove it with ease. A bouquet garni lends flavors.

The Use of Wine in Stock: The unfinished ends of wines are perfectly good for cooking. There are two ways of using wine in stock. You can simply add it after the water, in which case it is a flavoring element. Or, add the wine before the water. For example, I often pour wine into the pot with a bed of sautéed vegetables and roasted veal bones. Then I add heat to evaporate the wine. The vapors penetrate the meats and fats of the bones and help break down the proteins, which will leach into the stock and make it richer. However it is used, wine is a flavoring element that adds qualitatively to your stocks.

Your pot of bones and vegetables, bouquet garni, and wine is filled to about an inch above the level of the bones with cold water. It goes on the stove and simmers slowly for hours. It takes about 16 hours, for example, for veal to render all of its proteins. Chicken bones, on the other hand, give everything up in an hour; and fish yields what it has to offer in about half an hour. With denser bones, however, the long simmering causes the water to evaporate, and therefore additional water is required to keep it at the level of the original volume.

Water used to replenish stocks should be boiling or certainly very hot. If it is added cold, you must bring the stock back to a boil before it can simmer. Be careful—under the right conditions the addition of cold water can lower the temperature of the stock so that bacteria can invade, souring the stock.

To reduce stock to a true meat jelly, strain it very well through a china cap sieve, and very slowly cook it in another pan until it evaporates by half. Put it in the refrigerator to set and yield a dense jelly.

Reductions of stock require careful cleaning as they get more concentrated, and the cooking must go slower and slower. The tiny particles and scum in the reducing liquid roll to the surface of the simmering liquid and must be skimmed off constantly. If not, they stay at the bottom of the pan as the liquid becomes more dense. They can first scorch and then burn.

Remy was Josephine's companion and cared for her on a daily basis for a number of years. She phoned one day to say that Josephine was in the hospital and that she had suffered a stroke.

I went by Kaiser Hospital on Friday morning and found my way to Josephine's room. The day was remarkably beautiful and the room was full of sun. A woman was making the beds, but I had the impression no one else was there. The woman looked up at me and I told her I was looking for Josephine. She said, "Yes, she's here—in the chair by the window." I looked around, and behind the woman found Josephine sitting in the bright, warm light. She was asleep and looked like the smallest bird. I went to her and got down on one knee so that we would be face to face. I called out loud, "Josephine. Josephine. C'est moi." Slowly her head lifted and slowly her eyes opened. She looked at me squarely but gave me no outward sign of recognition. Then she asked me in a small voice and in French if I had any bad thoughts. I thought, "Oh my gosh, she's very far away." "No," I began, "I don't have any bad thoughts." "Good," she replied, "I don't either, because I'm in a place where everyone is happy." My mind was racing, trying to figure out if she even knew who I was. There was a moment of silence and finally, in the same soft tone, she said, "Tell me what you prepared at the restaurant last night." My whole soul smiled. I slipped her hand into mine and settled in to talk.

It was a long visit and we talked about family, the book, and everyday things. Sometimes she would drift away and become a little vague. I knew she was going to die. I didn't feel sad about that. I had to remind myself that she was not afraid to die. My father once told me that we have an obligation to those who are dying. He told me we have a responsibility not to interfere and not to block their way with our own fears. I asked Josephine about her brothers and she told me a story about them, recounting their names, discussing with me what they did, and which of them she felt closest to, which of them she knew the least. She finished her tale and said, "I just want to be with them." I felt in her response the hunger she sustained for her family. She had lived all of her life missing them. I had a very clear image while she talked about them, and to me it seemed that they were waiting for her. They were working to build a place where she would join them, and for everyone this was very joyful. Josephine would get everything that she wished for, in a place where everyone was happy.

I settled Josephine in her bed. It happened that the woman making up the room had taken classes with Josephine twenty-five years earlier. I wanted the people attending Josephine to know who she was. I wanted them to understand what made her so special, and why they should have a particularly good feeling for attending to her. She was in great pain, but she made no matter of it. Her mind was acutely active.

Josephine said, "My grandmother told me, *Robeirt,* it was all right for me to come." I felt the lightness of her being released; I sensed her joy. I said to her, "Josephine, I'm very happy for you. But I want you to know that I will miss you terribly." The happiness in my voice was genuine. Her face lit up; her cheeks got rosy. "I know, my dear, I shall miss you too. Come here and hold my hand." I went to sit with her. We looked directly into each other's faces for a very long time, saying nothing. She asked if she would see me again. I told her I would return the next day.

When I left the hospital to return to the restaurant, tears were streaming down my face. They were not the tears of sadness, because there was no way that I could be unhappy for her; she was going to get everything she desired. I knew that I would be deeply moved by her loss. She had made so much available to me. Our friendship inhabited a country, and when she left only I would know its dimensions. I also knew that I would rather have another afternoon in her company than anything.

The following day I went back to the hospital for another visit. I found her agitated. She worried about her daughter, about her grandchildren. I felt that we kept coming and going across a line from life to death, from where we were, to where she would be next.

When she was present she asked me what I would prepare at the restaurant that day. "We'll make a soup," I started. "What kind of a soup?" she asked. "Celery root," I told her. "Oh," she shivered, and said "I like that sort of soup." And so we went on to discuss the details of the menu I would prepare that day. "Can you bring me something to eat?" she asked. "Certainly, I'd be very happy to," I told her. "Today?" she wanted to know. "No, I have to go to work and prepare everything," I answered her. "Oh," she said, "that's too bad." "Why is that too bad? Aren't you planning to be here tomorrow?" "No," she answered "it's just that I'm hungry now. I'd love a cup of coffee." It pulled at my heart to hear her ask for coffee. She had told me any number of times how she could recall the pleasure of the coffee she had drunk in Italy in 1927, and her pleasure was vivid.

I returned to Le Trou and worked all afternoon. At about five o'clock, when the dishes we prepare at the restaurant start to take their final shape, my apprentice, John Campbell, put a bowl of celery root soup in front of me to taste. When I didn't respond immediately he said "Eat your soup." I looked at him and asked, "How can we get this to Josephine?" "Easy," he answered. "We pack it up in mason jars, and put them in a carton. You get on the motorcycle and bring it to her. We have more than two hours before anyone comes to dinner." We dropped everything and prepared the food for Josephine: a pot of *café filtre*— excellent, fresh, hot coffee in a jelly jar; a small pot of cream, a tin of cane sugar; a mason jar of soup; two crêpes wrapped carefully; a jelly jar of sorbet made from strawberries and red wine, carefully wrapped in newspaper to keep it chilled. I ran out the door, still dressed in my chef's white jacket, jumped onto the motorcycle, and drove rapidly across town to the hospital.

I arrived again at her room and announced in French, "Madame has requested dinner and the best restaurant in town has sent its chef personally to attend to you." Her face had a warm smile. I propped her up with pillows, recited the menu, and asked which thing she wanted first. "Coffee," was the immediate response. "Cream and sugar?" "Yes, please, some of each," she answered. I put a straw into the glass containing the hot coffee and held it for her. She relished it to the last taste. "Can I offer you a bit of sorbet to cleanse your palate before I offer you soup?" I asked. With her first taste of the soup, she rolled her eyes in delight and let out a satisfying, "Mmmmmm, that's the kind of soup I like." I fed her the remainder tablespoon by tablespoon and found myself reciting

in French with each spoonful that I fed to her: *"C'est la bonne nourriture. Ca c'est pour vous. C'est fait exprès pour vous. C'est la bonne cuisine."* It was as though with each taste I offered a prayer; with each tablespoon I brought her one step closer to La Mère Jacquette; and I was delivering her by this feeding to those who joyfully expected her. She had a ravenous appetite and ate everything with great relish. She said as she finished the soup, "Your food is always the best, *Robeirt."*

I offered her a crêpe to eat. It was thin and lacy and had the softness of flannel. She folded it in quarters and took a bite. It was made with the best ingredients: flour, sea salt, fresh eggs, light cream, and unsalted butter. She tasted them all with satisfaction—this, after all, was a Breton raised on crêpes. She had one bite left and suggested that the crêpe might like something sweet. "Like jam," I offered. "Yes, that would be very good." "I have some good cane sugar, Josephine." "No, dear, that's all right, I'm almost finished." "But you have some left, and the sugar is really excellent." "Alright," she said, "give it to me." I watched her expertly unfold the little bit of crêpe; she took a pinch of golden cane sugar and placed it inside. She refolded it with hands that moved with discipline and elegance, and which expressed the greatest control. She put the morsel in her mouth. "Oh," she said with delight, "that is very good."

Jacqueline, her daughter, told me that she visited Josephine the next morning. Sunday the 28th of October, and that she was in fine spirits. "Her only complaint," Jacqueline said, "was that she hadn't been fed yet." "It means, Jacki, that I was the last one who fed her." I was very glad for that. Josephine went to sleep after her daughter's visit; her heart failed, and she was gone to where La Mère Jacquette beckoned. After the funeral when we were all at the house, her grandson Danny best expressed how we all felt about her. "I'll turn a corner and be reminded of her suddenly and will feel her absence. It's like what happened the other day at the Cliff House." He proceeded to tell the story of being at the top of the Great Highway looking down the coast. He remembered the last time he had been there with Josephine. Danny's father had given him the use of a 1963 Austin Healey for a couple of weeks. One day he went to Josephine and he said, "Come on, Grandmère, I'm taking you for a ride." He took her to the car in a wheelchair and set her in the passenger seat. With the top down, he drove her down the Great Highway. "She thought it was great," he said. "I know I will miss her in little ways."

Index